Evolution of an
Unorthodox Rabbi

Evolution of an
Unorthodox Rabbi
John Moscowitz

DUNDURN
TORONTO

Editor: Michael Carroll
Design: Jennifer Gallinger
Cover design: Laura Boyle
Cover and interior images: Courtesy of John Moscowitz
Printer: Marquis

Library and Archives Canada Cataloguing in Publication

Moscowitz, John, author
        Evolution of an unorthodox rabbi / Rabbi John Moscowitz.

Includes index.
Issued in print and electronic formats.
ISBN 978-1-4597-3319-0 (paperback).--ISBN 978-1-4597-3321-3 (epub).--
ISBN 978-1-4597-3320-6 (pdf)

        1. Moscowitz, John. 2. Rabbis--Ontario--Toronto--Biography.
3. Judaism--Ontario--Toronto. I. Title.

BM755.M594A3 2015   296.8'341092   C2015-904693-9
                                                               C2015-904694-7

1   2   3   4   5   19   18   17   16   15

We acknowledge the support of the **Canada Council for the Arts** and the **Ontario Arts Council** for our publishing program. We also acknowledge the financial support of the **Government of Canada** through the **Canada Book Fund** and **Livres Canada Books**, and the **Government of Ontario** through the **Ontario Book Publishing Tax Credit** and the **Ontario Media Development Corporation**.

Care has been taken to trace the ownership of copyright material used in this book. The author and the publisher welcome any information enabling them to rectify any references or credits in subsequent editions.

— *J. Kirk Howard, President*

The publisher is not responsible for websites or their content unless they are owned by the publisher.

VISIT US AT
Dundurn.com | @dundurnpress | Facebook.com/dundurnpress | Pinterest.com/dundurnpress

Dundurn
3 Church Street, Suite 500
Toronto, Ontario, Canada
M5E 1M2

Contents

Foreword by Senator Linda Frum   9

Introduction   11

1 WHERE I COME FROM

Preamble   15

A Second Chance (2012)   16

What's with the "Jane Fonda" Part   26
in the Blog Title? (2011)

Memories of Mass (2004)   29

Remarks on the Installation of Rabbi John Moscowitz   31
by Rabbi Sanford Ragins (2000)

2 AT THE OPEN GATE: REMARKS ON THE HIGH HOLY DAYS

Preamble   37

When Change Is Religious (2013)   39

On Gratitude (2007)   44

We Jews Have Old Eyes (2004)   49

Surfing Against the Tide: Judaism and the   57
Information Age (1995)

Joy and Anxiety (1995)   64

Understanding Despair (1993)   65

Herodotus and History (1994)   72

3 ISRAEL: WHEN YOUR LOVE REMAINS THE SAME AND YOUR VIEWS CHANGE

Preamble	75
Kol Nidre and Truth (2012)	78
No Messiahs, Please, Just Peace (2010)	87
Of Rabbis and Imams (2009)	94
A False Symmetry (2004)	101
The Beginning of Hope? (2003)	104
Consolation and Destiny (2002)	106
Anguish and Hope (2002)	110

4 THE TORAH SPEAKS IN ITS LANGUAGE AND IN OURS

Preamble	121
What Do I Believe Happened at Sinai? (2009)	122
The Secret of Life (2011)	126
Noach: What Kind of Father Was Lamech?	132
The Haughty of Heart (1995)	137
Remembering Amalek, Thinking About Schindler (1994)	141
Absolutes and Ambiguities (1993)	146

5 ABOUT THAT MATTER OF EVIL ... (AND OUR EAST AFRICAN HOME)

Preamble	151
The Reach of Our Imagination (2001)	155
Evil — and Goodness (2001)	164
Making Good Out of Evil (2000)	165

The School Massacre Was Human Evil,   167
Not Tragedy (2012)

Rabbi Joseph B. Soloveitchik on the   169
Nature of Adam (2010)

6 JEWISH PRINCIPLES AND PUBLIC MATTERS

Preamble   173

Rabbis at Gay and Lesbian Weddings: 174
How I Changed My Mind (2012)

Barack Obama: Role Model for the Jews (2010)   184

Why *Munich* Still Matters (2006)   189

Terri Schiavo: A Personal View (2005)   192

Repentance: Learning from Clinton and   193
Rambam (1998)

Listening to Marshall McLuhan: 195
A Suggestion for Getting Shabbat Right (1996)

7 REMEMBRANCES

Preamble   199

Remembering David Hartman (1931–2013)   200

Watching Christopher Hitchens (1949–2011)   202

Eulogy for Joseph Rotman (1935–2015)   204

Eulogy for Morris Moscowitz (1914–2006)   206

Eulogy for Rabbi W. Gunther Plaut (1912–2012)   213

Her Character and Ours: On Jackie O (1929–1994)   216

Standing at Babi Yar (1994)   218

8 APPRECIATIONS

Preamble by Richard Rotman 223

Dr. Michael B. Oren 225

Laurie Sapir 226

Greer and Asher Kirshenbaum; Josh Saltzman 227

Fern and Stephen Morrison 228

Rabbi Ammiel Hirsch 229

Cantor Benjamin Maissner 230

Rabbi Naomi Levy 231

Marc and Craig Kielburger 233

Rabbi Jeffrey K. Salkin 234

Rabbi Karen Thomashow 236

Julie and Larry Schwartz 237

Rabbi Daniel Gordis 238

Michael and Janette Diamond; Jesse, Cole, and Ari 239

Rabbi John Rosove 240

Barry Borden 241

Michelle Katz 242

Rabbi Aaron Flanzraich 243

Yossi Klein Halevi 245

Books I Love 247

Afterword by Dr. Norman Doidge 253

Acknowledgements 257

Notes 261

Index 269

Foreword

In 1987 the board of Holy Blossom Temple, Toronto's oldest and most famous Reform synagogue, welcomed onto its pulpit a young rabbi from Los Angeles, California. As the title of this book declares from the start, John Moscowitz was an "unlikely" candidate for the rabbinate. Raised in a largely non-observant, progressive, and privileged home in St. Louis, Missouri, the adolescent Moscowitz rejected religiosity, including even the ritual of a bar mitzvah. He spent his college years in the thrall of the radical political ideology of the day, including that of Tom Hayden, his mentor at age twenty.

But after graduating from the Claremont Colleges there was a "twist." A transformation. John discovered a profound spirituality. And rather than apply his keen intellect and human sympathy to politics, academe, or psychiatry (as he earlier imagined he might), John chose to devote himself to the service of the Jewish community — wherever in the world that service might summon him.

The congregants of Holy Blossom Temple in Toronto were the fortunate beneficiaries of that service for twenty-five years, first as associate rabbi for thirteen years, then as the congregation's senior rabbi for twelve. Having found his calling, Rabbi Moscowitz earned eminence as one of the most cherished and effective rabbis Toronto has ever known. This book tells the story of those twenty-five years. It is part memoir, part tribute, and part social history.

Evolution of an Unorthodox Rabbi

I first encountered the new Rabbi Moscowitz shortly after his arrival at Holy Blossom. I was attending the funeral of a stillborn child over which he was presiding. Such funerals are controversial in Judaism, but by granting this wish to the baby's disconsolate mother, Rabbi Moscowitz had made a choice in favour of compassion.

It struck me then, as it has struck me every time since, whenever I hear John administer solace, or perform Jewish ritual, or offer up the wisdom of his soul, that he has a deeper understanding of the human heart — its sorrows, its nobility, its weaknesses, and its goodness — than anyone else I know.

Over the decades of friendship that have followed, I've had the pleasure of witnessing John's political and intellectual evolution. John Moscowitz's opinions and perspectives have shifted and developed over time. If there is one Jewish virtue I treasure most, it may be precisely the value we place on intellectual examination and re-examination and re-examination again.

You will find some of John's journey chronicled in the pages of this book. You will also find here respectful and affectionate tributes to John by friends, colleagues, and congregants whose lives have been made better for knowing him. I count myself among them. As a non-religious Jew, I've grown unexpectedly reliant on that wonderful brain and beautiful heart of his.

If it is the job of a rabbi to enlarge knowledge, relieve suffering, inspire goodness, and comfort the soul, then John Moscowitz is a rabbi for the ages. At Holy Blossom we were lucky he was ours. This book serves to tie rabbi and community even closer in understanding, memory, and love.

Senator Linda Frum
January 2015
Toronto

Introduction

In February 1987, while living in Los Angeles, I received a call one day from Rabbi Dow Marmur in Toronto. Might I be interested in a trip to Canada to interview as his associate? Then working on a doctorate in history at the University of California, Los Angeles (UCLA), I had another three years or so before finishing up. Upon completion of my dissertation, I planned to return to the congregational rabbinate.

Rabbi Marmur said he was calling at the encouragement of a mutual friend who suggested we really ought to meet each other. "After all," our friend observed, "both of you are acquired tastes."

I was fine with that, and judging by the delight with which he told the story, Dow Marmur was, too. Now I was curious — and besides, who didn't know of Holy Blossom?

I flew to Toronto a week or so later, and shortly thereafter Rabbi Marmur offered me the job. I changed course quickly, almost intuitively, and was in Toronto by July. I never completed the doctorate and never regretted my decision to leave UCLA for Holy Blossom. From my late twenties on, I wanted to be a rabbi more than I did an academic.

Some twenty-eight years later, I remain grateful to Dow Marmur for his invitation, and for providing a model of a rabbi engaged with ideas as with people. I'd seen some of that previously

— Sandy Ragins, Leonard Beerman, Harold Schulweis, to be sure — but such a rabbi was not the norm. At Holy Blossom I'd work closely with Dow Marmur and become office neighbours with Gunther Plaut. This was a pleasure. More than ever, I was galvanized to learn my craft, to know the tradition, and to teach its ideas and essence.

Among the things that became evident, first while watching Ragins and Beerman, then from observing Marmur and Plaut, was that when your job is a public one and involves teaching about matters that mean a great deal to people — well, if and when you change your mind and speak differently from before, you'll garner curiosity and comment. Sometimes other reactions accompany the curiosity: consternation and delight, to name two.

Nonetheless, because the matters are significant — both for the collective as for the individual — it's incumbent on rabbis, once having immersed themselves in study, to step forward and teach the tradition as cogently and forthrightly as possible. Indeed, rabbis are most fortunate to give expression to their learning and thinking, applied to ideas and to issues, and to do so publicly.

This was my privilege for twenty-five years at Holy Blossom Temple in Toronto. From beginning to end, I felt grateful to do so every day, even on those occasions when I knew my learning wasn't up to the needs of the moment.

As the years passed and my learning stockpiled, my thinking evolved. That, after all, is what learning does: it doesn't allow you to remain stagnant. Some changes surprised me, including on matters I thought I'd arrived at a fixed position about previously: Jewish tradition and its time-honoured boundaries, rabbis as "gatekeepers" of those boundaries, rabbis officiating at same-sex weddings, Israel and the possibilities of peace with the

Palestinians. What I learned and what I now thought, new or not new, I taught.

Some of those matters and the changes I underwent you will find in this book. Hence the title about an evolving rabbi who, while liberal in the classical sense, isn't necessarily typical of liberals, religious or political, at least as we use the term now a decade and a half into the twenty-first century. See "A Second Chance," "Rabbis at Same-Sex Weddings," and "Kol Nidre and Truth," in this regard.

However, my evolution as a rabbi is hardly the whole story. I'm not certain it's the main story. For, on most matters, I held steady to that which defined me from early on: the centrality of ideas and learning, the sense of the Peoplehood of the Jews, the efficacy of kindness and respect, high standards rabbis should hold themselves to. And all of it — the tradition and what we do to uphold it — is rooted in a profound experience of some four thousand years ago, one captured, mostly obliquely, in the Exodus story of this people called to God and obliged to live as if what is told there is true and timeless.

Perhaps that's why, while sifting through hundreds of sermons, writings, and all sorts of talks I gave over twenty-five years as a rabbi, little of it felt far away: not what I wrote many years ago, and not even those sermons I'm certain I wouldn't write today. I've changed over the years, but my past hasn't; it remains part of me, as it does for all of us. William Faulkner had it right in his novel *Requiem for a Nun*, after all: "The past is never dead. It's not even past."

February 2015
Toronto

... whosoever enters by the north gate ... shall leave by the south gate; and whosoever enters by the south gate shall leave by the north gate. They shall not go back through the gate by which they came in, but shall go out by the opposite one.

— Ezekiel 46:9

1

Where I Come From

PREAMBLE

The piece that follows this introductory preamble, "A Second Chance," says much about me, particularly what I held important over twenty-five years. It was meant to be autobiographical, yet also suggestive of matters far larger than one rabbi. However, while that sermon — almost the last I gave as senior rabbi — reveals what was crucial for me the last ten or fifteen years at Holy Blossom, it tells about me only in part.

For more on where I come from and what shaped me, see the Jane Fonda story of the early 1970s, a thin slice of my life then on the radical left. Equally, have a look at "Memories of Mass" and how Friday afternoons at Mass as a boy may have moved me to observe Friday night (and all of Shabbat) as an adult. I remain fond of both these times, and those experiences stay with me to this day.

I can't let go of this preamble without expressing gratitude to Sandy Ragins, my *Rav Muvhak* (one's special and pre-eminent rabbi) and eventually a close and trusted friend. Working near and for Rabbi Ragins as a rabbinic intern at Leo Baeck Temple in Los Angeles for two years in the late 1970s, I came to understand that the best rabbis possess two things that Sandy had in abundance and never showed off: integrity and knowledge. The first you might have to be born with, although I think you can hone it, almost like a skill; the second emerges from wide and deep enough reading to satisfy the curiosities of a roving mind. I never heard Sandy Ragins talk about either — it's just what he did and who he was.

Sandy installed me as an assistant rabbi in 1982 in Baltimore. He did the same in 2000 when I became Holy Blossom's senior rabbi. I was deeply appreciative for his words on the latter occasion in October 2000, included in this part of the book to close out a window on who I am and where I come from.

A SECOND CHANCE
Rosh Hashanah, September 2012

The late Israeli philosopher Ernst Simon often told the story of the last time Franz Kafka visited Berlin — in 1924, not long before the writer died a month short of his forty-first birthday. Walking through a park, Kafka came upon a little girl crying her eyes out. When he asked why she was in such distress, the girl sobbed that she had lost her doll.

Kafka was touched and saddened. He told the girl not to worry, that her doll had merely gone on a trip. In fact, he assured the girl, he knew the doll, having recently seen her as she was about to depart on a journey. Kafka promised that if the little girl returned to the park the next day, he would bring her a letter from her doll. And so each morning, over the next several weeks, Kafka brought a letter from the doll to his new friend, ostensibly written while on her trip.

During those weeks, Kafka grew more and more ill. He decided to return to Prague, but not before buying the girl another doll. Accompanying the new doll was a letter written by

Franz Kafka in which he insisted that, appearances to the contrary, this was indeed the doll that had belonged to the little girl. Admittedly, he told her, this doll looked different, but she had to understand that her doll had been on a long journey, had witnessed many remarkable sights, and had endured many difficult experiences. Life, Kafka wrote his young charge, had changed the doll's appearance.

Ismar Schorsch, former chancellor of the Jewish Theological Seminary, says that while there are various possible meanings to the Kafka parable, he prefers this one: "That a transformative experience alters us externally, as well as internally."[1] I suspect that Schorsch had Jews in mind here.

Schorsch's observation explains a good deal about us: who we are as Jews today and how circumstances have radically changed us over time, transforming not just our religious culture but more profoundly so ourselves. Like the doll in the Kafka story, we might wish we were the same, but we are not. Not at all.

I don't so much mean the externals of dress and language, where and even how we live. Or even this remarkable statistic (more than twenty years old now): approximately 98 percent of Jews no longer reside in the place in which at least one grandparent was born.[2] I refer to the deeper, the more telling metamorphosis: how we as Jews think, how we think about the Jews, how we think about other people, how we wish others to think about us.

This sermon is about our internal transformation — its costs, how to understand them, how to make up for them, maybe. And in the mix, more than usual about myself.

I begin in Jerusalem as I walked along Jaffa Road one bright summer day in 1976. As I did, a large man about my age — long, dark beard, *peyes*, *tzitzit* flying from his waist, bright white shirt, black pants — brushed past me. He glanced at me and smiled, almost as if we knew each other. I guess I didn't return the smile, and he continued on.

I forgot about the moment until a week or so later. While sitting at a restaurant in Jerusalem, the same man appeared at my side. He smiled once again. This time I asked, "Who are you?"

"You don't recognize me, do you?"

"No, I don't."

"I'm Danny Levin. We used to play touch football together in college."

Now I smiled. This was Danny Levin, who had been a kind of happy-go-lucky guy, hair down to his waist, always in white overalls and bare feet even when we played football? This was Danny Levin, now having discarded his college getup of a couple of years earlier for the dress of a Jerusalem yeshiva *bocher*?

Of course, Danny wondered the same about me. True, my appearance wasn't much different from before, but what was I now doing in Jerusalem? Why wasn't I still occupied with radical left-wing politics, as when Danny and I knew each other casually over football and campus hellos? Or at least in law school where many peers had headed? Danny Levin sat down and we spoke.

We had grown up in similar American backgrounds of that time and place: nice suburbs with lots of Jews and not much Judaism; grandparents who had fled Eastern Europe, but neither their Orthodox ways nor the inner city of their immigrant landings; and parents who had fled their parents' old-world ways for postwar American suburbia. Danny Levin and I had grown up in comfort and had gone off to college in hope.

Yet here we were in Jerusalem, each on our way back to a past, ours but not ours. We were consumed, possessed of a sense of confidence about what we were up to. We understood a lot actually, even as we yet had little knowledge.

Where I Come From

Our pursuit — Danny, a *baal teshuvah* yeshiva student, and me (I guess you might say), a *baal teshuvah* Reform rabbinical student — was, despite external differences, the same. We were chasing the religious inheritance barely bequeathed us, hoping to reclaim it. After that we didn't know, but the desire to take back our past was more than strong enough to propel us toward our futures.

What I did in going off to rabbinical school — a twist in life no one would have predicted even two years earlier — and what Danny Levin did in trading overalls for *tzitzit* was more than about the personal odysseys of two young men. It was a pursuit, a highly passionate one, born of a pervasive dilemma known to the vast majority of Jews in the contemporary world.

What do you do when you can't remember what was because you never knew it to begin with?

What do you do when what was once taught and absorbed at home — naturally, unselfconsciously, as part of the ongoing rhythm of daily life — no longer is?

What do you do when gaining literacy as a Jew, once a given, once a part of an older mimetic world, now means overcompensating to such an extent that family and friends say, "You want to do what? That's no job …"

What happens, what becomes of us, when being a Jew by virtue of what is taught and learned at the family table, the kitchen, the neighbourhood, on the way to synagogue, when a natural transmission of religious knowledge has long gone by the wayside?

What happens, what becomes of us, when the capability of parents, and grandparents for that matter, to teach Jewish values and rituals shrinks dramatically by virtue of ignorance or indifference, or even contempt?

Or to frame this dilemma in broader terms: what happens when a people, masters of a rich tradition, is catapulted rapidly and irrevocably from Tevye to Technology and emerges in the new world with but small traces of the tradition trailing, consequently believing that what Tevye knew no longer matters in the Age of Technology?

What had happened was modernity: its discontents and divisions fashioned by a radical sundering of a once-coherent and mimetic world, now forever gone.

What had happened in this sundering was that we Jews had lost our interior world: what we knew, the ideas that animated us and gave us coherence, even as our world was often rocked. We had lost our ballast; Judaism was no longer an anchor as the winds of change blew mightily, taking down everything in their way. And we would often come to identify more with other peoples and their pain than with our own people and our pain.

The sociologist John Murray Cuddihy, who knew the collective psyche of the Jews better then anybody else, brings the understanding of another sociologist, the great Talcott Parsons, to explain the essence of the problem for Jews: that of the modern phenomenon of "differentiation."

"Differentiation," Parsons observes, "slices through ancient primordial ties and identities, leaving crisis and 'wholeness/hunger' in its wake."[3] *Slices though ancient primordial ties and identities, leaving crisis and "wholeness/hunger" in its wake.* Doesn't that say it all?

What was the result of this radical sundering and slicing? The Jews were broken off from their past, from their ideas, from their wholeness — real or imagined. A strong sense of self, collectively and individually, the security born of being part of a people with a distinct place in the world — modernity emptied all of this out, leaving us instead with this wholeness/hunger gnawing away from within. There was little left on the inside. How could it be otherwise?

Where I Come From

Franz Kafka famously wrote in "Letter to His Father":

> You really had brought some traces of Judaism
> with you from the ghetto-like village community;
> it was not much and it dwindled a little more in
> the city and during your military service; but still,
> the impressions and memories of your youth did
> just about suffice for some sort of Jewish life ...
> Even in this there was still Judaism enough, but
> it was too little to be handed on to the child; it all
> dribbled away while you were passing it on.[4]

I was no different from Kafka, really, and perhaps neither were you. Off I went to rabbinical school, not to be a rabbi but hungry for knowledge and in search of the Jews. Over the next couple of years, I was enthusiastic to learn — yet also confused. Truth to tell, quite disappointed.

I loved learning Jewish texts and ideas. But where were they in the liberal synagogues in Los Angeles and elsewhere? They just weren't there — not the ideas, not the rituals, not the Hebrew, not even more than a faint smell of Peoplehood. Israel was routinely and roundly criticized — these were the Menachem Begin years — and I joined in.

Many Reform rabbis were knowledgeable, pious, and interesting. But the Judaism in Reform synagogues was emptied out, remedial, and thin. The gap was disturbing, and because I was then actually thinking of becoming a rabbi, I was more than a bit beside myself.

Bewildered — this is the fall of 1979 now — I approached my teacher, Rabbi David Ellenson, then a newly minted professor of Jewish Thought (later to become the president of Hebrew Union College).

"David," I remember asking more than a bit plaintively, "where is the 'there' there in Reform Judaism? I understand Reform and Conservative Judaism as effective strategies for keeping Jews within the fold. These movements, from the beginning, have understood that modernity causes the withering away of tradition — hence the liberal movements recognize that Jews need the help of synagogues in remaining Jewish. But I can't find the content in the liberal approaches. I hear the words — they're nice — but where are the ideas, the learning, and the guts behind the words? Is Judaism just confined to a private pursuit that rabbis engage in and that's it?"

As he listened, Ellenson at first frowned, and then as I concluded, he smiled. "You've named the problem exactly. Our way is more of a social strategy to keep Jews within the fold than it is a religious tradition. If by the word *there* you mean Judaism or its lack in the liberal Jewish world, you are correct."

"Great," I recall saying, "so what do I do now?" (My wholeness/hunger had just gotten worse.)

"Go read Joseph Soloveitchik and then read his student, David Hartman."

I did as Ellenson said. I read those two leading rabbinic thinkers, Soloveitchik and Hartman, again and again. That wholeness/hunger of mine got gradually replaced by learning, ideas, and intellectual and religious satisfaction. I had a core now — a Jewish one that allowed me to remain thoroughly modern all the while. I understood and respected the world Danny Levin wished to make his, but it wasn't mine. And neither was it an either/or choice: *frumkeit* and the ideas of the traditional milieu or nothing and forget the whole thing. That's a false choice, and Hartman in particular knows that.

Love for the Jews and Zion, Hartman's especially, and awe of and curiosity about God, Soloveitchik's especially, have changed me as a Jew and as a rabbi. Year after year I revelled in the intellectual verve of both Soloveitchik and Hartman. Their thinking helped me create my personal Jewish ballast — an interior religious sensibility that has proved satisfying and sustaining.

What I learned from them went way beyond me. I began to believe that the best way to respond to what modernity had emptied out was for liberal Jews to be challenged and changed and solidified by traditional and engaging Jewish ideas. You don't have to accept them all, but you do have to know them. I believe that more than ever today, and much of what I have done as a rabbi has been to make this happen for other Jews.

That moment with David Ellenson, the quest on which he sent me, explains more than anything else what I've tried to do as a rabbi for thirty years, including the past twenty-five at Holy Blossom Temple.

There have been successes and failures. There have been jaunts off the main path of this intellectual and religious road of mine. But it's all been the same pursuit: to provide, originally for myself and then others, a strong and robust internal well of knowledge on the way to a religious spirit and a fortified Jewish people.

I've hoped to help transform (maybe retransform) our interior by way of a deliberate infusion of Jewish ideas and intellectual knowledge, along with increased solidarity with our people. This hope impelled me, for instance, once the opportunity presented itself, to bring into our midst Jews who lived and eloquently expressed this kind of Peoplehood and love of Zion: former Israeli ambassador to the United States Michael Oren, novelist Amos Oz, journalist Yossi Klein Halevi, political commentator and columnist Charles Krauthammer, Israeli politician Einat Wilf, and prominent Israeli teachers like David Hartman, Daniel Gordis, Donniel Hartman, Yoram Hazony, and Noam Zion. And others, alive with ideas and different ways to think, to animate and teach us: the brilliant author Paul Berman, the late Anglo-American author Christopher Hitchens, former Canadian ambassador to the United Nations Stephen Lewis, U.S. ambassador to the United Nations Samantha Power, military historian Victor Davis Hanson, political commentator George Will, and political activist and one-time New Left leader Tom Hayden. One-of-a-kind figures — the radical theologian Arthur Green, public intellectuals like Leon Wieseltier and Michael Ignatieff, historical figures such as Elie Wiesel and Abba Eban — also graced our bimah and provoked our thinking.

Yes, I sought to bring our synagogue into the centre of the larger Toronto Jewish community. I knew this would provide the strength, the ideas, the knowledge, the sense of being part of a larger Jewish people that we as liberals require. We need this to fill in where we are deficient.

But I sought to do this as well so that Holy Blossom Temple could help open up the larger Jewish community as it so required — to open our more traditional friends and families to a liberal, egalitarian, more socially conscious spirit that can only strengthen our fellow Jews. Jews of disparate ways need to make one another better and not try to defeat each other.

No less, our Schwartz/Reisman Centre has been central to what I've endeavoured to do here to engender more learning, more exciting ideas, more change, more personal and collective religious sensibility. I'm most proud of our mainstay — the Shabbat Morning Torah Study, enlivened by ideas, learning, lively minds, great study and conversation — and sometimes the felt presence of God. A room often overflowing with dozens of Jews filled with joy and curiosity.

Over time I'd come to understand that the course I had set off on in the mid-1970s, one clarified by David Ellenson and then inspired by Joseph Soloveitchik and David Hartman, was a kind of latent response to the hollowing out of the core of the Jews, first by assimilation and then by massive murder. The world of our grandparents and their parents had been vanquished. A rebuilding and refashioning of Jewish life — more than in numerical terms — was required. I wanted to be part of that.

If in our liberal precincts, we could steady ourselves internally with ideas and learning, buttressed by a deep and meaningful attachment to Am Yisrael and Medinat Yisrael, then we might help steady and provide strength to the larger Jewish people.

Am I tribal then? Of course, I am! We have been decimated, we Jews in this twenty-first century. Much of our world, internal and external, has been destroyed in our lifetimes. Our Israel now is threatened as it hasn't been in decades.

Of course, I'm tribal. But that hardly means I'm illiberal, either in spirit or in deed. And so synagogues, ours and all others, must be open communities, treating well and taking seriously every member whether a part of us for ten days or for ten decades, whether known to us or not, whether recognized in our social milieu or not, whether strong of body or weak of spirit. Every Jew in our midst and beyond is worthy of our full regard. A religious community that does not honour this, in word and in deed, is neither religious nor a community.

This, too, is essential to cultivating a strong and transformed interior — to steady us personally with small acts of decency, to steady our people with inclusion of all in our midst, including those not Jewish who may wish to join the Jews. And, as much as anything, to strengthen ourselves with the literary and intellectual sustenance of the tradition.

There is a great deal more to say — that for down the road — but for now two final matters. First, I can't conclude without saying something very important to me: Holy Blossom Temple is one of a minority of synagogues that can and sometimes does embody the renewal of the Jew of which I speak. It is why I came to Toronto. It is why I stayed. It is why it has been a privilege to be your rabbi for twenty-five years. I am most appreciative for that, and I thank you, along with all members of our congregation.

Finally, let me return to the story of Franz Kafka, the little girl, her doll, and the inner transformation of the Jews. Ernst Simon, in telling the story, does so to demonstrate what he calls a "second naïveté" — that is, the sense of innocence necessary "to regain faith after having experienced the purgatory of secularization."

I understand this second naïveté as a chance to start over, to begin again without pretending you don't know what you do, without pretending what has happened hasn't happened. It's a chance to revive Kafka's experience and our own: to ensure the thriving of our own spirits and the survival of our own people. It's a way to provide necessary coherence, even as we understand the world is not necessarily coherent.

Kafka tried to do that for the little girl with a new doll. It is ours to do with learning, with ideas, with Peoplehood and the love of Zion. Ours is an extraordinary inheritance, a great gift. It belongs to every one of us, every Jew. It's ours for the taking, and take it we must — for our sake, more than we can possibly even understand.

WHAT'S WITH THE "JANE FONDA" PART IN THE BLOG TITLE? (2011)

For about three years (2009–2012), I wrote a blog. I did so at the urging of a true Canadian hero, Marc Kielburger, while in a long conversation one afternoon over a very bumpy road in East Africa in August 2009. Marc wanted to read what I was thinking about and was up to. Another friend, Richard Rotman, knowing my history, suggested the title "From Jane Fonda to Judaism." The Judaism part is familiar, the Jane Fonda one less so. Here then is a 2011 blog post — an abbreviated version of a larger story that I wrote to explain how I knew Fonda.

By the late spring of 1972, swept up in the political activism of that contentious time, I had left university after two years of study. I was certain I'd never return — I'd work odd jobs to support my political work, I claimed. I took note of my parents' studied nonchalance when they heard my intentions.

I then moved from the Claremont Colleges to the beach in Venice, California, to work with Tom Hayden, the New Left leader and anti–Vietnam War activist. It was at that time that Hayden fell in love with the actress Jane Fonda. Not long before, even while shedding the Hollywood life (but not necessarily its glamour), she had won an Oscar for her role in *Klute*. In the glare of the media spotlight, Fonda was morphing, earnestly if awkwardly, into a political activist.

Hayden quickly brought Fonda into the orbit of a dozen or so of us whom he had gathered that spring to form an educational campaign on the then raging Vietnam War. His aim — smart strategist as he was and remains — was to make the Vietnam War the pre-eminent issue as Americans debated the 1972 presidential election. We were his shock troops, organizing antiwar rallies, showing slide shows on the war at colleges and schools, taken up with endless meetings, and not a few celebrity sightings.

I got to know Jane Fonda over the next few months, most memorably hosting her (at Hayden's last-minute request while getting her from the Los Angeles airport) at my apartment at the beach, almost immediately upon her arrival back in California from Hanoi. Unless you were hiding under a rock in those hot August 1972 days, you couldn't have missed where Fonda had been and what she was up to. Two hours after Hayden called, there was Jane Fonda, sitting cross-legged and pretty on my threadbare "living room" floor, delivering the first report of her trip to Hanoi in front of a dozen or so hastily gathered antiwar activists. Her "infamous" trip, I should say, the one where news photos depicted her (pretending) to fire anti-aircraft missiles at U.S. warplanes, forever earning her the sobriquet "Hanoi Jane." Speaking to my parents later that evening, I casually relayed who had just been by. My father dropped the receiver.

For us Jane Fonda was a heroine — a little mysterious and somewhat distant, though sweet and friendly. That she was so graced with star power meant the distance was as much about our awe of her as her not quite knowing what to do with us.

I was then an idealistic twenty-year-old. In the year or so previous, I had discarded my generation's cultural, unreflective, and soft leftism, or "lifestyle," you could say. Now, joining my peers and inspired by Hayden, I followed a radical leftist con-sciousness: "Ho, Ho, Ho Chi Minh, NLF is gonna win!" we'd chant in street demonstrations, praising the "enemy" leader. In hindsight I'm not so sure my "consciousness" went terribly deep, but like many, I cared a great deal about what was happening in Vietnam. Nothing was more pressing to us than ending that war.

However, unlike many Jews caught up in the antiwar move-ment, I never hid my being Jewish, especially not my love for Israel. Side by side in my apartment were two posters, one of Madame Nguyen Thi Binh (the National Liberation Front nego-tiator in Paris), the other of Tiberias, Israel. This was confusing for most people, particularly for Jews, but to me it made all the sense in the world.

In the next few years, as my passions shifted from politics to Judaism and Israel, I made my way to rabbinical school but retained an interest in things political. My heroes remained, as they had been for years, even while on the hard left: Bobby Kennedy; the flame-throwing, take-no-prisoners St. Louis Cardinal pitcher Bob Gibson; Gregory Peck, or at least Peck as Atticus Finch in *To Kill a Mockingbird*; and Ari Ben Canaan in Leon Uris's novel *Exodus*, a stand-in for various Israelis I'd been taken with when in Israel as an eighteen-year-old in 1970. Ho Chi Minh fell by the wayside as I read differently from before, my eyes opening to the reality of life in North Vietnam. I've kept a respect and affection for Hayden, remaining in touch and bringing him to speak at Holy Blossom in 2008. I haven't seen Jane Fonda in many years now.

I've also kept a large file of notes about those days, specifically writings about, as Richard Rotman put it originally, "your journey from Jane to Judaism," which in broad strokes captures my migration from a twenty-year-old in Venice and Santa Monica in the early 1970s to a congregational rabbi today in Toronto.

MEMORIES OF MASS
From the *Globe and Mail*, April 3, 2004

As a young boy, I would periodically accompany my closest friend, Craig Sullivan, to Mass. In the early 1960s, the St. Louis Catholic world was a pre–Vatican II one, thick with Latin, ritual, and mystery. I couldn't take my eyes off the richness of it all — this foreign world that hinted at so much beyond my understanding.

I knew what not to do in church as a Jew, but I also knew how to experience the beauty of the Mass. I loved its unabashed preference for mystery, its old-world decor and ways, its clear sense that there was no more important place to be. God seemed real to me at the Annunciation Church in a way He didn't at my own synagogue, a suburban temple stripped of virtually all ritual.

Those times in Mass led me, in part, to search for the same experience in my own tradition. Craig Sullivan had more than a little to do with turning me into a Jew, even a rabbi, and I'm forever grateful.

More important, these same memories would later bring me to pay attention to the human need for religious ritual. I've never forgotten that, as the priests and their acolytes went about their devotions to God. I was transfixed by something I could neither quite grasp nor ignore, something powerful and present, beautiful but frightening.

Years later, no doubt with those afternoons at Mass still with me, I concluded that the religious experience is central to the human experience, that without an occasional gaze at the Power that sets everything into motion, the Power that makes life both more and less knowable at the same time, we are not fully human.

The rituals, the otherworldly Latin, the incense, the frocked and imposing yet friendly priests who chanted God's word at the Annunciation Church in early 1960s St. Louis, were human evocations of God's presence. The majesty of it made me feel most human, most curious about a God I had never glimpsed before and not all that often since.

I've never been able to get the memories of Mass out of my head. Somewhere along the way I realized that what I intuitively sensed forty years ago is no less true for Jews in synagogue: the deep and beautiful and unknowable mystery of God is best evoked by ritual and prayer and music that plays havoc with the rational and refuses to reduce God to the functional or the ethical. As a boy at the Annunciation Church, I thought God was real, and if there, why not in synagogue?

I learned from those days that only when God is almost felt and yet out of reach do we glimpse our deepest selves, and that public religious ritual can cultivate religious souls who, upon yielding some of the power of individuality and rationality, find the Unintelligible available, even if unknowable.

When God as the Unintelligible is available and maybe palpable, barriers between human beings begin to disappear; in feeling bound to God, we are moved to serve God's creatures. Being present at Mass as a boy provided me the gift of this knowledge, and I wonder if I didn't resolve then to help provide this gift to those within my own tradition.

Recently, I saw Craig Sullivan for the first time in more than thirty years. A long-lapsed Catholic, he is estranged from his own tradition and curious about mine. What I learned from his beautiful religious world eventually rearranged my life. There is a direct relationship between what I experienced then and what I now do with my life.

Having sensed then the godly and the tribal at the heart of another religion, I lean these days toward the tribal experience of my own people. Having once learned to be a Jew by going to Mass, I owe a debt to Catholicism that will always inform my love of ritual and prayer in Judaism. When two great faiths celebrate festivals of redemption in proximity, as Jews and Christians do now at Passover and Easter, we are reminded that without religious ritual the past will never claim us and the heart of life will always elude us.

REMARKS ON THE INSTALLATION OF RABBI JOHN MOSCOWITZ
By Rabbi Sanford Ragins, October 29, 2000

A couple of years ago John Moscowitz and I were at a synagogue in a London suburb for a meeting of the executive board of the

Central Conference of American Rabbis. The agenda was full, both exhaustive and exhausting. Rabbis tend to talk a lot, and when you get a lot of rabbis together in one place ... well, you can imagine.

Finally, after many intense hours of discussion and debate, there was a break in our proceedings, and at last we had some free time. It was a cool, overcast March afternoon. Grateful for the chance to be alone, I took a long walk to the two-storey house on a serene side street where Sigmund Freud spent the last months of his life after his escape from Nazi-occupied Vienna.

Now a museum, the house has many of Freud's mementos on display, as well as the famous "couch" left exactly where he placed it. As I wandered through the house, suddenly there was John at my side, unexpectedly, without plan. He was drawn to the place, as I had been, by curiosity and perhaps by our shared sense that the last home of a Jew who devoted his life to healing the spirit was worthy of pilgrimage.

There was John, once again in my life, as he has been so many times: quiet, thoughtful, a mixture of tenderness and strength. We walked back to our hotel together and talked along the way about our lives and our work, our frustrations and tsuris, telling each other the stories rabbis tell only to one another. John listened, as he always does, deeply, telling you by his eyes and his graceful body language and an occasional comment (not always in agreement) that he had heard you in trust, that you were understood and accepted, appreciated and valued.

A flashback to two decades ago. A young rabbinic student takes a job at my temple as an intern. He had been my student in a history class at Hebrew Union College, and now he is with me often. I learn about him for the first time as he teaches confirmation class, gives a sermon from time to time, connects with our kids, and hangs around, ever watchful, absorbing what he can of life in a synagogue and the work of a rabbi.

Where I Come From

What did I learn? That he is a terrific athlete, graceful on the diamond, alert and energetic; that he likes people and has a passion for Judaism, especially Jewish ideas; that he has a head of hair that drives those who, like myself, are follically challenged, into fits of jealousy; that he is rather reserved by nature, with a touch of shyness, but also that he has a subtle magnetism, a wistful charisma that bonds others to him because they sense, rightly, that in world of hype and hyperbole, he is a rarity — genuine, real, a person to be trusted, a mensch.

I learned that he is intolerant of phoniness, pretense, and arrogance in others and in himself; that he is impatient with surface phenomena and has a knack for going beyond appearances and down, down into the depths of an idea or a problem or a soul, that of another person or his own; that he knows how to laugh and how to think and how to suffer; that he wants desperately to be a rabbi so that he can teach and heal, assuage pain and bring hope to those in despair.

And now all that has happened. He has not only become a rabbi but a rabbi par excellence, seasoned and bruised by years of hard work, but not disillusioned, still driven by the need to be with and for others. Silver has invaded his hair, and his soul has been burnished, too. His professional skills have been sharply honed by decades of experience and trial and error. As he was on the ball field, so as a rabbi he has become adroit and nimble, responsive and there where and when he is needed.

His ability to listen is more penetrating, his compassion deeper, his calm way of reaching out to others in their suffering is stronger than ever. As you know, a conversation with John is never brisk or superficial but marked always by pauses: thoughtful moments of silence during which, without words, his connection with you ripens softly and becomes profound. His capacity for insightful, independent judgment, which in my experience has never been judgmental, is stronger than ever. Because he continues to study Judaism and read widely and voraciously, his knowledge and his wisdom have grown. And he has done this somehow without losing his *neshama*, his soul, his sense of self, his integrity.

There is an expression in the Talmud that describes such a person: *tocho k'varo*, "his inside is like his outside," the Rabbis say. *Tocho k'varo* is an antonym for "hypocrisy." In modern slang: what you see is what you get. And what you get with Rabbi John Moscowitz is most impressive: gentleness and power, wisdom and understanding, in a gifted, dedicated, sensitive, most private human being.

Private. I understand there is considerable curiosity in this community about that privacy, and that is how it should be: you should be curious and his privacy should be respected. You want to know: "Who is this guy?" But you will have to be content with the tip of the iceberg and accept that there is much below the surface and out of sight.

In Hasidism there is the phenomenon of the Nistar, literally, "the hidden one," the Tzaddik who does not reveal himself. Most Tzaddikim were public in a big way, fiercely competitive with one another, sometimes flamboyant and aggressive. But the Nistar, the hidden Tzaddik, was different. Such a Tzaddik has an ego of course, but it is so strong that self-advertisement and self-aggrandizement are unnecessary, indeed unthinkable. The Nistar is quietly solid and knows his limitations and his power. His disciples recognize this and are drawn to him with the surety that their rebbe is a person of substance, a teacher of profundity, a leader worthy of being followed. We Reform Jews do not often have Tzaddikim, at least not in the rabbinate, but in John we do have, and to its great good fortune this venerable congregation has a Nistar.

Where I Come From

I understand that in Italy, when there is to be a cross-country bicycle race, fans of one cyclist or another will paint words of encouragement along the course. If they support a racer named, say, Calamandrei, they will paint *FORZA,* CALAMANDREI in letters three feet high on walls and billboards so that Calamandrei can take strength from them on his way.

In three-foot letters then: *FORZA,* RABBI JOHN MOSCOWITZ! Or as we say in the synagogue: *HAZAK, HAZAK, V'NITHAZEK.* Be strong, be strong [my friend, John], and let us continue to give strength to one another.

2

At the Open Gate:
Remarks on the High Holy Days

PREAMBLE

Averaging about five sermons each High Holy Day season over twenty-five years at Holy Blossom, I delivered some 125 sermons during the Days of Awe. About a dozen are included in this book, most in this part.

I still like the majority of the Holy Day sermons and could comfortably speak them today. Others I like less so. Some (see "Surfing Against the Tide: Judaism in the Information Age") sound as if they're from another age, though still with something to say.

Writing for the holidays is different from writing for Shabbat. It's not that the number of people is greater; it's that the needs are more evident and press harder: at some point on Rosh Hashanah or Yom Kippur, what agitates or excites us (all the while our insides are being stoked by the Holy Day themes and music) is impossible to ignore, and maybe paramount. That we sit with many hundreds, family and friends included, yet are essentially alone, only heightens the significance of the *Yamim Noraim*, the Days of Awe. After all, it's all so starkly about life and death. What could press more than that?

Which is why I've felt from the beginning — you can actually feel this; it's just that physical — that Jews come to *shul* on Rosh Hashanah and Yom Kippur for the most important of reasons. No wonder we're uniquely receptive to the messages of those moments. No wonder the sermons are listened to more closely, the music felt more deeply, the passing parade of years and loved ones hurts the heart as it does.

If much of the time over twenty-five years, I believed I met the needs of the moment, other times I did not: rabbis also have to face the mirror then, and it's no less comfortable for us than for anyone else. Regardless, to speak on the holidays, to share what's most important to you as a Jew with other Jews — what a remarkable opportunity. You sense the uniqueness of these times all the more as the years slide into the distance.

One final thought. In reading over virtually every sermon I delivered on the Holy Days, I saw a pattern of which previously I had only had a glimmer: if earlier on I tended to speak more of public issues, later on I was inclined toward religious ones. Age? Experience? Did I know more (or less)? I don't know.

Oddly, but maybe tellingly, this migration coincided with another one making its way through me at the same time. Over the last decade or so, I grew less enamoured of rules, especially about observance and boundaries, and more responsive to what stirred the inside, the soul, the spirit — not of myself alone but of each of us. Especially so during the *Yamim Noraim* — then, when, acknowledged or not, much is on the line; then, when, willingly or not, the unbeliever, too, wondered about the judgment of the Divine. It's all the great drama of the Jews and of the Jew, and rabbis and cantors are fortunate for the front-row seats congregations afford them.

WHEN CHANGE IS RELIGIOUS
Rosh Hashanah, September 5, 2013

You may know that a couple of years ago Bruce Springsteen lost his close comrade, the one-of-a-kind charismatic sax man, his soul brother onstage and off, Clarence Clemons. Felled by a stroke, the "Big Man" died within days. Many asked how could the "Boss," who had leaned on Clarence literally and figuratively for forty years, go on. How might the E Street Band absorb the blow of Clarence's death and not be totally claimed by it?

Here is how Springsteen put it a year or so later while speaking to David Remnick in *The New Yorker*: "The band is like a little community up here. It gathers together, and we try to heal the parts that God broke and honor the parts that are no longer with us."[1]

To heal the parts that God broke and to honor the parts that are no longer with us. The E Street Band has been doing exactly that ever since Clarence Clemons died — for themselves, as well as for their devoted fans. Springsteen says they can only do this together, not alone and apart. Indeed, through the healing and honouring of these past few years, the band has changed. They've held on to their past, including the memories of Clemons and Danny Federici (also gone now), all the while moving on. Springsteen and his band have neglected neither their past nor their present, neither their brokenness nor their hopes. They can't; they want a future.

How do you do that exactly? How do you hold on to and honour who and what you've been all these years — your essential identity, your history, how everybody knows you, and how you know yourself — and all the while shift your gaze to the future, itself no less essential? When the past is fundamental to your being and your well-being, how do you seize the chance to change when your well-being requires that, too?

And to shed old skin in community? To think differently from before, to make noticeable changes in front of the curious eyes of family, friends, acquaintances, peers — those who have known you through it all? To walk a different path from the one you've travelled together with those most invested in you remaining the same? Not so easy. And I'll tell you why it's daunting to change among those closest. And then I'll tell you why at times doing so is the most important thing you can do. And not so daunting in the end, by the way.

Community is built into our genes. Hard-wired for millions of years now. By banding together in sufficient numbers, our early ancestors dramatically increased their odds of survival. Protecting themselves from attack, gathering enough food, propagating the next generation — early humans had to band together to survive. What was originally a physical necessity became a spiritual requisite. Being with other humans in ways large and small, intimate and social, was hard-wired into our existence.

And it still is. No other creature finds community so essential. We rely on one another. We define ourselves by others. We are enmeshed with one another. More than we can possibly fathom, you are me and I am you! Our Machzor so expresses itself: everything is in the "we" voice, very little in the "me" voice.

"Why was the [Rosh Hashanah] Confession composed in the plural, so that we say, We have sinned, rather than, I have sinned?" asked the sixteenth-century Rabbi Isaac Luria. "Because all Israel is one body and every one of Israel is a limb of that body; that is why we are all responsible for one another when we sin. So, if one's fellow should sin, it is as though one has sinned oneself ..."[2]

Back to that tricky matter — given that your limbs are mine and mine are yours, how will I enlist the strength to change when I'm so bound to you? Muster the courage to walk a different road from that which we've built together? Discover a unique voice within when I'm so accustomed to singing in the chorus?

The very nature of community is about stability, continuity, and mutuality. You are me and I am you. Your change may shake me up; mine might throw you for a loop. Big changes, large loops — who needs them?

Because sometimes change you must. Even as you might prefer otherwise, you may actually have no choice. We all know our own prisons, our sins, and, as well, those circumstances of our making or that of others that require us to change course, maybe even rearrange our very being. Repentance, *teshuvah*, means changing how you are in the world; it alone may pave the road, often a new one, toward healing. *To heal the parts that God broke and honor the parts no longer with us.*

In Hilchot Teshuvah (The Laws of Repentance), Maimonides — Rambam — describes what must occur for true repentance to take hold. That is, those actions that restore our order, moral and spiritual. In short, how we move from brokenness to healing, from sin to decency, if we so choose.

Hence, Rambam instructs as follows: you must give charity, you have to remove yourself from the sin you committed, and you have to change your behaviour. Then comes this, a kind of a kicker, at the end of the list: "One should also exile oneself from one's hometown — for the act of exile itself atones for sins, as it causes humility."[3]

Wow: to remove the stain of sin, to accomplish *teshuvah* — to heal, too, we would say — you must leave your community! Why such a drastic move? Why not just give *tzedakah* or ensure what you did you won't do again? Just travel the road most travelled and be done with it.

Not good enough. What Rambam is asserting, I believe, is that there are times when the sin is so egregious you simply must leave your community. No choice: no leave-taking, then no repentance and no healing.

Clearly, that sin might be committed by an individual who, to return home, must walk the path of deep humility. But if I'm reading Rambam correctly here and elsewhere, he is nonetheless also claiming that if the community itself has sinned, in such circumstances then, those who seek sanity and health may also have no choice; they, too must take leave of their community when it will not change its ways.

Where well-being, moral and spiritual, is not possible, you must leave that place. Is this an extreme situation? One hopes so. Is this an instructive teaching? One knows so.

When a poisonous grip won't loosen its grasp, then no healing will be had in the present, and not likely in the future, either. Sin, unaccompanied by *teshuvah*, inevitably trails fear and paralysis in its wake. That's the vise grip. What is true for the individual is true for the group — a family, a community of whatever kind. Under such circumstances change, even exile, is incumbent upon us. That's the only way to lessen the hold.

All in all, though, whether our change is small or large, noteworthy or not, this is not about change in and of itself. Rather, this is a matter of religious change. Religious change recognizes that, while sin is a deeply serious matter, to remove oneself from one's own sins or those of the community may not be as daunting as it appears. Religious change means that you and your community, you and your family and friends, can at one and the same time hold your past, know it, not pretend it away — *and* honour and encourage that move, that shift, that transformation that restores health and healing, wholeness and even happiness.

Religious change by its very nature is "to heal the parts that God [or, we should add, humans] broke and honour the parts no longer with us." This is exactly the nature of community at its best:

both in the remarkable community built by Bruce Springsteen, as well as in a religious community, which I believe Springsteen also inhabits and creates. Rabbi Jeffrey Salkin recently told me that a priest friend of his says Springsteen is the most important Catholic theologian in America today.

For religious change recognizes the difference between perfection and integrity. The first is never possible, the latter is always necessary. Religious change means you don't pretend away the truths, neither of your past nor your present, neither of your brokenness nor your hopes, because you want a future. Religious change can occur only within the individual, the family, the community keen for the future.

If Bruce Springsteen is one of my religious heroes, then, as many of you know, another is Rabbi Joseph B. Soloveitchik, the pre-eminent rabbinic authority of the twentieth century, it's fair to say. So permit me to conclude with a story about Rabbi Soloveitchik. On the surface it's a simple one, but upon reflection it's an anecdote that's also profound and telling, especially so for this moment when the mandate is *teshuvah*, repentance, which we should define as religious change, the only kind that matters.

You may know that upon arriving in America in the 1930s Rabbi Soloveitchik lived in Boston, but soon thereafter began to commute weekly to teach at Yeshiva University (YU) in Upper Manhattan. One day, while teaching the Talmud to his YU students, the door to the classroom opened and the man responsible for the Rav's travel arrangements popped his head in and said, "I'm sorry, Rabbi Soloveitchik, but there is no reservation for you back to Boston this afternoon."

"What name did you ask for?" inquired the Rav.

"I asked for Rabbi Joseph B. Soloveitchik."

The Rav laughed. "Oh, I never make reservations under that

name. It's too complicated and nobody can spell it, anyway. Just ask them if they have a reservation for Joe Solo!"[4]

Like the Rav, who wished to get from New York to Boston without complications, we are bid to move from last year to this in the most straightforward way possible. In our case, as our tradition so clearly implores now, it means making religious change; it means taking hold of the future we so fervently desire by owning the past without pretense; it means transforming ourselves by leaving that which keeps us in the wrong place — spiritually, morally, or physically. Then the broken parts may heal and all that deserves honouring — God, our lives, our communities, and the world about us — will be duly honoured.

ON GRATITUDE
Yom Kippur, September 22, 2007

About a dozen years ago Parkinson's disease struck my father. Slowly and relentlessly, he was robbed of his capabilities, physical and mental, and eventually of his life. Still, even in his last difficult years — he died thirteen months ago now — my father would often profess his good fortune. He enjoyed his family, he had known success and esteem, and he'd had a very good run for a long time — better and longer than most by far. About six months before my father died we, his sons, brought him to a wonderful Catholic palliative care home near my brother in Minneapolis, Minnesota. It had been a long and disorienting flight to get him there, but once at the Gianni Home, the nurses settled him comfortably in his small room. Exhausted, he took a long nap.

When our father awoke a couple of hours later, we were sitting at his bedside. He opened his eyes and looked groggily a couple of times around the last room of his life. He could no longer walk and could barely talk. Finally, he concentrated his eyes on his sons. Haltingly but clearly, he said, "I kind of like my new executive office."

Those words expressed our father's irony, his humour, his acceptance — most of all, his appreciation of what we had done to make him comfortable in his last days.

I wondered: Where did he get that ability for appreciation? Why was our father grateful, given that his body and his mind were badly ravaged by Parkinson's and he might have been sour?

About two months ago a long-time friend died. In early May, back pains brought Carole to her doctor, who told her she likely had a disc problem.

The mother of two young boys, a wife to her husband, Carole carried on until the pain was too much. The doctors then decided on an MRI. What ailed her, in fact, and would quickly take her down, was very advanced bone cancer.

The cancer was everywhere, and there was no hope. There would be no surgery, radiation, or chemotherapy. There would be nothing except waiting for death. And sure enough, within seven weeks, this vibrant, wry, hugely intelligent woman, who turned fifty in the middle of it all, was dead.

When I first heard of Carole's illness, knowing her fairly well, I feared that, so disconsolate would she be, she would literally turn her back on the world; she'd climb into bed, face the wall, and go silent. I couldn't have been more wrong.

As she progressed (if you can call that progression) from walking to a walker to bed, from being perhaps the best conversationalist I know to being unable to get words out, Carole remained hopeful in her last weeks. Not about her life — she understood she would die soon — rather, hopeful for her sons and for her husband, about what she was leaving behind. And she was optimistic and curious about what lay ahead for her. Carole believed that after death there was life in the world to come.

As I wondered about my father, so did I wonder, in the sense of being awestruck, about Carole: What allowed a dying mother with two young sons and a loving husband to feel grateful and at peace? Why didn't bitter despair consume her? I should say that as Carole was obviously a believer (she happened to be a rabbi), my father was most manifestly not a person of belief.

Regardless, what is it with gratitude and where does it come from? Especially when it ought to be otherwise and we have every right to "rage against the light."

Viktor E. Frankl, reflecting on the teachings of the biblical Prophet Habakkuk, writes:

> The unconditional faith in an unconditional meaning may turn the complete failure into a heroic triumph. That this is possible has not only been demonstrated by many a patient in our days but also by a peasant who lived in Biblical times, somewhere in Palestine. His were granaries in the literal sense. And they were literally empty. And yet, out of unconditional trust in ultimate meaning and an unconditional faith in ultimate being, Habakkuk chanted his triumphant hymn:
>
> "Although the fig tree shall not blossom, neither shall fruit be in the vines; the labor of the olive shall fail, and the fields shall yield no meat; the flock shall be cut off from the fold, and there shall be no herd in the stalls. Yet I will rejoice in the Lord, I will joy in the God of my salvation."[5]

We learn from the prophet that faith can emerge from suffering. The kind of faith that, while it can't cut away the suffering, enables those who suffer (and those who witness it) not to despair unbearably. The kind of faith that lifts up rather than lets down. The kind of faith that can enable us to maintain when we can do no more. However it is, faith is only possible because of something else present beforehand — gratitude.

Our tradition understands gratitude as the fundamental human need to give thanks to God. A God-given capability provided each of us because we require it. For gratitude is more at the heart of who we are as human beings and as Jews than we perhaps understand.

Our tradition believes that gratitude is owed and manifested first as thanks to God for those blessings we can see and feel (we human beings need to have things close by and verifiable), those things that make life better and sometimes richer. Second, gratitude is owed to God as the Rabbis viewed it, for the gift of sacred time. When time is set apart, as it is this day, we are struck differently how limited it is, and maybe, how better to utilize our hours and days. And finally, gratitude — *hoda'ah* — is a glint of recognition of the small daily wonders in our lives (some call them miracles) we are not to take for granted, noticing them only when they are gone.

But it all goes deeper than this even. For our word for giving thanks, *l'hodot/todah*, means also "to admit," "to confess," "to acknowledge," as well as "to express gratitude." By thanking someone — God or one of God's creatures — for what they have done for us, we admit that we require their gift to make us whole. In other words, an acknowledgement of gratitude is an admission of our incompleteness.

It goes further. For at the root of the word for *gratitude* — the Hebrew root is *yud, daled, hey* — is the very origin of who we are. *Yud, daled, hey* doesn't simply mean "to admit," "to confess," "to acknowledge." Remarkably, as well, this is the original root word for Jew, *Yehudi*, which means that first of all a *Yehudi*, a Jew, is one who both confesses and gives thanks.

Should we be surprised then that each of these actions — confession and expressing of gratitude — is integral to this day? This day of *vidui*, of our confessions to God of our sins of transgression. This day of *hoda'ah*/gratitude as we grow (once the confession has begun) increasingly aware of life itself. This day when we, the *Yehudim*/Jews, draw near to confess and to give thanks. In order to be more complete and most human. More at home, you might say.

On Rosh Hashanah I spoke about the importance of forgiveness and the opportunity to restore our relationships with one another, especially with those closest to us, but also with all of humanity and even with our God.

The companion to forgiveness is gratitude. If the capability to forgive allows us to open our hearts much of the way, then gratitude keeps the heart open. Gratitude fuels generosity and lubricates a loving heart. If forgiveness allows us to restore our relationships, gratitude is the guardian of that restoration.

Gratitude helps us to wonder, love, and appreciate. What is in front of us every day as *this* day. Our gifts that daily are our portion, as they say. You don't need me to name them; you know them.

Yet gifts bequeathed us hardly guarantee our gratitude. Hence our tradition teaches that upon arising in the morning a Jew says, *Modei ani lefanecha*, instructing us to give gratitude its due expression. The expression in itself is a gift: if I don't feel grateful, I am aided in getting there.

Literally, after the mini-death and the major darkness of nighttime and sleep, God is acknowledged for the restoration of life. Night is about fear, and day about hope, and God brings us from one to the other. The expression of gratitude provides awareness, if it wasn't quite there yet, that we can't do everything on our own. We don't live by our own hand alone. We weren't brought into a life on our own and we don't remain in life on our own.

Is this recognition itself not sufficient now during these Days of Awe, these days of wonderment and appreciation, to feel simple gratitude for what we have? Now, most of all, when we Jews come forward to confess and to thank — and thereby are restored into life. Perhaps that's exactly why the tradition understands Yom Kippur as a small death so that we, fortunate to be in life, will live with gratitude in our hearts and words of thanks on our tongues.

WE JEWS HAVE OLD EYES
Rosh Hashanah, September 17, 2004

After explosions devastated Middle School No. 1 in Beslan, Russia, in September 2004, investigators cautiously moved through the building to figure out exactly what had happened and why. In the school's library they discovered that various sections of the wooden floor had been pried up and removed and then put back well before the terrorists took over the school. This occurred, the investigators determined, weeks and perhaps months before the attack, maybe even during seemingly innocuous summer renovations at the school. That is apparently when the terrorists had hidden their weapons and other equipment necessary for their onslaught.

Hiding their weapons well before the attack enabled the terrorists to move in with precision and alacrity, and once in the building, to force their hostages to place explosives and to build barricades to forestall Russian forces.[6] That many children and others would die amid the horrific destruction was something the terrorists had obviously calculated well beforehand. In fact, that was the plan: to kill, to maim, to terrorize. No strategy was necessary once they got there — just good, thorough planning in advance.

Have we not been here before?

September has become a season of fear. We wonder: what will happen next, when and where and to whom? But fear and a sense of things spinning out of control aren't confined to one season or one place.

For we have — there is no other way to say it — a gathering jihad before our eyes. What we saw in Beslan, we saw in Bali; what we saw in New York City, we saw in Madrid; what we saw in Jerusalem, we saw in Moscow. What we saw in Jakarta, we will surely see more of: the massacre of many more innocents, either at the edges of the Muslim world or at the heart of the perceived enemy of the jihadists.

I don't want to be misunderstood or misquoted. Let me be quite clear. When I refer to "at the edges of the Muslim world," I mean specifically the fringes of Islam, the poisoned place from which a cult of death, fuelled by a radical version of Islam and an intense hate for Jews and the West, sends its shock troops out to terrorize and to wreak havoc.

And while they come from the periphery of the large world of Islam, these terrorists aren't fringe in their aim, nor in their capability, nor in their intelligence. This cult of death won't morph into a Good Neighbor Society if the West becomes more modest and less "boorish" in its ways. Or, for that matter, if Israel turns over the keys to the entirety of the West Bank. Or to all of the land of Israel. This cult of death won't disappear until it's been destroyed.

I wish it were otherwise and I wish I could speak of different matters on a day that celebrates life and beginnings and possibility. I would prefer, as well, not to sound like a broken record about terrorism, evil, and Israel, about Yasser Arafat and Radical Islam. Even for me, it's sometimes too much. Someone who knows me well says, "Well, it's in your bones."

I wish that were the only place it was. The problem is that it's in front of our eyes, this gathering storm of hatred and horror. And while we pursue the pleasures and routines of an apparently safe life, we and everyone else, it gathers its forces and its fuel. Our pleasures and privileges dull us from seeing what we prefer to wish away. In 2004, *New York Times* columnist David Brooks wrote:

> We should be used to this pathological mass movement by now. We should be able to talk about such things. Yet when you look at the Western reaction to the Beslan massacres, you see people quick to divert their attention away from the core horror of this act, as if to say: We don't want to stare into this abyss. We don't want to acknowledge those parts of human nature that were on display in Beslan. Something here, if thought about too deeply, undermines the categories we use to live our lives, undermines our faith in the essential goodness of human beings.[7]

It's understandable that we don't want to stare into the abyss of hatred. Who wants to look again and again at the wanton killings? Who wants to think about the kind of mind that would calculate how best to kill as many innocents as possible? Who wants to consider that it could happen close to home, especially if you believe that a non-judgmental stance of goodwill toward all will keep you safe?

While it is understandable for flawed creatures to look away, it is no longer acceptable. Too many lives in too many places have been snuffed out. Too many lives have been irrevocably ruined by maiming and loss. That we ourselves may not know those cut down by the jihadists can't blind us from what they've wrought.

After all, we Jews — as Rabbi Leo Baeck famously put it at the gathering of an earlier storm — "We Jews have old eyes." By which Baeck meant that because we are an ancient people, one whose tradition is as alert as it is venerable, we get fooled less easily. Fooled less by our wishes, fooled less by our social needs, fooled less by those who count on averted eyes to do their work. Old eyes aren't so easily deceived.

The ancient Greeks also had old eyes that enabled them to peer deeply into human nature. They understood, as many of us in the West do not, that people are driven and shaped ultimately more by fundamental primordial human feelings and less by conditions and circumstance. Too much poverty, too little opportunity, too much despair, too little money — while these are important and often overwhelming, they are not necessarily as determinative, said the Greeks, as the feelings inside the human heart, the thoughts calculated by the human brain. These finally animate us and our actions.

The Greeks taught that human beings are most deeply driven by these primordial feelings of hatred, envy, fear, and self-interest. People and their leaders are most likely to go to war not because their bellies ache with hunger but because they may otherwise lose, or not augment, their sizable fortune, their influence, the power they possess.

In writing about September 11, 2001, Victor Davis Hanson, the classicist and expert on ancient Greek wars, says: "In a single morning Americans also rediscovered the Hellenic idea that it is not wars per se that are always terrible, but the people — Hitler, Tojo, Stalin, Saddam Hussein, and bin Laden — and their repugnant ideas who start them."[8]

What the Greeks knew, our own tradition of venerable eyes knew earlier: that human nature is deeply flawed and is possessed of impulses to do some good and some evil. Moreover, our nature is adept enough at disguise to pretend away the rumbling and rampaging feelings of jealousy and envy and hatred and fear — to hide these human impulses behind conditions or context, behind matters of how much money we have or don't have.

These things — money, education, poverty, context — are important. And they do shape us. But our tradition believes they shape us less than do the impulses ingrained at the very deepest part of human nature from the very earliest moments of human existence.

In those earliest moments — in fact, in only the second generation of human history — there was the first murder. Genesis describes that murder with a straightforward banality, almost as if we had been there before: "And it happened when they were in the field, that Cain rose up against his brother Abel — and killed him." In other words, Cain ambushed Abel without any warning. Just like that, he took down his own brother.[9]

Where did the will to destroy, a brother no less, come from? Why did Cain rise up and kill Abel so quickly, so nakedly, and without apparent warning?

Ah, but the warning was there. Of Adam's two oldest sons, Cain, the farmer, and Abel, the herdsman, God, without giving any rationale, moments before had judged only Abel's sacrificial offering satisfactory. Enraged, Cain became "very angry and his countenance fell" (Genesis 4:5). The Hebrew suggests that his face literally fell apart and crumbled, as would the face of a child besieged by sorrow and shock.

And what does God do? Not much. "Why are you angry and why has your face fallen?" He asks Cain. "If you do well, will you not be accepted? And if you do not do well, sin is lurking at the door; its desire is for you, but you must master it" (Genesis 4:6–7).

At that point, does Cain then gather himself to master his urge to strike back? No, apparently not, for the demon of sin not only lies in wait but possesses his full body and full being, all the while he stares at his brother, Abel.

We have learned from earlier in Genesis that all human beings are of equal worth in God's eyes. Now we learn that, for better or worse, the opportunities and gifts given us are not of equal measure or reach. Whether God's partiality toward Abel is purposeful or not, it is real, it has permanent resonance, and it is consequential. We know, when we are willing to admit, that while human worth is distributed equally, everything else is not. Not opportunity. Not possessions. Nothing.

God (who knows why?) is arbitrary. Therefore so, too, is human experience. As author Karen Armstrong puts it, "Unless human beings can bring themselves to accept this early familial injustice and make their peace with it, they will remain fixed in vengeful patterns learned in childhood and will never progress to maturity and freedom."[10]

Hatred, jealousy, and anger are the primordial feelings that animate much of human existence. They're real, they're powerful, and they're necessary to master. Otherwise, first the face crumbles and then the world unravels.

But Cain didn't master these feelings; he didn't compose himself, neither inside nor on his face. Rather, "And it happened when they were in the field, that Cain rose up against his brother Abel — and killed him."

Was there no warning? Not explicitly, no, but in Cain's nature it was all there to see and foresee: the anger, the envy, the hatred against the very injustice of the world and therefore against the one — Abel — who seemed to be favoured by God.

What the Torah is drumming into us on this day of beginnings and possibility, I believe, is this: that while there are vast possibilities to be had, they aren't distributed equally, and the unfair distribution of what is good and possible in life animates, as from the very beginning, the primal human feelings that cause instability and unraveling, both on a small scale in personal life as well as on a large scale in public life. What was with Cain and Abel has always been and will always be as long there are human beings on this earth.

But the Torah also teaches that while the destruction wrought from acting on these feelings of jealousy and rage will play havoc in the community, and while this will engender alienation between the self and the other, as between the self and God, nonetheless, human beings can and must master the sin that crouches at the door. More than crouches — sometimes it stalks!

These old eyes provide deep knowledge. They allow us to see, perhaps best at moments like this when all seems open, something closer to the truth about the world and ourselves. These eyes allow us to be honest about what we've done and what we want to do, who we've hurt and how we've helped. These wizened eyes that peer through the lens of the liturgical and textural traditions of our people's experience can see the consequences of mastering, or not, the sin that crouches at the door — if we use them.

I don't mean to be so simplistic as to suggest that old eyes, their sights sharpened by prayer and learning, can alone eradicate sin, let alone terrorism. Rather, I would suggest this kind of sight-full wisdom makes us more vigilant to danger, it propels us to build communities of vibrancy and meaning, and has us on the alert to the nature of human nature, starting with our own primal feelings. Simply because, like it or not, human life of equal worth all the way around is not of equal weight in possibility and privilege. Our task is to come to terms with the gifts given us, to maximize them with hard work in service to God and others.

Consider what the High Priest in ancient days did as Yom Kippur approached. He first made expiation for himself, then for his household, and then for the whole community. Only then was there a chance at social stability. Only then was there the capability to recognize and contain those impulses that, if unchecked, make things unravel — and ironically and importantly, as we know from another dimension of the word *jihad*, through personal struggle to master the self.

Today, with the Temple long gone, with Rosh Hashanah and Yom Kippur having developed from sacrifice to reflection, from repentance by one High Priest to repentance by all Jews, our task remains the same: to seek Divine aid to contain the passions that rage and bring trouble; and to seek Divine help to imbue our humanity with the sense of God's awesomeness so that something like goodness, or at least modest decency, might prevail — this, even as iniquity, will always be real, and injustice and imbalance always about us.

Finally, just this: the high priest, as he would emerge from the Holy of Holies in the Temple as Yom Kippur was to begin, would say a special prayer for those in ancient Israel who lived at heightened risk from natural catastrophes — a prayer that "their homes might not become their graves." These ancient words were intended to anticipate trouble that could come at any time, expected or not — a natural catastrophe or a human-made one. A reminder that any place, including a school, we might say, could become a graveyard.

We are vulnerable, always. As we feel our vulnerability, both in our daydreams and in our nightmares, we intuitively understand what the high priest was saying.

And so on this day, especially, we would ask God that our homes and our schools, our places of worship and our places of work, wherever we are and wherever anyone is, that they may they be places of safety and security, protected from any inhumane passions of hatred and evil. And may our old eyes be alert to human nature and human-made horror, that the former may be constrained so that the latter can't gather forces. That is our simple prayer now as we ask to be written and sealed into the Book of Life.

SURFING AGAINST THE TIDE: JUDAISM AND THE INFORMATION AGE
Rosh Hashanah, September 25, 1995

Over the years you and I have learned to level with one another, especially at this wonderful Rosh Hashanah service. Let's do so again now. Let's acknowledge from the start the overriding concern before the *Yom Tovim*. It has nothing to do with what I or any other rabbi might speak about, or for how long; it has nothing to do with whether Cantor Maissner might be in good voice (some of us wouldn't know, anyway!). No, it's more serious than all of that.

The real concern before the *Yom Tovim*, of course, is with tickets. "Have I taken care of the tickets, already?" "Are tickets for dues a fair way to go?" "How dare they deny my six-year-old a ticket when I claim he's eight!" And so on.

Speaking of tickets, by the way, and I can admit this now, the first couple of years I was here I had trouble getting in the door on *yontif*. You see, it didn't occur to me that I would need a ticket, but as I tried to enter the Dewbourne entrance without one, I was stopped by the same usher for two years in a row. It was an innocent matter: I had never seen him before, and apparently neither had he ever seen me.

Now, in case you're wondering, I'm levelling with you, but surely not on the level that counts. For you and I know that the business of tickets isn't the real issue. It is, as the psychiatrists and their colleagues among us would say, the "presenting issue" that's easier to raise at the beginning before getting to more pressing concerns.

In this regard, then, a little story, about the late and immensely esteemed U.S. Supreme Court Justice Oliver Wendell Holmes. It seems that Justice Holmes was at times absent-minded. Once, while riding a train, he was asked for his ticket but couldn't find it. He searched everywhere — pockets, briefcase — but to no avail. Unable to find the train ticket, Holmes grew distressed.

The conductor, knowing the justice and his high reputation, told him not to worry. "Never mind, sir. When you find your ticket, I'm sure you'll mail it in."

Justice Holmes wasn't reassured. "Mr. Conductor," he replied, "you don't understand. The question is not 'Where is my ticket?' The question is 'Where am I going?'"

So let's speak this morning about the real matter: where are we going? I don't mean only as Jews but as a larger culture, and, most specifically, the impact of the culture, the society, on us as Jews, especially on the younger members among us. And since the question of where we are going addresses the future, I want to concentrate on only one matter, the very matter, the very reality, the very new culture, that dominates our unfolding future — the Internet and the Information Age.

Everywhere you go now, every conversation you have, every newspaper you read, television show you watch, job you do, future you try to imagine, what pops up everywhere, seemingly omnipresent, maybe omniscient, is the Internet.

Think for a moment about what the Internet does: it makes a huge planet much smaller; it makes our limited horizons vaster; it brings us into close contact with people we'll never meet; and it provides community when you're alone. What could be more impressive than that?

Think for another moment about what the Internet accomplishes: it brings information and more information — any kind of information one might conceivably need — quickly, conveniently, cheaply, without much regard for the usual obstacles of class, money, contacts. Anyone with access to the necessary hardware has access to this whole Information Age. What could be more impressive than this? Well ... let's think.

Listen first to what Clifford Stoll says. Stoll is one of the early online people. He is a security expert on the Internet, celebrated for cracking a prominent cyber-spying ring, among other things. Stoll has been online since you could be there and is also well known as an astronomer. He begins his book *Silicon Snake Oil* with the following reflection:

> Me, an Internet addict? Hey — I'm leading a full life, with family, friends, and a job. Computers are a sideline, not my life.
>
> Jupiter is rising in the east, looking down on the Connecticut farm where I'm vacationing. On one side, a forest; on the other, a cornfield. Three guys are talking about the Knicks in the next room; in the kitchen, several women are buttering popcorn. One of them just called my name. But I don't care.
>
> Fingers on the keyboard, I'm bathed in

the cold glow of my cathode-ray tube, answering e-mail. While one guy's checking the sky through binoculars, and another's stuffing himself with popcorn, I'm tapping out a letter to a stranger across the continent. My attention's directed to the Internet.

Tonight, twenty letters want replies, three people have invited me to chat over the network, there's a dozen newsgroups to read, and a volley of files to download. How can I keep up?

I see my reflection in the screen and a chill runs down my spine. Even on vacation, I can't escape the computer networks.

I take a deep breath and pull the plug.[11]

You know where I'm going with this. And especially if you know my history with computers, VCRs, voice mail — anything vaguely technological that requires reading an instruction Bible — you might think I'm cowed by the technology, intimidated into dumbfoundedness by the six-year-olds who operate these things with ease. Therefore, any criticisms are tainted by my own inadequacies. And you would be correct.

However, let me make something else clear. My criticisms, my skepticism, even to a degree my own incompetence (which is more resistance than incompetence), are born of something else: an understanding of the vast difference between gathering and exchanging information and thinking; the gap between smart machines and intelligent people; and the gulf between being used by technology and using technology wisely.

Look, this is the Information Age and computers are now what the wheel, the printing press, the combine once were, and that won't change. And there are significant benefits. So I'm not saying — and now I wish to speak most directly to the children here — I'm not saying don't use computers, stay offline. Rather, I'm saying, be cautious: use the computer, but don't make it your world, don't make it into something you worship or treasure.

You see, your world — our world as Jews — isn't about collecting data; it's about pursuing learning. It isn't about exchanging information or playing games on a machine; it's about thinking. Your world, our world, isn't centred on a screen, however miraculous it appears, but on a text, a sacred text that speaks to us of the miraculous gift of life.

I ask you very seriously, speaking not as a Luddite but as a thinking person: for all the benefits of being online, of having e-mail, of having access to the vast worlds of information, what good is all of that actually?

What does the Information Age tell us about what really matters? How does it help us live with purpose? How does it help us know God, know one another, know ourselves?

Clifford Stoll was recently asked the following question by an interviewer:

Q. Why is it that if I go home at night and sit down in front of the computer, I can't get up again before bedtime? Why can't I put it aside and read a book?

A. It's like switching from sweetened candy to vegetables. We all know that the vegetables are good for us and candy isn't but it's real easy to sit around and chew on candy for an hour. The result when you're done is you've lost that ability to eat vegetables. And you've gained no nutrition.[12]

And so I must ask all parents: would you, do you, allow your children a diet of mostly candy and sweets? Of course not. As loving and thinking parents, you take your children's nutritional needs seriously.

But what about their intellectual nutrition? What about our children's needs to learn to think, to reflect, to build lives on a solid foundation of knowledge and wisdom? Would you — would we — dare build that on the mushy and chewy foundation of intellectual candy?

Well, to a great degree that's what's happening. And that's my problem, our problem, with computer networks and the information highway: they simply "cheapen the meaning of actual experience,"[13] as Clifford Stoll has said. They can't teach how to perceive or know the world, they can't teach how to act in the world, and they can't teach obligations and community and dignity and grace. For all the benefits the Internet affords, it literally doesn't mean anything.

The historian Haym Soloveitchik makes this observation with regard to the difference between knowledge and information: "Knowledge [is] an attainment, something that has been wrested personally from the sources. Information, on the other hand, [is] something merely obtained, passed [along] like a commodity ..."[14]

It goes without saying that for Judaism, knowledge is the starting point of moral education, that is, "imparting the lesson of a reality deeper than the one actually perceived ..."[15] And so it should come as no surprise that when the Rabbis were asked what really is the purpose of learning scripture, they responded: "The function of wisdom is to do repentance and good deeds, so that [a person] should not study Torah — and then go and kick his father and his mother and his teacher."[16]

In this regard, please remember something crucial. Although

both learning scripture and operating on the Internet are intellectual endeavours in the broad sense, there is an important distinction: study of a sacred text evokes compassion, enriches one's emotional life, and makes clear what is important in life. It is instructive that Jewish law mandates that when in trouble sell the Torah. No kidding: if you require money to redeem hostages, sell the Sefer Torah. If there is an impoverished orphan girl who requires money to get married, sell the Sefer Torah to get her a dowry!

So knowledge, like information, isn't an end. But unlike information, knowledge — cultivating one's mind and responses through exposure to sacred text — most often leads to wisdom and most often results in doing right. Again, should we not ask, can sitting in front of a computer screen do the same?

I never tire of reiterating the rabbinic assertion that the intellect is an instrument of sanctification. The Rabbis intended by this assertion that the learning of sacred texts hones our thinking and heightens our appreciation of God. And, just maybe, it elevates our actions.

How can we not say and know, then, that the difference between thinking and knowledge and collecting and exchanging information is vast? Only this one last thing: we've been here before. We've been exposed to and tempted by toys before — toys and foolish things that distract from what matters.

The Talmud records the following discussion between the Jewish sages of the day and their Roman counterparts. The Jewish elders in Rome were asked, "If your God has no desire for idolatry in this world, why does he not destroy the idols?"

They replied, "If people worshipped things unnecessary to the world, He would do so, but they worship the sun, the moon, the stars, and the planets. Should He destroy this universe on account of fools?"[17]

Let us enjoy what we've been given — our lives in this remarkably interesting world. And let us do so with wisdom and in knowledge of what is significant and what is not.

JOY AND ANXIETY
Holy Blossom Temple Bulletin, September 15, 1995

Abraham Joshua Heschel (1907–1972) was a descendant of Hasidic nobility on both sides of his family. In his book *A Passion for Truth*, he writes of the two roots of his soul, each a compelling influence over him, each struggling within him for pre-eminence.

Mezbizh, a small town in Ukraine where Hasidism was founded, stood for joy. Kotzk, a town not far away, was about anxiety. Mezbizh was associated with the Baal Shem Tov, the originator of the joy of Hasidism; Kotzk was about Menachem Mendel, the Kotzker Rebbe, a daunting and severe figure.

Each town and each Hasidic approach had shaped Heschel's forbearers. In turn they shaped him. Heschel writes about these two powerful influences:

> [In my adult life] I realized that, in being guided by both the Baal Shem Tov and the Kotzker, I had allowed two forces to carry on a struggle within me. One was occasionally mightier than the other. But who was to prevail, which was to be my guide? Both spoke convincingly, and each proved right on one level yet questionable on another.
>
> Was it good to live with one's heart torn between the joy of Mezbizh and the anxiety of Kotzk? I had no choice: my heart was in Mezbizh, my mind in Kotzk.

> I was taught about inexhaustible mines of meaning by the Baal Shem; from the Kotzker I learned to detect immense mountains of absurdity standing in the way. The one taught me song, the other silence. The one reminded me that there could be a heaven on earth, the other shocked me into discovering Hell in the alleged Heavenly places in our world.[18]

The churning tension created inside Heschel by two dramatically different influences inhabits us all, sometimes quietly, sometimes not. These coming Days of Awe inevitably make this strain between our joys and anxieties uncomfortably real.

For many people this grows acute as the Holy Days approach; some are only so struck at a particular moment in the ten days; others, perhaps working hard to pay no mind to the goings-on, still feel a vague and disquieting pull from within and without.

Indeed how can any of us not know this tension at this time of year? The Days of Awe are as much about the joy and beauty and meaning of life, as the Baal Shem Tov dwelt on, and no less about the anxiety and struggle and yes, evil, as the Kotzker insisted.

The purpose of the Holy Days is not to resolve this tension but to recognize it. By recognizing our joys and our troubles, we inexorably bring ourselves back to our families and friends, to our community and to our God. Is this not where we belong?

UNDERSTANDING DESPAIR
Kol Nidre, September 24, 1993

I wish to approach what I will say tonight in the spirit of this brief but telling anecdote in the life of Avraham Yehoshua Heschel, the Apter Rav:

One day Rabbi Heschel, he the great-great-grandfather of the important twentieth-century theologian, received a visitor, a woman, as the story goes, known too well apparently for her conduct. Whatever people of loose and malicious tongues say about such a woman, they said about her. She approached Avraham Yehoshua Heschel as he sat among his disciples.

"Rabbi," she began, "I need your help, your intervention for me in heaven. I want to repent, I want to change my ways. Please help me."

The Apter Rav, known for his gentle and gracious ways, responded with anger. "You dare come to me? Shameless woman, you have the temerity to appear before me? Don't you realize that I have eyes to see and that my eyes see into your innermost soul?"

To prove his words, the Apter Rav proceeded to reveal certain things she had done. The woman blushed and then answered gently and sadly, "I don't understand you, Rabbi. Why must you reveal in public what God Himself prefers to keep secret?"

Later, the Apter Rav reflected on what he had done, troubled to his core. He said to his disciples who had witnessed his explosion, "This encounter has humbled me. It will remain a turning point in my life. It made me see that I was on the wrong path, for I chose *din*, judgment, over *rachamim*, compassion. [Our task] is not to judge other human beings, not to condemn others, but to understand them."[19]

I tell this story not for its own sake exactly but rather for what it suggests. There are times when, reflecting on life — its travails, complexities, sins, and secrets — we do so in compassion and understanding, not in judgment. Tonight is one such time. Let God judge, if He must. Let us understand.

Joyce Carol Oates wrote in a *New York Times* essay in 1993 that of the predominant human sins — anger, lust, avarice, envy, and so on — each carries with it an antidote, each has a way toward repair and forgiveness.[20] These are sins against others, sins eventually rather easy to be seen and judged. And therefore, because of the public nature of anger and the rest, because of the possibility of witnessing, judging, and sorting things out, forgiveness is possible.

However, wrote Oates, there is one human sin different from the others. This sin has no antidote; it has no clear path to repair. Unlike the other major sins, it doesn't impact in a direct way on other people. This sin is kept largely hidden from the view and judgment of others. This is the sin of despair.

Oates's frame of reference is the Catholic Church and its perceived frustration, even anger, at the person in despair. But, of course, we shouldn't be so confident to assume that her insight doesn't also apply to the synagogue, to Jews as well as to Catholics, to we who gather here this night.

Let me spell out this insight and its implications. Organized religion, tied up with the performance of ritual and ceremony, ever ready to proscribe ethics and quote scripture, by its very nature objectifies human experience. The result is the insistence that what happens out there in the world is of unquestionably greater importance than what goes on in here in the human spirit. In other words, despair, the least aggressive of sins, may be the most threatening to institutions that do better with public success than with private angst.

Now to ourselves. What Oates observes may explain, in significant part, the Jewish response to suicide.

We know that Judaism's argument with suicide is theological: it is expressly forbidden because life is only God's to give and God's to take. But in outlawing suicide, Jewish tradition may be responding to something far more visceral than the rational thinking of theology. This may be the human response of anger and fury — anger at the loved one who takes his or her own life, anger complicated and thickened by guilt or even a sense of failure; fury over what was so near and yet so unknown, the internal life of an intimate with whom we shared less than we knew.

Tradition, then, far more conversant and at ease with the performance of public ritual and the public face of the individual, far less at ease with private angst, private failure, the private face of the individual, declared the suicide "out of bounds." Literally out of bounds — to be buried only at the edge of or outside the Jewish cemetery, the mourners not obligated to normal mourning customs and duties. That this harsh response is invariably muted, even ignored, across the board by Jews doesn't temper tradition's severe decree. It doesn't hide the fundamental response to suicide: it is forbidden and most often judged with fear and contempt.

But my subject tonight isn't suicide. Rather it is that which, like suicide, is out of bounds, normally kept hidden from our view — difficult to speak about, but more than that, difficult to listen to. I'm referring to the private angst of despair. Whether the sin is in having the despair, or in not listening to one's despair, or in others not responding to that despair, we'll forgo for a moment. Let's speak about despair, bringing it into bounds, at least on this night and maybe beyond.

We do so because Yom Kippur begins in despair. The despair that, for all the good we have attempted to do, for all the decency we have learned, for all the acts of ugliness we have restrained ourselves from, that our lives don't add up, that our merit is not that noteworthy, that God might judge us harshly, not in compassion.

So on a night when tradition bids us to acknowledge despair, let us indeed do so. Not so much to gain merit but because tonight we are bid to afflict our souls, we are compelled to penetrate our private worlds, as we reckon with who we are. These actions are the first steps away from our despair.

We do this, you and I, whether we know despair or not, because if we don't now, we surely will again. Because there are those in our midst, perhaps in our own families, who feel what is difficult to articulate, difficult to listen to, easy to judge. Because, like the sins we confess tonight in the plural, despair, too, is our collective responsibility.

You and I together know the despair

- of aching loneliness;
- of being without friends or family or security or community or respect or contentment;
- of being locked in a marriage without love;
- of feeling life's frailty, of always being uncertain of what will be;
- of corrosive jealousy and unending hatred;
- of watching a loved one endure ravaging illness;
- of losing a loved one, wondering constantly if the ache, the awful ache, will ever be gone;
- of never having the material wants everyone else seems to have achieved or been given;
- of once knowing those material wants and then losing them;

- of life seeming to grow more and more complicated, less and less easy as we grow older;
- and of all our own private despairs, unknown
  to others, perhaps even to those most close.

I can't claim to know the despair of others, only my own when it's come upon me. But I do know the religious response to despair. I do know how we're to understand it on this night most of all.

We understand the religious response to despair in three ways. First, think about what the Bible teaches. When Israel fled from Egypt as a bedraggled band of hardened slaves, God made known His presence and saving power by way of a spectacular and immediate miracle: the parting of the waters so that Israel could make their way through. Once across that sea, Israel immediately gave testimony to that experience, pledging eternal loyalty: "The Lord will be our king forever," they sang. They were impressed.

But it didn't last — neither the loyalty nor the power of the miracle. Within three days Israel was ravenous, thirsty, frustrated, and in despair. They were furious at Moses, telling him that Egypt was far better than this and that they should never have left there.

What had God done wrong? Everything. He had provided Israel with a powerful miracle, but nothing of their more fundamental needs: how to have food, shelter, safety, community, love, purpose; how to be a human being in a complicated world; how to live with disappointment and despair; and how to find satisfaction and contentment. Without these more basic religious needs provided, Israel was vulnerable to expecting only miracles.

God learned. You can almost feel Him changing tactics at this point, from miracles that impress but don't sustain to commandments and duties that sustain and eventually impress in their own way. Human beings, perhaps especially when in distress, cope best through performing small acts of meaning rather than being bowled over by overwhelming religious experiences.[21]

The third way to respond religiously to despair is taught by Avraham Yehoshua Heschel, the Apter Rav. There is something in us, as there was in Heschel, that finds judgment easier than compassion. Consider this: did Heschel fear being tainted by this woman, not so much by her reputation as I think the story's tellers would have us believe but rather, as I suspect, by her despair? That her despair of having lowered herself, of knowing the dark side of life, of having no status or dignity or love was something Heschel couldn't face? Couldn't face because something of her was a part of him. And so he exploded in anger, afraid of what he saw in the mirror, pushing her away.

As there was something of this woman in Avraham Yehoshua Heschel, is there not something of him in us? When he saw into her soul, did he not see into his own soul? Did he not judge the woman because he judged himself?

But Heschel obviously learned. Looking at his disciples' faces, he knew what he had done. I suspect that when the afore-mentioned story of the woman speaks of his "humbling," it refers to Heschel's realization that he really was no better than the woman; perhaps at that moment he understood he was nowhere near as good as she.

In his humbling, in his recognition of himself in the outcast woman, in his stunned awareness that his despair — more disguised, more civilized, more acceptable to society — was greater than the despair of his visitor, Heschel knew compassion: for himself and for the woman. And then he chose the right path, responding to affliction, to despair, with compassion.

May we do the same. In this circle of community and care, may we respond, publically and privately, to affliction and despair with compassion. May we acknowledge that to feel despair is surely not sinful but to pretend that it doesn't exist, indeed, is a sin. May this be our vow tonight, tomorrow, and beyond.

HERODOTUS AND HISTORY
Yom Kippur, September 15, 1994

Herodotus, it is often said, is the "father of history," the first and most prominent in a long line of ancient Greek historians who shaped an approach to history still dominant in the Western world today. Neither these distinguished Greek historians nor the culture that produced them considered that history possessed any particular meaning. Herodotus and his colleagues recorded history and maintained a memory of the past for two essential purposes: to be inspired by past examples of ethical deeds, and to garner political insight that might assist or shed light on the present. Beyond this, history was presumed to offer no meaning, and its seekers shouldn't presume any lest they waste their time.

But if Herodotus was the founding father of history, as the West still largely knows it, then, as one historian, Yosef Hayim Yerushalmi, puts it, "the fathers [and mothers] of meaning in history are the Jews."[22] Unlike the ancient Greeks, Jews have, at least until the past century or two, never been interested in history, never been concerned with specific details or the exact recording of events, never worried much about chronology. In fact, as the Rabbis put it, *ein mukdam u'muchar baTorah* — there is no such thing as chronology in the Torah.

What the Rabbis were saying is: "History, chronology, that's only about human affairs. If that's all you pay attention to, you're going to come up wrong. You're going to miss, maybe even without a clue, what counts." What counts, they contended, is God's presence felt in history, in the affairs of human beings, in the events that give meaning and context to human life — and to death.[23]

What the Rabbis knew was that without memory there can be no meaning, and without meaning, memory is of vastly limited worth. So it's no accident that every important ritual event in Judaism recalls a specific past event, not for the purpose of recording history but rather in order to unpack, to relive, to retell the meaning and purpose of the original event.

The Rabbis weren't unsophisticated; in fact, quite the opposite. They were historians, but historians of meaning. They understood that ritual as simple recording rather quickly becomes the possession of a limited few archivists, but that ritual as reliving, as retelling, becomes remembering for the many. The former finds God entirely absent; the latter sees God as the force that gives meaning to memory.

And that is, of course, why we are here — to give meaning to our memories, those that surround us, haunt us, sustain us, and embrace us. Yizkor is a kind of reliving of our memories of those we loved and still do but who are more past than present — except now. Yizkor is, as well, a ritual of retrieving and retelling to ourselves the details, the moments of meaning and character. There can be no accident to what memory calls up now.

And Yizkor, as a ritual of remembering, brings us closer to loved ones, closer to our shared past, and closer to God who sustains us with our memories by the gift of meaning.

And now as God remembers, let us remember.

3

Israel: When Your Love Remains the Same and Your Views Change

PREAMBLE

I fell in love with Israel while I was there for seven weeks in the summer of 1970. Jerusalem and Tel Aviv, Hebron and Haifa, the kibbutz and the beach, the north, the south, even to the theatre to see the musical *Hair* — I went everywhere. Transfixed by the differences between life in the United States and that in Israel, I felt as if I'd gone to Mars that summer. I also felt very much at home.

My love for the country, typical of young North American Jews then, was fuelled by things that first took me by surprise and then just took me over: the tough and tender Israelis, the men and the women both; the still-hovering aura of the unexpected and the overwhelming victory in the Six Day War only three years earlier; Jerusalem, a place older than a young American could possibly fathom; and, as much as anything, the kibbutz, the idea and the place, still at the centre of Israeli life then. Nothing was more thrilling than to rise with the sun at 4:30, get out in the fields, and pick oranges and apples for hours while the day grew hot. I almost felt Israeli.

All I could do when I returned home at the end of August was to hole up for three days and consume Leon Uris's novel *Exodus*.

I was on fire from the summer and, once returned, forlorn to be back in a world bereft of Israel's significance and intensity.

I was eighteen that summer, Israel was twenty-two, and the young often have a thing for each other. My young love never left me, and over the decades it has ripened into an enduring love.

I've returned many times. I've lived in Jerusalem and have friends and family throughout the country. I've thought about making *aliyah* more than occasionally and have a small regret not having done so. My yearning to be in Israel never leaves me.

In the early 1970s, once I began to consider in earnest the vexing political matters embroiling Israelis and Arabs, my perspective was locked in with that of the left: novelist and journalist Amos Oz and peace activist and writer Uri Avnery were my lodestars, and eventually peace proponent and author David Grossman, too. I looked forward as much as anyone to Israel gathering its moral courage, as I was certain it must, and yielding land for peace. I took a back seat to no one in deriding the retrograde right of Menachem Begin and company.

From the early 1970s until the early 1990s, I sang the same tune as most everybody I knew. We were right, and time and facts would prove us so.

In September 1993, I joined the applause for the signing of the Oslo Accord. I hadn't read it, but if Israeli Prime Minister Yitzhak Rabin had extended his hand — however reluctantly — to Palestinian Liberation Organization (PLO) Chairman Yasser Arafat on the White House lawn, who was I to disagree? Anyway, more than anything, I wanted peace for Israel, and peace between Israelis and Palestinians. Who didn't?

But then things changed. Arafat, now ensconced in Gaza, stirred trouble and violence and breached agreements called for in Oslo.

If matters looked worrisome in 1994 and 1995, they got much worse in early 1996 when a spate of horrific bus bombings in Jerusalem, undeniably at the hand of Israel's ostensible peace partner, Mr. Arafat, reaped bloody carnage in the streets. Dozens were killed, the country badly shaken.

I, too, was shaken. It was then that I actually read the Oslo Accord. I wasn't so much stunned at what Rabin had signed as I was at my own willingness to shut my eyes in the hope that my wishes for peace would come true. I understood why Rabin had looked so grim that day with President Bill Clinton and Arafat in 1993. He'd had an idea about what he'd just done, even as he'd hoped for the best. I not only read Oslo; I read for the first time what the critics of Oslo had said. They seemed more in touch with reality than I did. It was sobering.

I knew then that I could no longer say what I once had because I no longer believed it. Of course, things were to grow worse with the onslaught of the Second Intifada, beginning in September 2000. More than ever, I felt compelled to speak differently from how I once had; I had no choice, since I had changed my mind in the face of a reality I'd wished away previously.

Still, none of what I've learned in the past twenty years or so has changed my mind about the requirement, practically and morally, of two states for two peoples. Whether it's achievable is another matter, but I do know it won't come from wishing it so.

The few sermons below, along with "A Second Chance" in "Where I Come From," the first part of this book, suggest how and why I came to change my mind about the possibilities for peace — at least for the time being, one should say.

KOL NIDRE AND TRUTH
Kol Nidre, September 25, 2012

The Kol Nidre appears to make little sense. First, with the exception of the last line or so, it's not a prayer. It's a legal formula, and a confusing and incoherent one at that. Next, the Sephardim assert that the vows annulled refer to last year's promises, while the Ashkenazim claim that the Kol Nidre cancels vows for this ensuing year. The confusion doesn't end there. Contrary to how things seem, the Kol Nidre is actually not chanted on Yom Kippur. It's said before the evening begins and isn't part of the service at all. In fact, this evening ought more properly to be called Erev Yom Kippur rather than Kol Nidre. Moreover, many medieval rabbis so detested the words that they got rid of the Kol Nidre — just threw it out. Early Reform rabbis did the same.

Sometimes the Kol Nidre is chanted once, sometimes twice, but normally three times. And should you bear down and read the text, its legalistic obtuseness will leave you cold. Furthermore, the obligations assumed in the vows — whether last year's or this year's — well, they do or they don't apply to the obligations between one person and another. And that's before we get to matters between ourselves and God.

So, all in all, the Kol Nidre seems a strange way to begin the holiest day of the year.

Yet tonight, once again, we are entranced. Those haunting sounds, like an undulating wave, wash over us, bathing our memories in its melodies. The intensity of which is such that when the *hazzan* finishes reciting the Kol Nidre, what happens next easily passes us by. But we shouldn't miss it. Immediately, we ask for forgiveness for all of our sins, which elicits God's response, *Vayomer Adonai el Moshe, salachti k'dvarecha* ("And God said to Moses, 'I have pardoned according to your request'").[1]

78

Why these words, "I have pardoned according to your request"? Words, by the way, lifted directly from the famous story of the spies in the Bible's Book of Numbers.

Remember those spies? Having been sent to assess the condition of the land and the strength of its inhabitants, the spies barely step foot in the Promised Land before turning right around! The task is too daunting, they say, and their fears go viral, spreading to their brethren who also turn tail.

Joshua and Caleb alone refuse the cover of numbers. No, the people aren't giants — we can take them, they proclaim. God has promised us this land, so let us go forward. But the larger Israelite community, having caught the fright of the majority, now recalls how good life was in Egypt.

God has had enough. "How long," He asks Moses, "will this people spurn me, how long will they have no faith in me despite all the signs I performed in their midst?" Moses then intercedes and somehow moves God from anger to acceptance. It's then and there — (Numbers 14:20) — that God says precisely the words we recite upon the conclusion of the Kol Nidre: *salachti k'dvarecha* — "I have pardoned according to your request."

Our question this night: why did the liturgical tradition intertwine the Kol Nidre with the story of the spies?

Our answer: human beings often vacillate between fear and courage, especially when it matters most. Escaping from the paralyzing clutches of fear and ignorance is no simple matter. At times, though, you don't have a choice. You must find and speak your truth. Caleb and Joshua knew that. God teaches us this. The Kol Nidre announces it.

What about us?

So this moment is for speaking that truth without regard for social cost. Because either your fears make you shy away from naming the fire before your eyes, in which case it will consume you, or your courage helps you rise up to speak truth and thereby have a chance to douse the fire before it becomes a storm.

Only Caleb and Joshua refused the cover of numbers. Will we?

And lest we forget, God and this day stand ready to help in truth-telling. And now to that truth. Now when the stakes are highest. For Israel and for the Jews.

The first truth: many Jews are in denial when it comes to the determination and the capability of the jihadists, allied with various forces, to destroy the State of Israel. That the current U.S. administration sloughs off this threat to Israel as an annoying political distraction, and that many otherwise well-meaning people wish to avert their eyes, should give us no comfort.

The first level of denial is psychological, as when you face a prospect too awful to take in. But the denial is more than that. It is also ideological.

Animating the liberal democratic West these days is the idea that nations and borders are antiquated carry-overs of the past couple of centuries and that one's primary allegiance now is to all peoples above one's own. This idea is compelling and has some evidence on its side. At its core this notion suggests that national security, patriotism, and defence of one's own are moving toward being unnecessary and even unhelpful in a global age; they are passé, even illiberal, in the new day.

But guess which particular people is vastly overrepresented in the promotion of this idea? And can you guess which is the one nation singled out every time as the prime example of such an antiquated age? None other than the Jewish state.

Worrisome to say the least. Maybe a pathology at work to say the worst.

The second truth: many Jews intuitively understand this situation but aren't accustomed to speaking up, especially if they don't feel in command of all the details. In the face of intimidation and social pressure, they grow fearful and quiescent.

Harvard professor of Yiddish literature Ruth Wisse tells of the start of the school term in 2008 that, while reviewing an assignment with a young woman, the student told Professor Wisse she was feeling guilty because of her work that fall for Barack Obama's campaign for the U.S. presidency.

Wisse assumed the student meant that her political work was taking a good deal of time from her studies, but she was quickly corrected. "No," said the student, "I'm feeling guilty because I'm working for Barack Obama, but I really support John McCain."

"If that's so," asked Wisse, "why are you working for Obama and not McCain?"

To which the student answered, "Because I wanted so badly to get along with my roommates and with everyone else."[2]

Amazing, isn't it, how the desire to conform trumps speaking one's mind?

Here is the third truth: if you go against the grain of the left/liberal Jewish consensus, especially if you're perceived as having influence, there may be a cost.

Let me tell you what happened in Orlando, Florida, in 1999. There, at the Union for Reform Judaism convention, the then Israeli deputy foreign minister, Yossi Beilin, the architect of the 1993 Oslo Accord with the PLO and a major foreign policy player in Jerusalem, gave the keynote speech.

It was a rousing, enthusiastic talk before several thousand leaders of Reform synagogues, in which Beilin assured his listeners that peace between Israelis and Palestinians was right around the corner — a new day of reconciliation was about to dawn. As he finished his speech, Beilin hit all the high emotional notes, and the roaring audience rose up and gave him a standing ovation.

I desperately wanted to disappear. I wasn't about to stand up — I knew enough to know that Beilin was way wrong — but I had hoped to avoid attention. Well, when virtually everybody else rises to their feet in enthusiasm, most glance around to make sure they have company. And if you're not part of the company, it's hard to hide.

I couldn't. I was easily noticed by friends and colleagues. One friend, a prominent rabbi, looked down at me, a combination of affection and disdain on her face. "Why are you spoiling our party?" she asked, annoyed and maybe a bit amused.

All I could do was mutter that Yossi Beilin was wrong. I then looked down at my feet.

I didn't say what I knew. I knew who Arafat was, I knew the worldview of the leadership of the PLO, I knew then the political strategy favoured by the Muslim Brotherhood. And I knew, strong as Israel was, that the Jewish state was in trouble. Why didn't my colleagues know this? Or maybe they did.

What happened in Orlando — a very small attempt at social and political intimidation — has happened in Toronto, as well, more than once and more than twice. I know what it means to be marginalized for what I say about Israel.

I've been told that Reform rabbis, after all, shouldn't speak about Israel and its enemies as I do. (As if "freedom of the pulpit" is only for one way of viewing the world.)

I don't see it as a matter of Reform or any other kind of rabbi, or left or right or centre, for that matter. Rather, it's a matter of telling the truth, at least as I'm best able to do. And knowing the difference between how we wish things were and how they really are. In this case the desire of Israel's enemies waxes hot still for its demise, while their capability to accomplish this increases almost weekly.

Once I refused to see this and sought the cover and comfort

of numbers. But by the late 1990s I began to understand Arafat's strategy as, in his words, a "stage by stage" destruction of the Jewish state — one turn diplomatic, next turn a military move, then another diplomatic one. And sooner, not later, you have Israel diminished, size-wise and politically, a sovereign, small nation on the run.

All the while I remained hopeful for a fair and secure two-state solution, a benefit for both sides. After all, what else will keep Israel both Jewish and democratic than living side by side a Palestinian state? I continue to believe and hope for this even, as with the majority of Israelis, I no longer believe it to be possible, at least in the foreseeable future.

About this wish of mine — over time the facts began to betray my wishes. As that occurred, I had a choice: remain silent and have more "friends" or speak and have fewer. As if there's a choice.

And while some Israeli policies and citizens have at times hardly helped things, the crux of the matter isn't that. The refusal to yield the Jews their history, their rights, part of their ancient land, is at the core of the matter. Yes, there are Palestinian moderates such as Sari Nusseibeh who seek compromise. But their numbers are small, their voices largely sidelined.

Of course, Israel is strong. More than ever, though, its enemies are strong and becoming stronger, a good deal more strategically at the advantage. Does anyone believe the Arab Spring is anything but winter now? Does anyone believe the Muslim Brotherhood is of a moderate inclination, interested in incremental change? Does anyone believe Tehran is anything but serious and near capable in its desire to annihilate the Jewish state?

More often than I care to say, speaking as I do tonight gets me called "right wing." Let's be clear what such name-calling (almost always out of my earshot!) is about. It's nothing less than an attempt to place somebody who so speaks beyond the pale politically — their view of the world deemed irrelevant at best, deserving of demonization, if need be. It's an attempt at a political takedown.

Just so we understand: I speak, in the American context, as a Jack Kennedy, Scoop Jackson, Bill Clinton, Joe Lieberman Democrat, a believer in the exercise of a strong America abroad, including the defence of Israel, but I am moderately left on economic matters and libertarian/liberal on social issues. In the Canadian context I don't quite have so ready a political home, but I do have an abiding admiration for Canadian Prime Minister Stephen Harper.

Now to truth number four, the most painful one. That is, America is no longer a resolute and unwavering defender of Israel. President Obama's wavering support of Israel isn't a matter of a personality clash — Barack and Bibi as oil and water — but an antipathy that Obama has toward Israel, one long visible and now all the more so. Yes, we know the Obama administration claims unprecedented support for Israel, but these are military commitments made in the George W. Bush era and still in force today.

Obama's worldview is simply a different one from those of his predecessors: America is no more exceptional than Japan; Israel is but one of many nations; the Muslim Brotherhood and the Iranian mullahs are best engaged rather than isolated and defeated.

Canada currently stands essentially alone in the world as the defender of the State of Israel. Prime Minister Harper towers above the crowd — alone. Inspiring as are Harper and Canada, it's hardly sufficient. Strong as Israel is, alone, it can't ensure its survival without the shoulder-to-shoulder support of the United States.

All of this is difficult to say out loud. All very stark. All very true.

In a moment, then, the fifth and final truth.

First, though, let's look at why all this matters so much, how the threats of a highly militarized Iran, joined by various emboldened jihadist forces inadvertently aided by a distracted and somewhat indifferent American administration, fits within a larger context of the state of the Jewish people.

Here I borrow from what Charles Krauthammer observed in the late 1990s in *The Weekly Standard*:

> The return to Zion is now the principal drama of Jewish history. What began as an experiment has become the very heart of the Jewish people — its cultural, spiritual, and psychological center, soon to become its demographic center as well. Israel is the hinge. Upon it rest the hopes — the only hope — for Jewish continuity and survival.[3]

In other words, the obvious: the combination of demography, the birth rate, and the assimilation in North America means that Israel is now the exceptional part of the Jewish world. It alone possesses the power, the numbers, the substance affording Judaism the ability to survive and thrive. Without Israel the Jewish world, the Jewish people, it would all prove radically different in less than a generation, maybe two.

Our final truth isn't political, psychological, or intellectual. It's a religious truth, the most important one. When God says, *salachti k'dvarecha*, He is saying, "I want a future with you, the Children of Israel. I want this future for you. Despite your fears and subsequent behaviour, I forgive you. Now is the time to look to the future." God is saying, "Caleb and Joshua will bring you to that future and to your land. Like them, be strong and of good courage."

God is now saying to us, in effect: the Kol Nidre will rock your boat. It will slice in two your desire to conform at the cost of speaking truth. Listen. Listen carefully and deeply to the Kol Nidre, to that which you hear within and you see without.

As for us, the Kol Nidre's haunting melody keeps us in mind of what's most important. That's why the Rabbis, try as they did, couldn't keep the Kol Nidre away from Yom Kippur — the Jews wouldn't allow it. And that's why the night is called what it is, and why, despite appearances, ultimately, there is nothing confusing about the Kol Nidre: it speaks not in the words but in the melody, the deepest and most abiding religious truths, and it does so loudly. And it helps our truths ring loudly within.

Here is that truth: if at Rosh Hashanah, arrayed before the Divine Judge, we are fearful, if we don't know then what the year will bring, if we feel ourselves at the mercy of the Divine Court, then the Kol Nidre announces a very different kind of day. Not at all a day of fear.

The Sefat Emet, the great Hasidic master of the late nineteenth century, believed this evening and this day gives us confidence, even credibility. Like a nursing mother, Yom Kippur provides nourishment for the rest of our days, literally encouraging us toward claiming our future. Today is a day, the Sefat Emet taught, when we know exactly who we are and what is our truth. *Hayom t'amtzeinu*: today is the day to renew our courage. Today is the day to be confident in what we know to be true.

This is what the Kol Nidre announces. This is its truth. This is our truth. Now we name the world as it is and as it must be.

Does not the Kol Nidre, said tonight, coursing through us still, make all the sense in the world?

Now let us make sense of the world. Let us speak the truth as we know it. Unbowed, unafraid, in service of a bright future for Israel, and for our people.

NO MESSIAHS, PLEASE, JUST PEACE
March 20, 2010

Some weeks ago a prominent public square in Ramallah in the West Bank was dedicated to the memory of a woman named Dalal Mughrabi, one of the terrorists who killed thirty-eight Israeli civilians and injured many more in the Coastal Road massacre in 1978 on the road from Haifa to Tel Aviv.

Who was in attendance at the square in Ramallah during the ceremony? The president of the Palestinian Authority (PA), Mahmoud Abbas, along with the prime minister of the PA, Salam Fayyad. In particular, Mr. Fayyad's presence is worth remarking on, since he is a respected international figure who has bona fides as an economist and diplomat. He enjoys a reputation as a mature and wise political leader, someone with whom the Israelis can talk and negotiate. As far as we know, neither Abbas nor Fayyad protested the public honouring of the memory — and the deed — of the Coastal Road massacre terrorists.

Another dedication took place not very far from Ramallah, this one just last week in the Jewish quarter of Jerusalem. The Hurva Synagogue, destroyed in the 1948 war by the Arab Legion, has been for these sixty-plus years not much more than a shell. In ruins for decades and finally now rebuilt, it was rededicated last week.

How does the Palestinian Authority, run by Abbas and Fayyad, respond when, in the wake of the rededication, rumours are deliberately spread that the rededication of the synagogue is a harbinger of the Jews' plan to destroy the Dome of the Rock on the Temple Mount and to build in its place the third Jewish Jerusalem Temple? Again there is silence on the part of the Palestinian leadership, and hence the "days of rage" in the Palestinian streets last week.

What was the response from the United States to the synagogue rededication in Jerusalem and the spreading of false
rumours to incite people in the Palestinian streets? Did *New
York Times* columnist Thomas Friedman write something and
then go on television's *Meet the Press* to say to Hamas and Salam
Fayyad: "Stop driving drunk! Friends tell one another not to
drive drunk. You can't go out and incite your people. Otherwise
you're destroying the peace process." No, that didn't happen.

Did White House adviser David Axelrod, apparently burdened with great sorrow, also appear on *Meet the Press* and say:
"It's high time for the Palestinian leadership to get serious once
and for all about peace." No, that didn't happen, either.

Did U.S. Secretary of State Hillary Clinton ring up Abbas
or Fayyad and harangue either one in a forty-five-minute verbal
slap in the face? No to that, as well.

Of course, another matter took place last week: a major
insult, a foolish announcement that by virtue of its timing caused
embarrassment for the Americans and for the Israelis.

During a visit to Israel by U.S. Vice-President Joe Biden, a
mid-level bureaucratic staffer in the Israeli Interior Ministry
announced the fourth step out of seven in a process of approval to
build sixteen hundred new housing units in Ramat Shlomo. This
area is in northern Jerusalem between French Hill and Ramot,
across the 1949 armistice line, across the 1967 border, and now
in an area of Jerusalem more northern than eastern, far from
Arab neighbourhoods but nonetheless in East Jerusalem, a section of town everyone knows will be part of Jerusalem in any kind
of peace settlement in exchange for appropriate land swaps. The
international community knows this, the European Union knows
this, the Americans know this, and the Palestinians know this.

So this mid-level staffer makes the announcement. Everyone agrees that Benjamin Netanyahu didn't know about it

beforehand, that he should have known about it, and that this was incompetence and stupidity on the part of the Israeli government (and/or an attempt by the interior minister to force Netanyahu's hand, which isn't clear). And everyone also knows this was and is fully consistent with the agreement made last summer by Obama and Netanyahu to freeze any settlement building in the West Bank, with the deliberate exclusion of any freeze on Jewish building in Jerusalem. Again, both were explicitly agreed to by the Israelis and the Americans.

In this regard let us remember: no Israeli prime minister, not from the left or right, not from Likud or Labour, has or would forgo building in the Jewish sections of Jerusalem. And none — not one prime minister — has agreed to a freeze on settlements in the West Bank until Netanyahu. So, following the insult to the U.S. vice-president comes, as it should, a full apology by the Israeli prime minister, both to the vice-president and the president. Offered and accepted.

But then one day later, almost out of the blue (but not really), David Axelrod makes his statements on *Meet the Press*, and Hillary Clinton delivers her verbal slap to Netanyahu. Both, quite clearly, directed by President Obama.

Why did the Americans ratchet things up when they knew there was an agreement not to freeze housing in Jerusalem, that Netanyahu has gone further than any other Israeli prime minister on the settlements, that this was an inadvertent insult, and that an apology had been made and accepted?

Some say the U.S. president has a habit of accommodating those with whom he should be toughest, all the while roughing up his closest allies. Maybe. Others say the Americans were just waiting for an opportunity to realign the relationship between the United States and Israel. Maybe. Or, at least as likely by the look of things, this was a chance to realign the Israeli internal political alignment, to push out the right wing of Netanyahu's government and bring in those more or less on the left (Tzipi Livni and others). The Americans, angling for an Israel government more to their liking, sought to pressure Netanyahu, not from his right but rather from his left.

About all of the aforementioned the journalist Yossi Klein Halevi writes:

By placing the issue of building in Jewish neighborhoods in East Jerusalem at the center of the peace process, President Obama has inadvertently challenged the Palestinians to do no less.

Astonishingly, Obama is repeating the key tactical mistake of his failed efforts to restart Middle East peace talks over the last year. Though Obama's insistence on a settlement freeze to help restart negotiations was legitimate, he went a step too far by including building in East Jerusalem. Every Israeli government over the last four decades has built in the Jewish neighborhoods of East Jerusalem; no government, let alone one headed by the Likud, could possibly agree to a freeze there. Obama made resumption of negotiations hostage to a demand that could not be met. The result was that Palestinian leaders were forced to adjust their demands accordingly.

Obama is directly responsible for one of the most absurd turns in the history of Middle East negotiations. Though Palestinian leaders negotiated with Israeli governments that built extensively in the West Bank, they now refused to sit down with the first Israeli government

to actually agree to a suspension of building. Obama's demand for a building freeze in
Jerusalem led to a freeze in negotiations.[4]

All of the above brought Halevi to further observe: "In turning an incident into a crisis, Obama has convinced many Israelis
that he was merely seeking a pretext to pick a fight with Israel.
Netanyahu was inadvertently shabby; Obama, deliberately so."[5]

(A parenthetical note: when I speak like this — that is to say
exactly what the Palestinian Authority is up to and to be critical
of a popular American president — some write me [or say to
their friends] that I am just "a right winger." It's clear that, rather
than provide an account of whatever I believe politically, this is
merely a tactic to undermine my message. And it's fascinating to
observe that the tactic is employed only by Jews; I actually never
hear it from non-Jews. In any case, if you want to know what I
believe about the outline of an Israeli/Palestinian peace, see the
next sermon in this book, "Of Rabbis and Imams.")

Charles Krauthammer has a different view of why all this
is happening. He's written much over the past couple of years
about his belief that Obama is an American president with a
messianic complex. By Krauthammer's telling, Obama, by virtue
of his intellectual capability, his rhetorical capability, the way he's
positioned and possessed of personal/political desire to change
and fix virtually everything (from domestic to international
matters), may fancy himself beyond normal human limits.

I don't know if Krauthammer is correct or not with regard to
Obama. However, I do know something about the messianic —
and most specifically for our purposes today, how the nature of
our tradition is fundamentally anti-messianic.

One example: three times the Torah employs the phrase
Vayikra Adonai el Moshe that God calls to Moses. Normally,

the Torah states *Vayidaber Adonai el Moshe* — "God speaks to Moses" — but three times God *calls* Moses. The first time is a moment of historical mission: the beginning of Exodus when God comes to the previously obscure Moses and says, "You're the one to help liberate your people from Egyptian slavery."

The second moment is found in Exodus 19 as God says to Moses, "I call you to go to the Mountain and receive the Ten Commandments to deliver to your people." (Now let's be clear about something here: if anything could give you a messianic complex, it's likely having God come to you not once but twice and say, "You're the man. You're the man to liberate your people, and you're the man to deliver my laws." That indeed would give anyone a messianic complex!)

Then God calls to Moses a third time — in fact, in our Torah reading this morning. At the very beginning we read and hear: *Vayikra Adonai el Moshe* — "God calls once again to Moses." Here, instead of the great moment of liberation and the exalted moment of revelation, what does God do? He gives to Moses all the minutiae of the sacrificial rites!

Why after the great calls when God gives Moses the opportunity to heroically liberate his people and then just as heroically be the agent of the great Torah, why here in the third call is it only about the minutiae of the sacrifices, something so utterly small compared to previous moments?

Our tradition asserts this is so because, if at the beginning God needed Moses's leadership and then his assistance at the moment of Sinai, now God is conveying something of an entirely different nature.

Now God is saying, "Don't get caught up in the drama of the bigger moments of life. The reason is because any possibility of holy life is lived in the minutiae, the largely unseen and unheralded moments of daily life. You're not the man on the

Mountain any longer. You're not the man who freed the slaves any longer. Rather, you're the one who will deliver the details, the learning as to how to live day by day in society, one person mixing with another." Real life is lived very little at the top of the Mountain and mostly much lower down.

What does this mean exactly? It means we are fundamentally an anti-messianic people because life isn't lived — it can't be any other way— in some ideal place. Rather, life is lived with real human beings who will engender conflicts that can rarely ever be solved to everyone's satisfaction.

But there is a possibility, one born of the understanding that real life is lived where people live in conflict, with stress, with hopes that can only be partially realized. The greatest gift, therefore, is the gift of the knowledge that you actually can live in some decent peace with your neighbours, with your history, and with your hopes. This kind of living isn't easy, but it's the only possibility for something approaching peace. This is living in history, not on holiday, as Charles Krauthammer has written.

Therefore, our hope at this moment is to get beyond all the drama, beyond the messianic, beyond the destruction of life and of hopes, and maybe, just maybe, with capable Israeli leadership, with capable Palestinian leadership, with capable international leadership (unburdened by the fantasies or the needs of being messianic), and without any attempt to bring a messianic time, God willing, there will be the possibility of peace, of dignity, and of normality.

May these hopes be realized sooner and not later.[6]

OF RABBIS AND IMAMS
November 14, 2009

At the outset of this week's Torah reading, once Abraham has prevailed in all the trials sent his way, once he has sired a progenitor to secure the future — indeed, even as Abraham has done all that God has asked — still, not before taking several more actions, does Abraham step aside.

First, he buries his wife, Sarah, at a marked and public location; second, by virtue of this burial, he arranges a legal foothold in the land (the cave at Machpelah); third, he makes certain that his son, Isaac, will marry; and, finally, Abraham himself takes another wife who gives him six more sons (who, together, turn out to be the more or less friendly nations neighbouring the Israelites — the Midianites, the best example — no small matter in a rather tough neighbourhood).

Abraham is so energetic precisely now because, believing in the justness of his life's work, he protects his investment against an unknown future. He isn't shy to act on his own behalf, to say nothing of that of his descendants.

Later, the first-century BCE sage Hillel placed Abraham's instincts into a canonized dictum. Hillel asks, "If I am only for myself, who am I?" Then he remarks (it is actually more of a statement than a question), "But if I am not for myself, what am I?" Hillel, too, was hardly shy in protecting his essential interests.

Likewise, the Rabbis designed the primary *mitzvah* incumbent on Jews in the treatment of others (*Gemilut Chasidim*, deeds of social mutual responsibility) out of similar thinking: "Deeds of social mutual responsibility" for them meant, in effect: "I will give to you, in part, so that you will give to me; that is, when you are in need, my obligation is to serve you; likewise, one day down the road when I am vulnerable, I may count on you."

Both by nature and by intent, deeds of goodness (as our tradition has it) are rooted neither in selflessness nor in selfishness but rather in enlightened self-interest. Likely originating in an early human strategy for survival, this impulse became refined and integrated into Judaism's moral imperative requiring that human life be held sacred.

Religion at its best (ours included) takes the natural inclination toward self-centredness and makes it constructive. As Abraham preserves his self-interest, he does this; as Hillel asks his questions, he does this; likewise, our rabbis.

Indeed, could our people have survived, even thrived, without this kind of thinking? Could any people?

If once Jews knew this, if this had long been in our bones, it isn't clear that today this is so. One contemporary example this morning: the nature of "dialogue" between Jews and Muslims.

I raise this matter in particular because this Shabbat, this weekend, some synagogues and mosques (more specifically, rabbis and imams) across North America are meeting with one another. Spurred by a New York City organization, rabbis and imams are trading pulpits, as it were.

Part of the larger phenomenon of Jews and Muslims in dialogue — almost always initiated by Jews — this meeting recently drew the attention of Rabbi Daniel Gordis. Noting the presence of an American rabbinic delegation in Jerusalem last month, Gordis asserted that no society can do well without criticism, and no nation will better itself without serious public debate. He wrote in *The Jerusalem Post*:

> But on the other side of the divide [some Jews are] so insistent on dialogue that it's no longer clear to what they are most fundamentally committed. When a group of American rabbis visited

Jerusalem last week, one of them remarked that it was unfortunate that Ramallah wasn't on the itinerary. "Why visit Ramallah?" another member of the group asked. "Because Ramallah is also part of our story," was the response. "More than Holon? Are you distressed that we're not visiting Holon?" was the question that followed. To that, the first rabbi had no response.

Why, indeed, should Ramallah matter to us more than Holon? And why hide our pro-Israel position (if that's really what we are) simply to appeal to more college students? Had Theodor Herzl adopted that stance with the sultan, or had Chaim Weizmann been bashful in London, would we have a state? Had Golda Meir been self-conscious about her convictions in the face of an American community not entirely certain that a Jewish state was a good idea, where would we be? One shudders to imagine.[7]

Back now to this Shabbat, to this congregation. If other rabbis have invited imams to speak today, why haven't I? Not because I don't want to do so; indeed, I would much prefer to be hosting an imam today as other colleagues are so doing.

Here, then, is why that isn't the case. In September I received this invitation: would I be willing to host an imam of a Toronto area mosque on a Shabbat morning later in the fall? In turn the imam would host me the same weekend. We were invited to bring along interested members of our respective congregations. Hence, this "Weekend of Twinning."

My response: yes. One question: does the imam accept Israel's right to exist as a nation among other nations? Our coming together, I indicated, wasn't contingent on agreement on Middle Eastern borders and policies, on Jerusalem, even on "right of return." Simply, that Israel has a right to exist as a Jewish state, a nation among other nations. I wouldn't publicly parade the imam's acceptance of Israel's right to exist, I hastened to add.

The organizer, a Jew heading a New York City institute seeking to make his program available throughout North America, indicated he would get back to me. Three days later came his reply: what you're asking violates what we're about; we can't include you in the exchange with the imam.

Here, in part, is my e-mail response to this gentleman:

> Your response amazes and disappoints me. A basic acceptance of the other is fundamental to any dialogue. Otherwise, there is no trust, and no real relationship…. [Acceptance, not even agreement!] is central to any relationship, whether between two individuals, two institutions, two nations.
>
> The State of Israel as a Jewish state (which entails providing full citizenship for those not Jewish) is fundamental to Judaism, and the vast, vast majority of Jews. Not to have that on the table and accepted from the beginning, as essential to dialogue, is not only a mistake, it flies in the face of any kind of meaningful relationship.
>
> It works both ways. Muslims have their essentials, what is crucial to Islam and Muslims today. My view is that the essentials of both groups must be understood at the start, as communicated and worked out between (in this case) the rabbi and the imam. This doesn't mean

agreement on everything, especially political matters. That's impossible and it too flies in the face of reality.... It does, however, mean that both sides get one another and are willing to say so in order to begin a dialogue, in hopes that a relationship would ensue....

All of this is why, by the way, I have said for many years — since about 1970 as I began to think about this — that for peace, for the essential dignity of both Jews and Palestinians, there need be two states: a State of Israel and a State of Palestine, each with territorial integrity (meaning historic integrity and geographic contiguity); as well as the kind of economic, political, social infrastructures which undergird successful states.

This means compromise by both Jews and Palestinians: Jews to give up the vast part of the West Bank (including many areas that resonate most deeply of Jewish history and religious tradition, i.e., Hebron, Tekoah, parts of Jerusalem); and, Jews (the State of Israel) to help ensure the viability of a Palestinian state through appropriate measures (financial support among other things). And I believe, as well, that once Israel's right to live in peace is an integral part of Palestine's political and educational culture, a State of Palestine has every right to arm itself, defend itself, as does every other nation.

And, in return, all that over 80 percent of Israeli Jews ask is for peace and an end to violence. Which obviously means as well to cease

working with any party seeking the destruction
of Israel (whether through violence, or Arafat's
"stage by stage" strategy — still favoured by
many as the best way to achieve Israel's demise,
and essentially the way of Tony Judt, Jimmy
Carter, and others toward one state, in which
before very long the Jews would be a minority,
and a very vulnerable one at that).

Do you think that is a lot to ask? Do you
think that is (only) "Netanyahu thinking" as
you said to me on the phone when I said these
things? Do you think that without these com-
promises there will be any possibility of peace
in Israel/Palestine? Do you think that any relationship between Muslims and Jews can be
devoid of deep acceptance of the other, whether
we have been wired for that or not?[8]

Ironically, this very Shabbat, when the imam and I might
have come together, Abraham purchases the gravesite for Sarah
upon her death. What is behind this very public and protracted
negotiation? Even just a glance at the Genesis 23 story makes
very clear that when Abraham stands up for his interests and
those of his descendants, he does so not only out of respect for
the other but no less out of respect for himself and his own.

The bottom line for Abraham, as for us, is that self-preservation
is born in significant measure of enlightened self-interest and
deep self-respect. Anything else is inauthentic, counterproductive,
and ultimately self-destructive. Ironically, too, self-preservation
and self-respect are essential to relationships with the other,
whether as individuals or peoples or nations. If you don't respect
yourself — what is essential to who you are, what you are at the

core of your psychology, your being, your history, your values — you won't respect the other and their integrity.

Abraham was about that. Hillel was about that. The Rabbis knew and taught that. But I don't think we're about that, at least as Jews. I don't think we act out of enlightened self-interest. All too often we run to show our sensitivity to others and in so doing run over or run by our own interests, often the most important ones. When I was told by the organizer out of New York City that raising the matter of Israel's right to exist "violates" what the program is about, could there be a more dramatic example, a more painful example, of our running over our own interests, our own needs and truths?

Daniel Gordis, in criticizing the typical dialogue thinking of these days, puts it like this:

> Have we become so utterly addicted to dialogue with our enemies that we would rather visit their cities than our own? Have we lost the ability to say, "If you breathe new life into the age-old blood libel, we will shun you"? Would we invite Alfred Dreyfus's accusers here for dialogue, were they alive today? We have real enemies. Have we so lost sight of that that we forget that anything we say, to paraphrase Miranda, "can and will be used against us"?
>
> If those who insist on silencing any critique of Israel fail us because their passion threatens to squelch the debate we desperately need, those passionately committed to open debate suffer from the opposite problem — they do not recognize that they are unwittingly playing right into the hands of those determined to destroy us.[9]

Why then are we so unsteady and unknowing of enlightened self-interest, so wavering in a stance of self-regard? Why be in dialogue with those who refuse to recognize what is at our very core as Jews? Are we really so willing to jettison the centrality of Israel as a Jewish state for something so expedient as the self-deceiving good feeling we achieve when we're applauded for being "open"?

The full answers to these questions are for another day. I raise the questions and speak of rabbis and imams today to signal that something is wrong in the state of Jewish self-regard, something not small and, indeed, potentially self-destructive.

I would love, one day soon, to host an imam here at Holy Blossom Temple. I would love our synagogue to be in a relationship with a mosque so that our congregation and a Muslim congregation would know and speak with each other in a meaningful way. But as we are obligated to respect our Muslim neighbours for what is important to them, let us do so out of respect for what is essential to us as Jews. Let us then speak the truth with one another, a truth that reflects our respective histories, one that because it begins with enlightened self-regard can engender genuine regard and respect for the other.

Nothing else will do. And, ironically, nothing else is more likely to do more justice to the needs and causes of the respective parties. That's exactly what Abraham did even as his life seemed spent all those years ago. Should we do no less today?

A FALSE SYMMETRY[10]
From the *Globe and Mail*, February 12, 2004

No one knows how peace might eventually come to Israelis and Palestinians. And no one perspective — not a pro-Geneva Accord one, or an anti-Geneva perspective; not the view from the right, or the view from the left — can claim absolute understanding of how peace might unfold.

Yet one belief, rather casually assumed by the vast majority across the political spectrum to be at the heart of the conflict, is utterly out of sync with reality. We must understand the falseness of this thinking, so at the very least not to be fooled by it.

This assumption presumes a relentless symmetry in which Israelis and Palestinians — their sins as well as their capabilities to assume responsibility — are weighted more or less in balance: The Israelis have their fallibilities, and the Palestinians theirs; Ariel Sharon is Israel's extremist and Yasser Arafat is the Palestinian's extremist; the Jews produced Baruch Goldstein, the Palestinians gave the world Hamas and Islamic jihad; Israel does not accept the Palestinian narrative, neither are the Palestinians sympathetic to Israel's story.

In reality a troubling asymmetry exists that suggests why Israeli society is significantly prepared for peace while Palestinian society is not. That is, Israeli society today is roughly divided among the following groups, from the far left to the far right: Israel's far left has accepted the legitimacy of the Palestinian narrative over that of the Israeli narrative. This is a small group, although influential (i.e., Avram Burg) because it includes the artistic, media, and intellectual elite who enjoy significant say in public opinion.

Next on the spectrum, the moderate left in Israel accepts the equal legitimacy of the Palestinian and Israeli narratives. Moving over more, the moderate right of Israel can be said to accept the right of Palestinian statehood (although it probably believes that the Israelis have something more of a right). Finally, on the far right of Israeli society, a small minority insists that only Israel enjoys national legitimacy.

And on the Palestinian side? There are nuances among three camps: those who believe Israel should be destroyed through violence; those who believe it should be destroyed through territorial concessions and demographic changes; and finally those Palestinians who believe that Israel is simply too strong to be destroyed, that its existence is permanent, and that the Palestinians must reconcile themselves to this reality.

But these are nuances. In none of these camps — including the third one — is there an acceptance of what is normative in the vast reaches of Israeli society today: that this struggle is between two national rights, and there must ultimately be two states. This includes even Sari Nusseibeh who belongs in the third category.

The gist of the asymmetry is seen most clearly in two imperatives, which are necessarily in balance politically and utterly out of balance in numerical popular social reality: to achieve peace, Israelis for their part must recognize the national rights of the Palestinian people, which at least 75 percent of Israelis do; and on the Palestinian side for matters to resolve themselves, Palestinians must recognize the need for a secure legitimate existence of a Jewish state, which arguably something under 20 percent of Palestinian society does today (and even then that 20 percent is in the third category that recognizes Israel's legitimacy by virtue of its power).

It is this imbalance — this deep social, political, personal asymmetry — that is the heart of the matter. In sum the problem may just come down to this: that for the Israelis to accept the narrative most dear to Palestinian society, it must imagine its own demise.

However, for Israel to achieve security and stability in a rough neighbourhood, it must also help imagine how the rough parts of the neighbourhood can be straightened out, at least to some extent. Therefore, to achieve security the Jewish state must help Palestinian society reimagine itself as a mature state side by side with Israel. As the stronger power, Israel must help in this endeavour — but no less so than the nations of the world and the Palestinian people themselves.

Only then will the crippling asymmetry resolve itself into a possible peace.

THE BEGINNING OF HOPE?
Holy Blossom Temple Bulletin, January 2003

Washington Post columnist Charles Krauthammer recalls that when he first heard about the Oslo Accord in 1993, he immediately called an Israeli friend and asked, "What happened?"

His friend responded, "We won, we finally won. They have accepted us."

Krauthammer was shocked but knew his friend's view reflected the view of the majority of Israeli and American Jews.[11]

I thought of Krauthammer this past November when a Fatah terrorist (part of Yasser Arafat's gang) burst into a home on Kibbutz Metzer and pumped bullets into Tina Damari, her three children, and another kibbutz member, murdering all of them. Members of Kibbutz Metzer, most of whom were strong advocates of peace negotiations, were shocked. They were shocked by the murders, but almost more shocked because the terrorists had come through the nearby Arab village of Meiser, which they thought was friendly to their Jewish neighbours.

One kibbutz member said, "Something of special value has been broken. We thought that if good people sit and talk we could change the world. The reality is different. We will no longer be naive."

I thought, too, of Krauthammer's observation upon learning that a Jewish organization I once supported enthusiastically was among the sponsors of a crude and anti-Semitic propaganda piece produced by the Israeli branch of Physicians for Human Rights. Filled with ugly stereotypes of armed Israeli soldiers (unmistakably depicted as Second World War Nazis) oppressing innocent Palestinian victims (unmistakably portrayed as the Jews of the Holocaust), the picture was clear: the Jews are now the brutalizers, the suicide bombers nothing but hapless victims.

What has happened? Why has the shock of the past two years come upon most of us, seemingly out of the blue? Why do we Jews twist ourselves intellectually into pretzels in order to be liked by all, often undermining our own self-interest?

I suspect the beginning of an answer is found in what writer Amos Oz recalled recently. His father, upon leaving Germany in the 1930s, was haunted by signs saying JEWS GET OUT — GO TO PALESTINE. Upon returning for a visit to Europe in the late 1960s, Oz's father was haunted once again, this time by signs reading JEWS GET OUT OF PALESTINE.

Krauthammer refers to the experience of being so shocked as "taking a holiday from history."[12] We Jews of modernity, imbued with a kind of messianism, one more secular than religious, believe that previous history can be annulled; that human nature can change, that all conflicts can be resolved. Hope in this view is based on human wish rather than human nature.

Nonsense, says Krauthammer. History is made by real people who engender conflicts, some containable, few fully resolved. This kind of history doesn't end. That's why Judaism is fundamentally anti-messianic; messianism is dangerous and unreal; and history is where people have lived since Eden and it won't stop.[13] "There is nothing new under the sun," says Ecclesiastes.

This doesn't mean there is no hope. Rather it means that hope is based on real life, on containing problems rather than looking for perfection. Such knowledge is hopeful. The fact that we are now more knowledgeable than two years ago might be the beginning of hope.

CONSOLATION AND DESTINY
Yizkor (Pesach) Reflections in Crisis, April 3, 2002

A few minutes ago we stood — as our ancestors once did — as words of gratitude and praise and relief were recited for God's salvific hand. Shortly before this moment in our history, the Book of Exodus records a matter that requires our attention now.

Our Torah reads: "When Pharaoh let the people go, God did not lead them by the way of the land of the Philistines although it was nearer; for God said, the people may have a change of heart — *pen yinachem ha'am* — when they see war and return to Egypt."[14] Many commentators have asked, "What is the meaning of the phrase *pen yinachem ha'am?*"

Is it, as is often translated, "lest the people have a change of heart, or that they would change their minds" — in the sense of repenting over the original intention (to move forward as God was directing them)? Very probably. After all, God worried that the Israelites, faced by the threat of war, might well change their minds. They might return to Egypt rather than move forward toward the land. And yet, a closer look at the word *yinachem* suggests that, ultimately, this phrase isn't about a change of mind or heart or even about repentance. Rather, it's about consolation.

Why is *pen yinachem ha'am*, at the deepest level, about consolation? Because, as Leon Wieseltier has pointed out in his book *Kaddish*, "to be consoled is to repent, that is, to change one's mind [specifically] to agree to have one's attention diverted from one's sorrow, to admit another object, another motive, another desire into one's consciousness." Wieseltier adds, "For sorrow wants nothing but sorrow."[15]

Sorrow wants nothing but sorrow. And consolation is about changing one's mind to admit another object, another motive into one's consciousness.

Why does this matter now? For this simple reason: that as central as is our mourning now for our loved ones — those who once sat with us side by side, those whom once we could see and touch and love — still, these difficult days we have admitted another kind of sorrow into our souls. That is the sorrow of the larger Jewish people unfolding before our eyes; the sorrow that is wafting through the land of our ancestors and the land of our brethren; the sorrow that fills us with despair as homicide bombers slaughter our people and a foul wind of hate blows across Europe; the sorrow we believed we would never know again; the kind of sorrow we prayed the State of Israel would always protect us against; the sorrow we fear may grow larger, deeper, more inconsolable.

And so as we seek consolation for personal sorrow now, we also pray for consolation for this larger sorrow burdening our people. We now admit one kind of sorrow into the place we normally reserve for the other. We do so because "sorrow wants nothing but sorrow" in the human heart; yet, also because we sense that this kind of consolation — communal, historical, the personal with the Peoplehood — will best move us forward. Forward in identification with our land and our people; forward out of the clutching grasp of helplessness and powerlessness; forward, somehow, some way, to once again stand together, to sing of our gratitude and praise and relief on safer shores, our sorrow then abated but not forgotten.

And so, as individuals and as a congregation, we take into our hearts many and much: our own loved ones, the details of whose lives we knew intimately, details we still remember daily; as well, members of our larger people, the details of whose lives we don't know, yet whose destiny we share.

And so permit me to ask: that, as each of us says Yizkor for our loved ones, let us also remember those of our people whose lives are now cut short, not in surrender to God but by the brutal calculation of the hand and mind of the terrorist.

For when "we admit another object" into our lives, we find consolation; when we identify with the sorrows of others, our sorrow is softened; when we see ourselves as part of something larger, we move forward — from helplessness to praise, from despair to gratitude.

For we require this "mingling of our consolations" now when our souls are burdened, not only by the normal memories that always rush back at Yizkor but also by the foul wind of hate that seeks to destroy something essential to us: our collective memory, our deeply felt history, our identity, our homeland, our land where it all began, where we were nurtured and exiled from, this land to which we have finally returned in our lifetime.

The endeavour to destroy and divide us, the willful attempt to deny our claim to our land, then and now; the hate that fuels this is kicked up by a war criminal, Yasser Arafat — oddly, even as we seek to share the land. As Fouad Ajami has written, "[in waging this brutal war] Arafat is [aiming] for Israel's soul, to wear it down."[16]

And why does Arafat, along with the "Arab street," think he will succeed? Because as Ajami writes, "a foul wind blows through Arab lands [now] that Israel is on the run, that perhaps the verdict of the 1948 war ... could be undone ... [that perhaps as the fantasy goes] the Jewish state was not destined to last ... [that Israel would be like the] Crusader Kingdom that had risen in the Levant, lasted for almost 200 years ... then pulled up stakes, and left on the soil its castles and bridges and ruins."[17]

So let it be said clearly: we surrender to death, but not to terrorism; we yield finally to God's will, but not to the hand of terror; we have known destruction, but it has never been our destiny.

We have been around far too long to be felled by such a foul wind. Our memory is too deep to be severed or distorted by the fools on the television, its cords cut or denied by Arafat's lies. And I believe our collective will and backbone is too strong to be broken by hate or by indifference. As Shimon Peres said two nights ago, "This is not a war of images. This is a war for existence."

Therefore in this war we must take our place, not as physical warriors (that is up to Israel to do, we hope wisely and smartly), but rather as spiritual warriors, Jews, whose mothers and fathers have given us a place at the heart of Jewish history; whose mothers and fathers have given us the privilege to help make that history live in the present; whose mothers and fathers have handed us the responsibility to ensure that it sustains in the future. This is our role as Warriors of the Spirit — in our land and in other good lands, too.

So here now at this place and time of memory, public remembrance of our loved ones counters the helplessness that death must ultimately bring. Likewise, mingling our personal sorrows with the larger sorrow — making our voices, our passion, our will for Israel and her survival known and public — counters the helplessness we feel.

This mingling will ensure that once again we and our people will come to safer shores and stand together. We will once again offer gratitude and praise and relief to God for guiding us to these shores. Our relief will then mingle painfully with our regret of loss of life of our people and other peoples, too; yet, to sing God's song in safety is the primary — and primordial — imperative at this moment when consolation is less about loss and more about saving life and our land.

This is how we shall move forward. This is how we must move forward. This is our consolation and our destiny, as it was once that of our ancestors.

ANGUISH AND HOPE
March 16, 2002

The week I recently spent in Jerusalem was bracketed by two Saturday night bombs. The first, outside a synagogue in Jerusalem's Beit Yisrael Quarter, destroyed the lives of a whole family, killing ten in all; the second bomb killed eleven young Israelis relaxing at a popular Jerusalem café.

I happened to arrive in Jerusalem the day after the first bombing, and I left the day after the second. Coming out of a café at about 10:30 p.m. this past Saturday night, I heard that bomb explode several hundred yards away. Its noise reverberated around the city; almost immediately ambulances and police filled Jerusalem's streets. All else came to a halt — most particularly the lives of those eleven young Israelis.

This was the deadliest seven days in years. It left many shaken. But not all.

The havoc wreaked that week was both physical and emotional. There were too many funerals of too many young people; there were those soldiers picked off one by one by a Palestinian sniper, aided by a kind of arrogance that would leave a hillside above that checkpoint unchecked; there was an unbearable pain and a shaken nation.

No parent went unrattled. Children were unusually quiet, while Israeli teens had a different look in their eyes.

What do you tell your children, many Israeli parents asked, that you can go to the army, but you can't go downtown? That's the odd thing: parents feel safer with their children in the army than they do with them out on the streets, going to school, shopping in a mall, or going over to a friend's house.

It all feels unsettled and elusive as if no one quite knows exactly what's happening, even as we know that everything has changed. As bombs explode everywhere as if they were merely firecrackers, we have trouble putting the right words to what has occurred. However, Ari Shavit, writing in *Haaretz*, does try and name what's happening:

A name is needed. This war needs a name. If you don't give your war a name you can't fight it. If you don't give your war a name you can't win it. You will lose. And in losing, die. One possibility is the Al-Aqsa Intifada. But that is the Palestinian name, not the Israeli one. And for a long time now the point hasn't been Al-Aqsa. Not only Al-Aqsa. Nor is there an intifada here. There are no mass demonstrations, no popular uprising, no stone throwing. So those who say intifada are lying. Merely laundering words.

Another possibility is the End of the Occupation War. The Palestinians' war to end the occupation. But this war broke out immediately after the Palestinians were offered the end of the occupation. By exchanging Ehud Barak for Ariel Sharon, this war itself actually perpetuated the occupation. And in large part, this war is being waged outside the areas of the occupation. It makes no distinction between Israelis of occupation and Israelis of outside the occupation. So anyone who speaks about the End of the Occupation War is lying. Merely laundering words.

Perhaps the Peace for the Settlements War. The war of Ariel Sharon to perpetuate the settlements. But this war broke out immediately after

Israel agreed to dismantle about a hundred settlements. The war broke out immediately after
the Palestinians ostensibly agreed to accept the
existence of the remaining settlements. And
in none of their ideological platforms do the
Palestinians posit the settlements as a sufficient condition for ending this war and estab-
lishing peace. In none of their war cries do the
Palestinians posit the goal of dismantling the
settlements as a final goal. So anyone who says
that this war is the Peace for the Settlements
War is lying. Merely laundering words.[18]

The anguish in Israel now, and in ourselves, grows steadily
as we grope to name what has happened and to grieve over the
ongoing loss of life. Yet it is also about the moral ambiguity of
the situation.

We hate that Israeli tanks rumble through Ramallah and
Beit Jalla. We hate that tanks are rumbling through Gaza. We
hate the arrests of hundreds of Palestinians, these young men
bent on destruction as many are, humbled by blindfolds. No one
likes that innocent Arabs are killed at the hand of Jews. Indeed,
we hate this and hate that it is happening to us and our people.
We hate that any of it happens at our hand, even if that hand is
forced and there is no choice.

But even as our eyes watch tanks roll over cars in Ramallah,
let our gaze not be averted from what drives the current
unravelling: a Palestinian campaign of terror, a Palestinian
guerrilla warfare against Israel and against the Jewish people,
fought by a Palestinian leadership bent on the destruction of
Israel and on the denial of all Jewish claims to our homeland.
We hate everything that is going on, but we hate it less, far less,

than the potential catastrophe that too many Palestinians would now love to see unfold.

When survival is at stake — and let us not kid ourselves, strong as Israel is, its survival is at stake — then moral ambiguity is the moral imperative. The moral imperative now is to live and survive; secondly, we shall do it as best we can.

We have a small example of that kind of moral ambiguity here in the synagogue. I refer to the fact that for two or three weeks now, when we say Kaddish, we remember not only our own beloved dead but also those Jews killed in Israel each week by terrorism. And so one might ask: why remember just the Jewish innocent alone without also remembering the Arab innocent?

We do so for this reason: much of the blurring of this situation is fostered by a fraudulent suggestion of moral equivalency that proposes to apportion blame equally on each side. They deserve each other, goes this attempt at moral equivalency: there has been Israeli death and destruction and there has been Palestinian death and destruction; there are the settlements on one side, and terrorism on the other. A plague on both their houses!

This is absolute nonsense.

Journalist Yossi Klein Halevi put this phony moral equivalency into perspective when he wrote in the *Los Angeles Times*:

> One side has religious fanatics who are violent and hateful but discredited by the mainstream public and repudiated by most of its religious leaders. The other side has religious fanatics who are violent and hateful and celebrated by the mainstream as holy men.
>
> One side is ready to compromise for peace and has abandoned its dream of complete

possession of the contested land. The other side insists on absolute ownership of the land.

One side is prepared to stop arguing about history and give precedence to the future. The other side is still fighting medieval wars against infidels.

One side has painfully concluded that both sides in this decades-long conflict have inflicted and suffered injustices. The other side believes that only it has suffered injustice and attributes all wrongs to its enemy.

One side believes that this is a tragic conflict between two legitimate national movements. The other side believes this is a conflict between native sons and foreign interlopers.

One side was so sickened of being occupiers that it empowered its archenemy and armed his terrorist forces and offered him shared sovereignty over its capital city. The other side rails against the injustice of an occupation that the occupier offered to end.[19]

So, as we name reality clearly, let us say unequivocally: Palestinian lives are worth every bit as much as Jewish lives; their deaths are as much a dent in God's image as are Jewish deaths. However, equally unequivocally, let us also say: when the survival of our homeland is at stake, when our people are in peril, we will put ourselves first. Therefore, when we say Kaddish here in synagogue, while we value the lost lives of all innocents, we shall mention the Jewish innocents in this horrible mess alone.

We don't pretend away our moral ambiguity then. And we certainly don't celebrate it. In fact, we hate it because it goes against the grain of the Jewish moral imperative to make the world better. However, we live with it, because the only other choice at the moment is to die with it. (I should say, as well, that our moral ambiguity is expressed by the fact that while we name Jews killed by Palestinian terrorists while reading the Yahrzeit list, we don't name Jewish soldiers killed in fighting that war. That is a different matter).

I said earlier that many were shaken and most were rattled, but not all. Here is what I was referring to, and this is what mitigates my sense of despair significantly.

I refer to heroes and heroines in Israel. And there are many.

Most of the heroes manifest their heroism in the quiet and courageous ways they live daily life, adamant not to succumb to the stunning terror of terrorism, even as they fear what is around the corner or down the block or on the radio.

Their courage is clear and is shown in many ways. When a suicide bomber was caught at a popular café on Emet Refayim Street last week, the very next day Israelis filled the café to show solidarity with its owners and with the neighbourhood. When there are suspicious bags about, Israelis are alert to report them and move people toward safety. When a suicide bomber has left death and destruction in his wake, many rush to help the injured and care for the dead, while others pursue and take down the terrorist. We don't usually know the names of these Israeli heroes, but they are us as we are they.

There are public heroes, too, Israelis who by virtue of their political leadership have the ability to bring Jews together both inside and outside Israel. One is Shimon Peres, who were he a citizen of another country, would long ago have been named the secretary-general of the United Nations. Israelis hold Peres at a distance, perhaps feeling that he seems more at home in Paris than in Tel Aviv. Nonetheless, he has been a coalition builder in a country that badly needs commonality in its political leadership. He and Ariel Sharon form an important partnership at this time of crisis, and I believe history will judge Peres as one of the great leaders of Israel. Ironically, the fullness of his greatness is, I believe, unfolding now before our eyes as he approaches eighty years old.

Another such person is Yoram Hazony, president of the Shalem Center, a Jerusalem think tank. Dr. Hazony, whom I invited to speak here at Holy Blossom Temple in 2001, like Peres, is bringing Israelis from the left, centre, and right together in common understanding and common defence. An architect of the Kinneret Agreement to articulate a new understanding of the importance of Zionism and democracy as the foundations of the state, Hazony also now forges this new public understanding: that while Oslo was a mistake, so, too, the settlements as a requirement of Zionist ideology had us travelling the wrong road. Probably 80 percent of Israelis agree with this analysis; it is Yoram Hazony who is driving the national debate.

Hazony is courageous enough to say in public that he was wrong to hold the settlements up as a fundamental requirement for the State of Israel. He is slowly bringing together a surprising coalition of people toward a common political and social understanding of how to sustain the state and the society. Therefore Peres and Hazony, separated by two generations and apparently by political ideology, are nonetheless driving Israel toward a common political centre that is Jewish and democratic. They seek to galvanize many to stand with them — and stand for the state.

But in my mind the most compelling Israelis are those who are seventeen, eighteen, and nineteen years old — teenagers with a different look in their eyes.

The night before the café blast, sitting at the Shabbat dinner table of friends, I spoke with three eighteen-year-old Israelis, the third or fourth occasion I had to talk with eighteen-year-olds that week. Each had attended funerals of friends that morning, each was in the broad Zionist and observant camp, each was impressive, resolute, bright, and respectful. They buoyed my spirits, as I know they buoy the spirits of their families and of their nation. I left my friends' home that evening with great hope in the midst of grinding despair.

The next afternoon at the home of other friends, I met and spoke with some more eighteen-year-olds. One spoke for all the young people I encountered that week when he said as follows. That while he had long been in the peace camp, he had now made a significant shift. His shift occurred at Rosh Hashanah in 2000, he told me, when Yasser Arafat, after earlier rejecting that extraordinary offer at Camp David, started the Second Intifada and this ongoing spiral toward violence, chaos, and murder that we know all too well.

"At that moment I understood that Arafat wanted not the territories, not land, certainly not peace, but us and our country," he said. Then he looked straight at me. "I would have traded territories and land for peace, but I will not trade our lives. This is my country and I will fight for it and I will defend it."

No words could better reflect my own sentiments. I, too, shifted significantly not long ago. I, too, finally woke up to the fact that Arafat, whether by hook or by crook, whether by violence or diplomacy, wants to destroy the State of Israel, and nothing short of that. I, along perhaps with many others, was fooled, not so much by Arafat but rather by my own desire for peace and resolution. It once obscured my view of reality. It no longer does.

Because for all the criticism that Israel brings upon itself in dealing with Palestinians, it is Israel that has compromised to make peace. And it is the Palestinian leaders who continue to call for "death to the Jews" and for the destruction of the Jewish state. While the huge majority of Jews — inside Israel and out — believe the land belongs to two peoples and should be fairly divided and secure, one can no longer say that about Arafat and his henchmen. In fact, we never could say that, even while we went on doing so for years.

I want to come back to Ari Shavit, since he does, in fact, finally name this situation. In his *Haaretz* article, he writes:

> Only one name comes to me: the War of Sovereignty. Maybe the War of Israeli Sovereignty. Maybe the War of Jewish Sovereignty. Because this is the goal of the war: not to bring about the collapse of the occupation but to bring about the collapse of Jewish sovereignty. To deny the Jews the right to be sovereign in any part of the Land of Israel. And this is also both the strategy and the tactic of this war: by means of killing in cafés and killing in restaurants and killing in malls and pizzerias and in night clubs, to show the Jews that they are no longer safe any place in Israel. By generating fear and sowing separation, it wants to isolate the Jews in separate political and geographic cantons that are alienated from one another and turn away from one another and devote all their efforts to mutual gratuitous hatred.
>
> By means of murder and massacre, this war is trying to force the Jews out of every public place and deny them any feeling of public order, to insulate them in terrified, helpless individual life. In order to disrupt completely all the workings of their common life. In order to void of content

their political independence. And in order to demonstrate to them, by means of bombs, that they are no longer sovereign. That the Jews are not sovereign anywhere in this country.[20]

Where does all of this leave us and our people then? Quite near the very moment when everything changed in Jewish history, when we learn that all is possible, just as everything seems the darkest.

For what is Pesach about, really? The God-given capacity to name reality clearly and the God-given capacity to imagine a world different from the one we have. God gave our ancestors the daring gift to be capable to say: the world I live in now doesn't have to be like this; indeed, shouldn't be this way. We can break every expectation and the world can change radically. The point of Pesach, and this is our task at the Seder, is to shake up human complacency and to imagine differently.

That's what those eighteen-year-olds are about. That's what's in their eyes — gentle but firm, fierce in their determination both to fight for their country and for the moral ideals of their people and their tradition. They don't pretend away reality, and neither do they abandon hope that things can get better.

"[Exodus] becomes a call to revolutionary hope regardless of the conditions of history," says David Hartman.[21] So this is the essence of what it means to be a Jew: to know and name reality and imagine differently, to not despair because of what is, and to not abandon hope for what must be. This is our mission and our purpose, and because we are a people of memory, we know we have seen worse, we know we will see better.

Still, this we know at this hour: Israel and Israelis need us to be there face to face, to stand with them in their, and our, difficult hour. Judaism commences, Hartman says in effect, not with spiritual transformation of personal identity, not with *mitzvah*, not with a leap of faith, but rather with a leap of solidarity with Am Yisrael.

The eighteen-year-olds whom I met in Jerusalem remain with me. Their clear words, their resolute and passionate eyes, their humour and their hope have made their way into my head and my heart, I suspect for a long time to come. I will stand with them as best I can, and know that you will, as well.

4

The Torah Speaks in Its Language and in Ours

PREAMBLE

Early on in rabbinical school I learned the famous adage of Rabbi Ben Bag Bag (possibly a cover for his real name, in any case, likely a disciple of the famous Rabbi Hillel): "Turn the Torah over and over for everything is in it. Delve into it, grow old and worn over it, and never move away from it, for you will find no better portion than it."[1]

No words better describe the satisfaction acquired in growing into something once foreign but eventually elemental (as it proved for me): the life-enhancing, wisdom-filled waters of the Torah, including that work's vast corpus of accompanying commentaries and literature. Absorbing this by learning it, slowly and surely, text by text, idea by idea. Not all of it, not even most of it, but enough to change your life.

While the intellectual core of Judaism beckoned uniquely as I considered rabbinical school, I didn't know that what I would come to understand as "Jewish ideas" was quite so rooted in Torah. Alas, I couldn't have been more fortunate than to learn the ideas and the worldview embedded in the Torah, and then, best as I could, to convey what I learned. All of this from the delving and delving into the thrilling, if sometimes slow in yielding, sources of the tradition. In fact, entering Hebrew Union College in 1976, I was far more committed to learning than to being a rabbi — the latter would come to be by virtue of the former.

To dig deeper: the rabbinic tradition gets at the centrality — really, the joy — of learning in telling ways. Noting that the great Rabbi Akiva asserts that, "The father merits the son with beauty and strength and wealth and wisdom and years,"[2] Menachem Azariah says, in effect, "Wait, not so fast, you've missed something crucial — in fact, the crux of it all." Menachem claims, through a brilliant exposition of interpretation, made almost spine-tingling by Leon Wieseltier in his book *Kaddish*,[3] that "wisdom" isn't inherited, at least the bulk of it. Yes, Menachem says, your looks and financial circumstances, your physical strength and length of days, can be passed along to a great degree. But not your learning.

How revealing is that? I didn't come across this text and its rereadings for some time, but once I did I understood the notion that to acquire learning (this kind, anyway) is to acquire life.

Included here are a few of my reflections (as Ben Bag Bag's word for "delving" is sometimes translated) as I attempted, like all of us, to swim in the waters of the Torah and no less in those of contemporary times.

WHAT DO I BELIEVE HAPPENED AT SINAI?
Erev Shavuot, May 28, 2009

Permit me to begin autobiographically as the link between autobiography and theology, between the personal and the philosophical, is undeniable. I didn't much think about God growing up and into my twenties. I didn't believe and I didn't not believe. But something was stirring, so off to Hebrew Union College I went at age twenty-four. Not to be a rabbi, or so I told myself, but certainly enthusiastic to drink at the intellectual wells of a venerable religious tradition. What would come later, I hadn't a clue.

While the stirring wasn't about God, my spirit was full and ready. Already in love with Israel and drawn toward the satisfactions of community, I was anxious to be competent at ritual matters and keen to handle Jewish texts in the original. So I headed toward the heart of things Jewish. And rabbinical school, if not being a rabbi, seemed a pretty good route there. In short, I was passionate for Jewish knowledge, meaning, and a place in the world.

Once at the rabbinical seminary, I realized that, regardless of what I believed or didn't believe, I should make myself decently conversant about theology, God, commandments — the very things that animate Judaism. However, God and matters of spirit weren't much at the centre of Hebrew Union College life in the late 1970s and early 1980s. As well as I can remember, only Eugene Borowitz and the late Michael Signer spoke this language.

Moreover, what I was exposed to in rabbinical school (and more so in the larger liberal Jewish milieu) perplexed and disappointed me. What passed for religious discourse was the oft-stated banal mantra: how you observe and what you believe doesn't really matter as long as you can be said to be making "an informed choice." (Informed by what exactly? I kept wondering. A course or two in Judaism? A bit of Hebrew? A mantra may mean never having to think about what you say!)

That few wished to make demands and that little was required were indications that the larger culture was winning easily: it was more important to please than to require; more important to be nice than to ask after truth.

In any case, in my circles I heard next to nothing about what God was, what God did, what God demanded. Not from a traditional point of view, nor from a contemporary one. I did hear a great deal about the God of "choice," the watchword of radical individualism.

Fortunately, though, two professors — Eugene Borowitz and David Ellenson — directed me to the writings of two rabbis whose thinking has influenced me ever since: David Hartman and his teacher, Joseph Soloveitchik.

Reading Hartman and Soloveitchik, I first encountered normative and traditional ideas in Judaism. I found these ideas compelling and substantive and discovered that by temperament and philosophy I was (and remain) partial to ideas like God as creator and redeemer, like the world to come, like reward and punishment — especially as discussed with sophistication by the rabbis.

I was quite comfortable that, while my own practice didn't reflect the ideas I was learning, nonetheless, these ideas held as real, as anchors, for my developing theology. For it seemed rather clear that without the tradition and its animating ideas, we are, more or less, floating about and lunging at one intellectual life raft after another. I wanted to swim and not sink in the life-giving waters of the Torah and related literature. I absolutely revelled in the compelling ideas of the rabbis and others. I sought their ideas as friends and teachers — as the best ideas can often be for intellectual seekers.

More than anything else, I learned in reading Hartman and Soloveitchik that ideas matter; they help us to understand our world and our place in it; they help organize our thinking about how and why we live in the image of God. Put simply, my way toward religiosity, as well as my belief in *Torah mi-Sinai* ("Torah from Sinai," which I came to slowly over time), developed through learning the ideas fundamental to Jewish tradition. The intellectual door into the House of Judaism was my way toward the centre of Jewish life.

I also learned from Hartman and Soloveitchik, albeit indirectly, that religious practice needn't necessarily be reflective of religious belief: what you believe may not necessarily lead to a practice consistent with those beliefs. (My practice wasn't and has never been so consistent, and I have never been anything less than comfortable with the contradiction.) Finally, I learned not to judge Judaism by what individual Jews do or believe; Judaism exists on its own, and we are, most of the time, fairly inadequate embodiments of the tradition.

So, in the end, what do I believe about the Ur-idea of our tradition, that the Torah itself was revealed by God on Sinai? It became clear early on, at least to me, that either the fundamentals at the heart of the tradition — God is real, God has commanded, God has commanded His people — are either real or not. Related: matters of belief aren't measured by the normal terms of evidence; belief need bear little resemblance to what the world looks like. Put differently, there is no direct relationship between faith and consequence, between deed and reward. That I learned from the Rabbis and from life.

And so, with regard to what happened on Sinai, I have faith that it occurred, and this faith was a conscious choice, made over time, because the opposite means not only no faith and not only no God, but it also makes far less sense.

I have faith that God was present and real at Sinai. I have faith that then and there God set in motion a very different kind of history and direction for a particular people at a particular time. There the Jews were given the unique mission to testify to God's word and way on earth, to spread these truths to others for the benefit of all humans.

Specifically, I believe that God revealed the Torah to the Israelites on the Mountain, and over a fairly short period of time a few with capability at writing recorded what was "revealed" in their presence. As with any communication, what was said wasn't necessarily exactly what was heard, and therefore the contradictions in our Torah are of no surprise, nor of concern (at least to me), with regard to the matter of faith.

And, finally, I believe that a commanding God spoke at Sinai. Consequently, Jews have been a commanded people ever since, as well as a responding people. Whether we respond or not, and how we do so, these are entirely different matters; they don't provide evidence one way or another about God's presence or nature.

Do I believe this way in part because, as suggested, as a young man, I wanted a strong Jewish identity, more Judaic knowledge, and a place in the world? No doubt.

Do I also believe as I do because, as suggested, the opposite means that the whole thing — God, revelation, commandments — is a fairy tale, meaning that Judaism is *entirely* created from the human mind and experience? To me this renders our religious tradition a *plastir*, not even a Hebrew word but rather a Greek one that Moses cunningly employs to slam God when God bars Moses from the Promised Land. At that moment Moses says to God, as the Rabbis reconfigure it, that his Torah is *plastir*, that is, "plaster," a cover, something essentially phony.[4]

So, in the end, I believe in *Torah mi-Sinai* because, while the palpable experience of God has never been my lot, faith, slowly growing, episodically deepening, has been. For that I count myself fortunate, among the faithful, and for that I thank God.

THE SECRET OF LIFE
June 4, 2011

On Shabbat morning, June 4, 2011, I addressed my remarks to the Confirmation students. That morning marked their graduation from grade ten at Holy Blossom Temple.

The Torah Speaks in Its Language and in Ours

I hope everyone will forgive me if I concentrate on our Confirmation students this morning. I want to speak directly with you, though I don't mind if others overhear. I speak to you now because you are our future: the future of Canada; the future of the Jewish people; the future of Holy Blossom Temple; the future of your families.

Which means we are invested in you. Your parents have invested in you: with their hearts and their hopes, their time and their resources. We, your rabbis and cantors, we, your teachers and your congregation, are also invested in you. In fact, we need you. We need you to be smart and kind. We need you to be happy and to have hope. We need you to be Jews.

With this in mind I want to tell you the secret of life. Three secrets, actually. Three things that, if you get them right, or even right enough, means you'll do well and you'll live well. I guarantee it. I can offer you no guarantees about how long you'll live or how much money you'll make. But I can guarantee your happiness — better, your contentedness.

And, by the way, these actually are secrets. They must be because, even though they're right in front of all of our eyes, most of us don't get them.

Will you understand these secrets? Will your hearts and minds tell you what your eyes see? I don't know. It depends on whether you're prepared to actually open your eyes, really open your eyes — to perceive, to know, to feel the world about you. It depends on whether and how well you learn and think. It depends on how each one of you trusts your soul. Most fall short of this. I hope you won't.

I'm not the teller of secrets. A man named Shimon HaTzaddik, Simon the Just, is the secret teller. He likely lived in the third century BCE and was a popular teacher and rabbi in the Jerusalem area. He had many disciples. You may have heard his most important teaching. However, I suspect you don't know it in the way I'm speaking of now.

Al Shelosha Devarim haOlam Omeid: al haTorah, al haAvodah, v'al Gemilut Chasidim, Simon the Just taught.[5] The world — notice, not the Jewish people but the world itself — is sustained by three matters: Torah, *Avodah*, and *Gemilut Chasidim*.

What are these things exactly, these secrets to a good life?

Secret number one: the Torah means how and how well you think — whether you're discerning, whether you perceive the world as it is, not as your peers or others tell you it is. There is a difference: the first way you learn and figure things out by hard work, by diligent thinking, by being prepared to think differently from the crowd. To do this you must avail yourselves of the wisdom of our Torah and our other holy books. You see, our Torah is the very sharpest lens possible through which to view the world. It's as if we need glasses in order to see most clearly. Our Torah is our necessary lens.

The second way you don't really learn, though you think you do. Instead, you repeat what others say. You hear things and take them in without giving much thought to the wisdom or the rightness of what you've absorbed. The first way of learning means you think for yourself — with the help of those wiser, for sure. The second way, in effect, you let others tell you what to think.

More than that, when you think for yourself, you think better. Actually, you feel better, too. There is great satisfaction in well-earned independence. The same kind of satisfaction is found in clarity. Trust me, or at least hear what I am saying. Deep learning of our holy books, accomplished over time and with regularity, brings both. But it takes effort. And discipline. And time. And as much as anything else, being willing to stand out from the crowd. None of this is easy. But doing it and doing it often enough changes you. You're better able to see the world, both for what it is and how you would like to remake it.

So figuring out what really is — by thinking and working hard at it and then by looking through the sharpest lens there is (our Torah) — is secret number one to a good life, a contented life. All of this because the Torah has the touch of the Divine. That touch, God's grace, is what deepens our learning, sharpens our thinking, and generates unusual brain power — and makes us most human.

Secret number two from our friend Simon the Just is this: *Avodah*, prayer, by which I don't mean the rote saying of words — those prayers and blessings Jews have said for centuries. *Avodah* means how you understand your place in the world, where you fit in with things. It means not assuming that you or any of us are at the centre of the world. Never, never assume that. I will tell you why. Because unless there is room left for God, there is no room for anyone at all. This is the fundamental thinking of *Avodah*.

Avodah is, therefore, humbling. Modesty, self-restraint — these are great things. If you pull back a little, if you leave room for others, not only is there room for God but, ironically, you leave room, real space, to grow, to be who you are, who God needs you to be.

So to participate in such a community provides you with an understanding of your place in the world, something, by the way, that took me a long time to learn because I was never part of a praying community until my mid-twenties. You'll experience here a kind of contentment found nowhere else. In such a regular praying synagogue community, you get reminded — by the prayers, by the learning, by God, by your fellow Jews, actually just by showing up — of your place in the world, and, no less than that, Who is at the centre of it all. That's our second secret to a contented life.

Here is the third secret from our friend, Simon the Just: *Gemilut Chasidim*, normally translated as deeds of loving kindnesses, or as I prefer, deeds of social mutual responsibility. Here we focus on the main part: *Chesed*.

Chesed, first of all, means kindness. So I would say to you, be kind. Be kinder than you think you have to be — to your families, to your friends, and to those nearby. And be even kinder than that to those who have less, to those who hurt, to those who have fewer friends, to those who are on the margin. Be kind to your fellow Jews; be kind to all fellow human beings.

Chesed also means loyalty, which means treating people well when no one else is watching; loyalty also in the sense of having someone's back, exactly as your parents have your backs because they love you so powerfully. You must have the backs of others — family and friends, and others who are well beyond your immediate circle. Watch out for them because there may be no one else doing so. Giving of yourself in all ways and doing more of that than you think you should: this is how you put loyalty and kindness together.

Kindness and loyalty put together are best exemplified by what the writer Christopher Hitchens has observed. Reflecting on his likely fatal illness, Hitchens implored his readers as follows: "If there is anybody known to you who might benefit from a letter or a visit, do not *on any account* postpone the writing or the making of it. The difference made will almost certainly be more than you have calculated."[6]

If you make this way of thinking integral to who you are, I promise that the rewards, the satisfactions, and the contentedness will be large in your life. You'll be smart in the most important of ways. Don't assume for the moment that intellectuals, those who read the most books, those who have the highest degrees, are smarter than you are. The kind of intelligence that our tradition affirms is what Simon the Just points toward: intelligence that makes us better because we think better and because we treat others well precisely because we understand who they are — God's creatures, no less than are we.

If you do those things, I guarantee your contentedness, I guarantee your parents' pride, and I guarantee your congregation's satisfaction. But more important than what we feel, you'll help make the world, one act of kindness after another, better than before. You'll do this as Jews, as human beings, as citizens of the world.

None of this can be measured, not a bit of it can be calculated. It's all far larger than that.

You need this. We need you to cultivate and possess this kind of intelligence, this kind of learning, as a foundation for how you act in the world.

We need you to be like this. Again, my guarantee: if you act like this, if you think like this often enough, your satisfactions will be much larger than otherwise; your successes will be more than can be measured; your parents will rest contentedly; your congregation will take pride.

Most important, so will you know contentment if you live a life of hope and generosity, of intelligence and kindness — you who will stand for the Torah, for *Avodah*, and for *Chesed*.

Nothing could be more important than this. No secret is better hidden from unseeing eyes and unknowing hearts, yet more available to be revealed. Go and find it. Go and live by it. Go with God. Go do good for all, yourselves included. Doing so, you will build contented lives and help to sustain the world.

NOACH: WHAT KIND OF FATHER WAS LAMECH?[7]

From *The Modern Men's Torah Commentary,*
edited by Jeffrey K. Salkin

Noah was a righteous man; he was blameless in his age.

— Genesis 6:9

At the birth of his son, Lamech predicts, "This one will provide us relief from our work and from the toil of our hands, out of the very soil which the Lord placed under a curse."[8]

Noah's name, Noach, heralds comfort for a beleaguered world. His great accomplishment, the saving of humanity, will inspire Midrash Tanhuma to acclaim, "Before Noah's birth, what was reaped was not what had been sown. Where wheat or barley was sown, thorns and thistles were reaped. But after Noah was born, the earth returned to orderly growth. What was sown was reaped ..."

Such eloquent testimony aside, Lamech's announcement is worrisome. What is promised is more daunting than restoring nature's harmony, more far-reaching than righting the order made wrong by human beings; Noah is, in effect, enlisted to rearrange the very nature of humanity. As Karen Armstrong writes, he is charged to do nothing less than "reverse the curse of Adam's sin and bring relief to both humanity and the afflicted earth."[9]

Unfazed, endowed with decency, and attuned to God's will, Noah augurs hope as devastation looms. His father appears prescient.

Once the flood rampages and the waters recede, God, relenting of his promise to destroy the world, renews life through Noah and his sons, Shem, Ham, and Japheth. Now Noah can finally do what his name actually suggests: rest. (The etymology is askew; Noach more properly means "rest," not "relief" or "comfort," as Lamech's naming implies. This is only a curiosity and not yet an agitation. After all, Noah has indeed provided comfort and relief and is justified in unwinding inside his tent.)

Still, startlingly, as Noah rescues humanity, he can't save himself. Once inside that tent, Noah becomes undone: "Noah, the tiller of the soil, was the first to plant a vineyard. He drank of the wine and became drunk, and he uncovered himself within his tent."[10]

Whatever "uncovered" means — the speculations abound — Noah is done, spent morally and physically, his impressive résumé in shambles. Why could Noah save humanity but not himself? Why does he unravel so quickly, unbound from any moral compass or psychological core to hold himself at bay?

Is it, as the eleventh-century rabbinic commentator Rashi and others hint, that while Noah is more decent and less corrupt than his peers, he is more ordinary than he appears? That is to say that while Noah may be at ease following God's instructions, he is ill-equipped to internalize the implications.

Or does his personal undoing (mirrored in the telling actions of his son, Ham, who deliberately stares at and then almost gleefully tells of his father's uncovered nakedness), in fact, belong at Lamech's feet, or, more precisely, with his fathering? Perhaps the undone son possesses insufficient internal paternal ballast to buoy himself when storm-tossed and adrift. Maybe too much is expected of a son by a father who provides too little.

Regarding fathers and sons, most especially what fathers do for sons, we begin not with Noah but rather with Sigmund Freud. And not with Freudian analysis but rather with the childhood story Freud often told about himself and his father, here recounted in *The Interpretation of Dreams*:

And now, for the first time, I happened upon the youthful experience which even to-day still expresses its power in all these emotions and dreams. I might have been ten or twelve years old when my father began to take me with him on his walks, and in his conversation to reveal his views on the things of this world. Thus it was that he once told me the following incident, in order to show me that I had been born into happier times than he: "When I was a young man, I was walking one Saturday along the street in the village where you were born; I was well-dressed, with a new fur cap on my head. Up comes a Christian, who knocks my cap into the mud, and shouts, 'Jew, get off the pavement!'"— "And what did you do?" — "I went into the street and picked up the cap," he calmly replied. That did not seem heroic on the part of the big, strong man who was leading me, a little fellow by the hand. I contrasted this situation, which did not please me, with another, more in harmony with my sentiments — the scene in which Hannibal's father, Hamilcar Barcas, made his son swear before the household altar to take vengeance on the Romans. Ever since then Hannibal has had a place in my phantasies.[11]

No wonder Freud, now in his seventies and summing things up in *Civilization and Its Discontents*, observed, "I cannot think of any need in childhood as strong as a need for a father's protection."[12]

The Torah Speaks in Its Language and in Ours

We know of Jacob Freud's parental inadequacies from his son's observations. Yet how can we claim that Lamech, likewise, can't be a "big, strong man" holding his son firmly hand in hand?

While the biblical text is mute on Lamech's paternal ways, Leon Kass, an astute contemporary observer of biblical personalities and events, paints a picture of Noah. He sees Noah as a son without a proper father, and as a father who, in coming unglued in front of his sons, can no longer claim paternal authority:

> [His] drunkenness robs Noah of his dignity, his parental authority, and his very humanity. Prostrate rather than upright, this newly established master of the earth has, in the space of one verse, utterly lost his standing. Worse, instead of escaping from his origins, Noah in fact returns to the shameful naked condition of the aboriginal state: "he was uncovered in his tent." Stripped of his clothing, naked, exposed and vulnerable to disgrace, he appears merely as a *male*, not as a father — not even as a humanized, rational animal. Noah will not be the last man who degrades and unfathers himself as a result of drink. Paternal authority and respectability are precarious indeed.[13]

So there it is: Noah, stripped of any patina of civility, shorn of any claim to the mantle of fatherhood, is reduced to his animal self. Flat on his back, Noah returns to the origins he can't escape — his father and his father's ways.

Who, then, was Lamech, and how might the son be like the father?

While the Bible is circumspect on Lamech, the Rabbis, perhaps intuiting in the son's eventual undoing something of the ways of the father, are not. Noting Genesis 4:19 ("Lamech took to himself two wives"), they remark on the male ways of that generation: men would invariably take two wives at a time, making of the first almost a widow, while turning the second into something of a harlot. In other words, Lamech literally turns his back on one wife and uses the second one, more or less, for sexual pleasure alone. So Lamech was no stand-up man — not for his women, not for his son. Given what Noah observed at home as a young man, need we wonder more about his moral compass?

This doesn't mean, however, that Lamech is without a certain kind of discernment. As fathers often do, he knows his son well. He understands, specifically, that Noah has the stuff inside to be counted on, to bear any burden out in the larger world — and, indeed, he will become the protecting father to the mass of humanity. Nonetheless, the father, knowing something about himself, is well aware that his son — this world-class hero-to-be — is possessed of an internal hollowness. As great as Noah will be in the world, he will be just as suspect at home.

So, indeed, Noah is no stand-up father to his own sons, and eventually he becomes a first-class fool at home. Perhaps Lamech was prescient. He sensed that Noah could be heroic, kind, and decent for the world to see; yet inside his tent for none but his own sons to know, Noah will be unable to stand up straight, neither as a man nor as a father.

Lamech, knowing himself to be a bit crooked with his women, also knows he can't be straight with his son. He therefore deliberately twists his son's name. Noah is the one who can never rest and will always be taunted by having a name that suggests he's restful, perhaps the very reason he becomes twisted. But Noah can also be the one to bring relief and comfort for all humanity. Indeed, this is no misnaming at all. Rest is about stability, normality, continuity — achievements for which Noah lays the foundation by saving humanity. Nevertheless, these are accomplishments beyond the reach of his character, yet they aren't necessarily beyond the double meaning of his name.

THE HAUGHTY OF HEART
August 19, 1995

The Torah often inspires us and brings us the word of God. And sometimes it bedevils and discomforts us — intellectually, morally, and otherwise. Such is how it is with this week's *sidra*.

I say this because, for all the fascinating riches of Parashat Ekev — the blessings that flow from obeying God's Laws, the sheltering protection offered by God to a loyal Israel, the promise of the land and more — we can't escape the fact that two themes prominent throughout the Bible, obsessions really, hold centre stage in Ekev.

On the one hand, the *sidra* speaks in this voice: "You shall devour [and destroy] the people the Lord delivers to you, showing them no pity ... The Lord your God will deliver a plague against them until those who are left in hiding perish before you ... The Lord your God will deliver them up to you, throwing them into utter panic until they are wiped out. [God] will deliver their kings into your hand, and you shall obliterate their name from under the heavens ..."[14] There is more, but you get the point: the Torah speaks with the voice of anger, legitimizing and commanding the conquering and destruction of other peoples.

And, on the other hand, the *sidra* speaks in a very different voice, one we liberals are most comfortable with and proud of, one we would wish to promote as the Torah's "true" voice and spirit: "[Remember:] the Lord your God upholds the cause of the fatherless and the widow, and befriends the stranger, pro-viding [the stranger] with food and clothing — You, too, must befriend the stranger, for you were strangers in the land of Egypt."[15] This voice — compassionate, concerned for the vulner-able, commanding care for other peoples — is radically different from Ekev's angry words.

What do we the students of this Book do with these two opposing voices and commands? How can they be understood in relation to each other? Can they, should they, be reconciled one with the other?

First, the obvious from the point of view of the Bible itself: the striking divergence between these two thrusts has a lot to do with power. The stranger to be befriended was presumed to be among the vulnerable, the demoralized, those without power, a perpetual reminder of the enslaved Israelites in Egypt. Meanwhile, those whom the Torah seeks to demonize and commands Israel to conquer and wield power over serve as an ever-present symbol of the ruling Egyptians.

Very much related to this issue of power is this fact: the Canaanites and the other peoples the Torah seeks to destroy were viewed as idolaters who worship deities infused with their own power and will, competitors in Israelite eyes with the only source of power in the world — *Adonai*. The stranger to be taken in, meanwhile, was by definition "godless" — therefore without a power to back him up, not a competitor, not threatening. The stranger, the *ger*, could be brought in under the wings of *Adonai*.

Of course, the biblical foundation for responses — the idol intoxicated, powerful enemy, and the godless and vulnerable stranger — was God. The love of the stranger was a direct result and reflection of the love of God. Likewise, the will to conquer the Canaanite reflected and expressed the desire to love and pro-mote none but the Israelite God, walking in none but His ways.

God as the source of the response to both the powerful and the powerless, the spur to conquer and destroy as well as to love and befriend, may well point toward the nature of the contradictory reaction to the proverbial "other."

Yehezkel Kaufmann, the eminent biblical scholar and for many years professor of Bible at Hebrew University, noted that biblical religion, unlike contemporaneous and later developing religions, simply couldn't accept the notion that another power in the universe might overcome God and usurp His authority. The reason the Bible so hates this possibility is because it then allows, as competing religions teach, for other powers, other gods, to serve as a source of evil. Consequently, said Kaufmann, Judaism transferred evil from the metaphysical to the moral realm, that is, the realm of human beings sinning. Therefore, other competing deities are stripped of much of their power, specifically, the capacity to create and promote evil. And not unrelated: if the Israelite God is not regarded as the source of evil, how else, after all, can human beings exercise free will?[16]

And so it may be, and here let's speculate that this exaggerated and contradictory obsession with the other — anyone not within the Israelite fold — was rooted in the matter of sin.

To further speculate: what might that sin be exactly? Can we identify and understand it? To do so we first step back from the biblical context and into that of later tradition, most particularly that of modern scholars who presume that this total annihilation of the Canaanites never actually happened. Moreover, of course, modern scholarship asserts that Deuteronomy and other such texts were produced once the Israelites were well settled in their land. It follows, then, that these aggressive and angry threats were furious warnings about following the ways, including sinful ones, of those other peoples already occupying the land.

But what was the sin of those people who trafficked in local idols, who hadn't experienced the awesome, liberating hand of the Israelite God, who hadn't heard His commanding voice at Sinai?

Listen now to one of those furious warnings in our *sidra*: "You must not bring an abhorrent thing into your house — otherwise you will be rejected as it is. You must despise it as abominable and abhorrent — for it is rejected."[17]

What do the Rabbis do with this warning? Do they think it's really about conquering the Canaanites and about their sins only? No. They go and quote Proverbs: "An abomination of the Lord are all of the haughty of heart."[18] To which Rabbi Yohanan says in the name of Rabbi Shimon bar Yochai: "If one is haughty of spirit, it is as if he serves idols."[19]

So there it is: the "haughty of heart" is the one who thinks he's like God, who considers himself superior to others. This, then, is Israelite idol worship — every bit the sin of the Canaanites who actually worship their idols. In the eyes of our Rabbis, the Israelite, the Jew who forgets the true power in the world, who forgets the God of Egypt and Sinai, is every bit as sinful as the Canaanite who denies it. So the powerful, God-denying other is greatly demonized, in part as a projection of fear of what Israel might become: haughty, forgetful, assimilated in destructive ways. The stranger, meanwhile, could easily be befriended as a reminder, not a forgetting denier, of Egypt, therefore of God's ultimate and true power.

The Bible, on the surface vexing and disquieting, is finally instructive, inspiring, and just maybe revealing of the word of God: when you're obsessed with the other, when you demonize others, when you focus on the sins of others, be warned — the first sin to acknowledge may be your own. It is, inevitably, perhaps a combination of forgetfulness and haughtiness that tempts all of us, that denies God, that spoils the spirit. If, as Shimon bar Yochai taught, you are spoiled or haughty of spirit, your actions are no better than the one who worships idols.

As the month of Elul approaches, and God beckons and waits and watches, and we shall decide how and who to be, is there any better inspiration?

REMEMBERING AMALEK, THINKING ABOUT SCHINDLER
February 19, 1994

In the prologue to his book *Zakhor: Jewish History and Jewish Memory*, the historian Yosef Hayim Yerushalmi writes that memory, as used in the religious sense in Judaism, is neither a genetic matter nor a psychic structure along the lines of the Jungian archetype. Rather, Yerushalmi says:

> Contrary to a theory widely held as late as the seventeenth century, a child left in the forest to its own linguistic devices would not speak Hebrew spontaneously, not even were it a Jewish *enfant sauvage*, and neither would it "remember" that Abraham journeyed from Ur to Canaan. Only the group can bequeath both language and a transpersonal memory.[20]

The implication here, therefore, is that even, perhaps especially, individual memory is learned, organized, given meaning through a social framework, by which we are also to understand that as Yerushalmi puts it, "collective memory is not a metaphor but a social reality transmitted and sustained through the conscious efforts and institutions of the group."[21]

What else is the Seder, for instance, but a transmission of a specific memory and its lessons? What else is Purim but a transmission of another memory?

That this is the case, that collective memory is a social reality transmitted to and by the group through various ritual means, is an acknowledgement of a serious problem for the group: history only happens but once. Later generations not on hand for the event don't have the eyes or the ears or the smell to know first-hand what took place.

The biblical figure Amalek must have been frightening. What he and his people did to the Israelites upon their exit from Egypt must have been worse. We know this because the Bible hates Amalek, imploring those within his grasp to remember him and what he did to the Bible's people.

The animosity aroused by Amalek caused him to be Israel's archetypal enemy. After all, by attacking the Israelites so soon after Egypt, he was their first enemy; therefore, he is recalled with a certain prominence. Israel, still uninformed as a people, naked to the world, as it were, was unusually vulnerable; Amalek's actions made him the eternal foe. He would stand in later memory not only for himself but for other enemies, as well.

Therefore, this Shabbat, as is custom for the Sabbath preceding Purim, is Shabbat Zachor. We are bid, in anticipation of the Book of Esther, to once again remember the original foe, Amalek.

We remember him through three brief verses recorded in Deuteronomy:

> Remember what Amalek did to you on your
> journey, after you left Egypt: how, undeterred
> by fear of God, he surprised you on the march,
> when you were famished and weary, and cut
> down all the stragglers in your rear. Therefore

> when the Lord your God grants you safety from
> all your enemies around you, in the land the
> Lord your God is giving you as a heredity por-
> tion, you shall blot out the memory of Amalek
> from under heaven. Do not forget![22]

This isn't the only passage about Amalek. In fact, it's the second of two extended pieces, and significantly different from the
first. The first episode involving Amalek is located as the historical
event apparently takes place: in the Book of Exodus, soon after the
liberation from Egypt, just before the giving of the Torah on Sinai.

The Exodus account provides the entire story, including
that famous moment as Moses raises his hand and Israel grows
stronger; and when tired, he lowers his hand and Israel falters.
Finally, his supporters hold up his hands and Israel prevails.
That was Amalek who Moses and the Israelites were fighting
and finally defeating.

In this original Exodus description, there is no sense of
aroused anger, no exhortation to remember — rather, a seemingly straightforward rendering of the event. It's followed
interestingly enough by God telling Moses to write down in a
document what had happened to serve as a reminder. But that's
it. No need to plead with those there to remember; they were
there as history broke out.

The Exodus passage, then, is dramatically different from the
Deuteronomy passage. Deuteronomy, addressed to a much later
generation, one far removed from the battle with Amalek, isn't
concerned with details but with meaning. Therefore, there's the
sense of anger, the exhortation to remember, that is, to be mind-
ful about a past they never knew but must know.

What was it that this later generation, apparently now settled in their land, apparently prosperous, must know exactly?

Why did Amalek leave such a lasting imprint on Israel's memory? Why was it necessary that this later generation know this?

Text and tradition emphasize two things about the original events. First, as Exodus makes explicit, was Israel's vulnerability: "[Amalek] surprised you on the march, when you were famished and weary, and cut down all the stragglers at your rear." The biblical scholar Benno Jacob puts this vulnerability into context, saying, "The emigrant and the fugitive bore a certain degree of sacredness; as they were seeking a special goal, and a new home, they deserved humane treatment.... [Israel's] treatment, good or bad, during this period of need, would never be forgotten ..."[23]

In other words, there is a strong relationship between how one is treated in a time of vulnerability and memory itself. In effect, the worse you are treated when vulnerable, the more duty bound you are to remember. Likewise, humane, decent, even unexpected treatment in such circumstances brings equal obligation to remember.

This relationship between vulnerability and memory is expressed linguistically in the two passages on Amalek. In Exodus, Joshua and Israel "disable" Amalek (*vayachalosh*); while the much later Deuteronomy passage reminds its audience that Amalek had been treacherous in going after *hanecheshalim*, those who, famished and tired, were "lagging behind," those least able to fend off an enemy.

They *were* finally fended off, immediately avenged by the wrath of Joshua and other Israelites, and later remembered by those not there. Amalek must always be disabled because he went after Israel's most vulnerable flank.

There is one other matter text and tradition stress in accounting for Amalek's lasting impression on Israel's memory: He was, again as Deuteronomy says explicitly, "undeterred by fear of God" in his assault on Israel.

The Bible goes to great lengths to underscore the binding tie between the fear of God and humane conduct. As Nahum M. Sarna puts it, "'Fear of God' ... acts as the ultimate restraint upon perfidy and inhumanity, particularly in situations in which self-interest might tempt one to exploit the weak and disadvantaged ... Conversely, it also functions positively as the motivating force for decent behavior, and it imposes obligations and duties."[24]

Fear of God means not only fear of Divine retribution but also respect for God's creatures. Fear of God, therefore, is a civilizing and moralizing agent and can bring about courageous, unexpected, and even mystifying behaviour. Lack of this fear, as Amalek exemplified, is indeed the most arrogant and potentially brutalizing behaviour.

My remarks this morning are in response to two matters: Deuteronomy's plea to its audience and all future generations to "remember Amalek" and what he did to our ancestors; and, second, to tradition's assertion that he symbolizes anyone who would unjustly assault Israel, from Haman to Hitler. But in a small way, too, these remarks are a response to the movie *Schindler's List.*

Of all the questions and controversies surrounding the movie, the only one I find of interest is the obsession (or in its milder forms, just plain wonderment) as to why director Steven Spielberg chose not to spell out Oskar Schindler's metamorphosis from Nazi lover to Jewish protector. Many critics want to know: why the change? Why doesn't Spielberg attempt to draw it out?

Stanley Kauffmann, film critic for *The New Republic,* writes about this issue and how it's approached in the film: "... never is there a Moment of Truth, together with an angelic choir, on the sound track. Spielberg's artistic triumph is that he refuses to explicate, to interfere with what is actually known. He leaves the mystery of Schindler's goodness as finally inexplicable as the mystery of 'human savagery' around him."[25]

Well, of course, Kauffmann is right: Spielberg beautifully refuses to tell everything, this kind of question being too profound to pretend that we can know everything about it. But Kauffmann isn't entirely right. There is, after all, that one moment when Schindler is first confronted with the Nazis' full brutality and fury at the expense of the Jews, unprotected and vulnerable.

You watch Schindler watching. He doesn't need to say anything. He doesn't need to explain. Probably he couldn't, anyway. We can only guess that, for reasons beyond our understanding, he may have been deterred by the fear of God, his actions may have been a modern playing out of both lessons of remembering Amalek: where God is not, evil may reign; where God is, goodness may just prevail.

Let us then remember Amalek. And Schindler, too.

ABSOLUTES AND AMBIGUITIES
May 8, 1993

The following episode is found at the very end of this morning's Torah portion: a man whose parents were identified as an Israelite mother and an Egyptian father found himself in a fight. His opponent was another man, both of whose parents were apparently Israelite. In the course of their fight, the first man spoke God's name in blasphemy, likely using His name in some kind of explicit curse.

At that point he was hauled away to Moses and then placed in custody, while Moses went off to consult the Lord about an appropriate punishment. The Lord then spoke to Moses as follows: "Take the blasphemer outside the camp and let all [who heard his cursing] lay their hands upon his head, and let the whole community stone him."

God then announces for all to hear that the punishment for blaspheming His name is death: the whole community, stranger

146

and citizen alike, are to take collective responsibility for the punishment. The episode concludes with the community taking the blasphemer beyond the camp and bombarding him with stones.

This story provokes numerous questions, but two are most important: why does the Book of Leviticus, which has very little narrative material and concerns itself predominately with the sacrificial cult, take the time to relate this obscure story? And, second, why is the Bible so harsh, so apparently extreme in response to a man using God's name as part of a curse?

Now as to the first question — the story's inclusion in this book with regard to the sacrificial cult — two more pieces of information are significant, both related to the identity of the blasphemer's mother. Whereas the blasphemer's name isn't given, his mother's name is. She is Shelomit, the daughter of a man named Dibri, he of the tribe of Dan.

That isn't irrelevant information. The tribe of Dan, way up north in the ancient land of Israel, had its own cultic centre, did some of its own sacrificing, and was held by the Jerusalem Temple's priests in utter disrepute. It's likely that the blasphemer's Danite lineage is more troublesome than his Egyptian background.

Second, note his mother's name: Shelomit, the daughter of Dibri. "Shelomit" is from *shalom*, while "Dibri" is from *daber*, "to speak." In a story about cursing, such a name can hardly be ignored.

With this story set before us, then, and its important questions asked, here are reflections about its meaning even for later generations that may feel removed by time and repulsed by content. First, this is a story about oral culture. Specifically about *speaking* and about *hearing*.

About speaking: the Bible is, after all, about the word of God, whether understood literally or metaphorically, or both. Words emanate from God and are imbued with meaning and value. When human beings speak, it is out of the knowledge that this is a Divinely given capacity; when one opens one's mouth to speak, one is imitating God in a tradition that has no higher aspiration than the imitation of the Divine.

So the power in speaking words is great. At no time is this power greater than in the act of blessing, or in the act of cursing. That is as true today as in the Bible. The Bible understood that both blessings and curses were an integral part of speech, both played a role in human life and expression, and both were at their maximum when God's name was included. We can therefore conclude that if a blessing backed by God was to be taken seriously by those who heard it, it would be no less so for a curse that also evoked God's name.

If speaking has consequences and responsibilities, so, too, does hearing. That the act of hearing wasn't passive, and, in fact, bore its own responsibilities must be seen as originating at Sinai: God spoke and Israel heard. But Israel, of course, didn't simply hear; Israel heard God's words and responded, underscoring forever that to hear is not to disclaim responsibility but rather to be part of a circle of active participation.

Look at our biblical story: all who were within hearing of the blasphemer's curse were enjoined, like it or not, to include themselves in his punishment. The reason is clear. In the Bible, hearing is, like seeing, a way to witness something. One hears blessings and provides witness by responding "Amen." Likewise, to hear a vow or a curse makes one a witness — literally, a party to an event, owing response and testimony.

In this story, therefore, once the punishment was announced, all who witnessed the original cursing through hearing it — everyone, the citizen and stranger both — were to come forward, lay their hands on his head, and then stone him. Just as the blasphemer's uttering of this curse brought him to this horrible moment, the happenstance of hearing his curse obligated others to take part in his death.

So important is speaking and hearing in the Bible, so tied to God are both, that in the most extreme situations the results aren't easy to accept. Nothing was apparently as extreme as cursing God's name — using the God-given capacity to diminish God, and along with Him, one's fellow human beings.

And, therefore, as well as commentators can estimate, the stoning by death of the blasphemer was a one-time occurrence included in the text as a reminder of the significance of words, especially employed in the most debasing and demeaning (literally, "de-meaning") ways.

We can't conclude a look at this story without noting the following facts:

- that Moses is unsure of what to do, how to rule, and goes off to consult God about the punishment;
- that the man is taken outside the camp to be stoned and to die — the camp being a place not to be defiled by death;
- that this man had a mother, who though she's from Dan, is named as a "speaker of peace"; and
- that this man is an outsider to the camp, not a full Israelite, with ties to Egypt, a past enemy, and Dan, a current competitor.

All of which underscores the fact that the Bible, even *as* it is absolute in teaching the significance — the Divine and therefore human significance — of speaking and hearing, is deeply ambivalent about this episode. So much so that it puts the curse in the mouth of an outsider shaped both by oppression and war and by words of peace, but who, nonetheless, has violated the sanctity of God by his words.

In other words, laws are absolute in the Bible because Divine principles are. Nonetheless, human beings aren't so consistent, are far from perfect, and the Bible is caught here between both realities. May we, the Bible's readers, learn from both its absolutes and its ambivalences, knowing our ancestors did just that.

5

About That Matter of Evil ...
(and Our East African Home)

PREAMBLE

As well as I remember, I spoke about evil publicly for the first time in September 1995. The wretchedly awful behaviour of Paul Bernardo and Karla Homolka had preoccupied Canadians that summer. In the wake of the court revelations of the sadistic torturing of Leslie Mahaffy and Kristen French, I spoke about evil on Rosh Hashanah — that of Bernardo and Homolka, and potentially of all human beings. I rooted my remarks in the Jewish tradition's understanding of evil as a human reality — always latent, sometimes realized. We rarely talk of God's agonizing regret at the creation of the human (see Genesis 6:5), but I did so that Rosh Hashanah.

Since then I've spoken on a number of occasions about those who calculatedly rip apart innocent lives and terrorize societies, who kill and maim and do so deliberately. In December 2000, at a memorial service marking the 1989 Montreal massacre of fourteen women, I offered some reflections (see "Making Good Out of Evil" in this part of the book). In December 2012, on the heels of the Newtown massacre in which twenty schoolchildren were gunned down, I published a piece in the *Globe and Mail* (see "The School Massacre Was Human Evil, Not Tragedy"). There I criticized the ever-present habit of employing the word *tragedy* instead of naming it clearly — *evil*.

Over the years, when I talked about evil done by individuals, while there was some discomfort, there was little pushback. The likes of Bernardo, their crimes so inhumane and despicable, were easy to despise. When I spoke about evil done by groups, including religious ones, the response was often different.

The spate of horrific bus bombings in early 1996 in Jerusalem riveted my attention, but it wasn't until the out-of-the-blue-sky horrors of September 11, and the regular terrorizing of Israelis during the Second Intifada of the early 2000s, that I first addressed the evil committed by Islamo-Fascists (Christopher Hitchens's term). I did so initially in a sermon on Rosh Hashanah just five days after the September 11 attacks (see "The Reach of Our Imagination," the first piece in this part).

Unlike the reaction to evil wrought by an easy-to-demonize "lone wolf," when I spoke about groups perpetrating heinous crimes, the reaction was of a different order. Then the upset was significant, the kickback intense and even personal. I had, it was claimed, attacked Muslims as a whole. When that proved demonstrably untrue, it was suggested instead that maybe I just sounded too much like a "fundamentalist" for a liberal rabbi in a liberal milieu.

That I think is demonstrably true. I'm aware I don't always speak like most liberal rabbis.

Here's why. Although raised in a home with a deeply psychoanalytic bent, and while a strong believer in therapy and psychoanalysis, I long ago refused the temptations of the therapeutic rabbinate. I thought my job was to be a rabbi, not a therapist. If to some ears that sounds "fundamentalist," I'll live with it: my intellectual religious roots are with the Torah and the Rabbis, not the *New York Times.*

The dissonance is real. Ours, after all, is a therapeutic culture that prefers to locate "problems" (and their solutions) within the uneven wiring of the human psyche or amid trying social circumstances. There are such things, as there are very real traumas. Life isn't an easy way, and there are bumps on everyone's road, sometimes bad ones, and a rabbi's task is also to bring comfort to those who ail (without fail, every single one of us at some point). But Osama bin Laden's childhood was by all accounts happy enough, his family among the wealthiest on the Arabian Peninsula. And Mohamed Atta, too, and his compatriots — they had it okay, as well.

No, sometimes evil is just that — evil, *rah*, as Jewish tradition (actually, God) calls it very early on. And, yes, evil can grow from the poisoned stem of any religion or any group's ideological roots, as it can sprout from the venom of the jealously enraged human heart.

In the early 1960s, I knew something about evil, even without a ready vocabulary. It began when I couldn't take my eyes off the movie screen while watching *To Kill a Mockingbird.* The awful wickedness of Bob Ewell hurt my ten-year-old heart as surely as the kindness of Atticus Finch and then Boo Radley swelled my heart. When I left the theatre that day, I knew something inside had changed.

Much, much later I began to see such behaviour as within its own category, whether at the behest of an individual or a group. Once a rabbi, and once capable, I felt an obligation to say what I knew, always as tested and understood by a tradition possessed of the kind of eyes unafraid to take in what is happening, even if painful and vexing.

For some people I spoke about evil more and differently

from what they preferred; for others I was too reticent and pulled my punches on occasion. I respect both views and have learned from each, though neither changed my essential conviction of the requirement, borne uniquely by rabbis but nonetheless incumbent on all, to name and to confront evil when it raises its head openly or when it "crouches [hiding] at the door," as told in Genesis 4:7.

So, too, my belief hasn't changed that, alongside naming evil, must go our active recognition of goodness. I set this out in the last part of a Holy Blossom Temple Bulletin (see "Evil — and Goodness") one month after September 11.

Finally, and related, my own evolution as a rabbi was also about evolution itself — an unanticipated change that occurred when I went to East Africa the first time in 2009. I didn't return to Canada the same person.

The experience on the savannahs of old, watching animals exhibiting behaviour suspiciously human and then reading extensively about evolution, made me think about humans differently, about our complex nature in particular.

I taught the tradition, early Genesis especially, with new eyes: in part, eyes widened by a deeper understanding of our profound relationship to animals; and in part a newly sharpened perspective on an ancient text (the Bible) that reveals sophisticated thinking about how we came to be God's Divinely imprinted creatures who, too, were once part of the animal kingdom (and still are). The Bible, early Genesis specifically, isn't estranged from notions of evolution!

Being in the Great Rift Valley (I've since returned twice) spun my head around about God's pinnacle creation — the creature our tradition would first name *Adam*, that is, "one from the earth." I learned things on the beautiful and haunting savannahs of Kenya and Tanzania about our common and remarkable history that I hadn't paid attention to previously. I'd always assumed evolution to be "true," but until I set foot in our most ancient home, I had no idea how true, how profound, and how thrilling it all is.

Read the blog post at the end of this part of the book to discover what I learned from a close reading of Rabbi Joseph Soloveitchik, once back from East Africa in 2009. You'll understand better my deepening (and maybe evolving) view of our flawed but fascinating nature. And, no less important, why I say that, while Jerusalem is our eternal home as Jews, the Great Rift Valley, on and around those savannahs where it all began, is our original home, as it is for all people and for every People.

THE REACH OF OUR IMAGINATION
Rosh Hashanah, September 16, 2001

Five days ago our breath was sucked out of us, even if only for a day or so. Not so for almost three thousand people in New York City, in Washington, D.C., and over Pennsylvania farm country. Cut down and obliterated in the morning light by forces more real, more cunning, more potent than most imagined, their life force forever gone. All parts of them extinguished in an instant or two.

Some say the world is now forever changed, but I don't think so. Rather, the horrors of September 11 make reality crystal-clear for those whose vision had been fogged by illusion. What crashed through glass, steel, and concrete on Tuesday shattered our illusions, too.

While some who perpetrated this horrifically brilliant and evil act will likely stand trial, so, too, shall we go on trial. Ours, though, is a different kind of trial. And it begins now.

Their trial is about their work of September 11. Ours is about how we respond to what they've done. After the shock subsides and the dead are hard to rest in some fashion or another, and once the cleanup is at hand, and after the markets rebound and normality returns, what then?

What shall we do once the stark face of Satan has faded from television screens and from our minds? What shall we do when children are no longer afraid and adults are no longer shaken? What shall we do when hope wends its way back into our hearts and when impressive plans are announced to rebuild Manhattan's financial district? What shall we do once Israel is again front and centre as the target of Radical Islam and when the phrases "necessary restraints" and "unnecessary provocation" ring out from the pundits and politicians as they surely will?

How do we understand what happened? And how shall we respond?

Let's begin with our Holy Day. The words of our liturgy — the ideas of sin and forgiveness — aren't adequate for this moment. After all, these Days of Awe concern themselves with lives mostly restrained by basic decency. Yours and mine: we who lie a little, cheat here and there, hurt one another some, don't live as well as we should, sin against one another, against God, against ourselves. Masters of the small stuff: a little cheating, some convenient lies, lots of corners cut. These days of reflection help us be less petty, more generous, less cruel, and kinder. We seek renewal, and we might just find it.

But that's not what this September is about. Not this one.

Out liturgy isn't up to this moment for another reason. We've tailored the liturgy bequeathed us by those who lived at a different time but whose natures can't be that different from our own, and we've made it nice. Very nice — we've incorporated the courtesies, the pretenses, and the squishy thinking of our time.

Evil is mentioned, yes, but as an old-time idea with no staying power. It isn't represented in our nice prayer books for what it is: a force, the work, and machinations of specific people with a poisoned and hard ideology that's crashed in on us.

This week isn't the first time such horrors have been visited by some humans on others. The old liturgy knew that well; the modern liturgy wipes the slate clean of evil.

If our liturgy has abandoned reality, not everybody else has. And so let us turn to a piece of recent literature, a horror novel of the late 1980s, Thomas Harris's *The Silence of the Lambs*, later made into a movie of the same title. As Andrew Delbanco sets the scene in *The Death of Satan*, there is

> an exchange between an imprisoned madman, a psychiatrist who bites his victims to death and subsequently cannibalizes them, and a young female FBI agent who seeks his help in pursuing another serial killer. The mad doctor stands, straitjacketed, inside his Plexiglas cage and addresses the young woman outside it, who is soft-spoken, methodical, and named for a small bird.[1]

The mad psychiatrist, Hannibal Lecter, then says to the FBI agent:

> "Nothing happened to me, Officer Starling. *I* happened. You can't reduce me to a set of influences. You've given up good and evil for behaviorism, Officer Starling. You've got everybody in moral dignity pants — nothing is ever anybody's fault. Look at me, Officer Starling. Can you stand to say I'm evil?"[2]

Delbanco, discussing Lecter's dialogue, comments: "These words are an epitome of modern horror — the horror of knowing that we cannot answer the monster's question."[3]

When Osama bin Laden says, "We can defeat America — it is much weaker than it appears," that's precisely what he means. He believes we're incapable of responding to the monster's challenge because we're unwilling to name evil. We don't wish to see it or know it, and therefore we will never name it. Bin Laden knows what we refuse to know.

He knows that our thinking is more of a match for the value-free thinking of Officer Starling than that of a complex religious tradition that names evil as unequivocally as it names good. We Jews and we of the liberal democratic West have lost the language for evil. We're most often rendered confused and silent in the face of evil. The petty and common are our fare for judgment and quick response, not the man-made horror show that comes out of a beautiful blue September sky.

We have neither the vocabulary nor the stomach for evil. Bin Laden and his ilk know that and count on it. That's nothing new, though.

In *The Death of Satan*, Delbanco writes: "We live in the most brutal century in human history, but instead of stepping forward to take the credit, [the devil] has rendered himself invisible." The very notion of evil, Delbanco contends, seems to be incompatible with modern life, from which the ideas of transgression and the accountable self are fast receding. Yet despite the loss of old words and moral concepts — Satan, sin, evil — "we cannot do without some conceptual means for thinking about the sorts of experiences that used to go under the name of evil." Delbanco adds that his "driving motive" in writing his book is "the conviction that if evil, with all the insidious complexity which Augustine attributed to it, escapes the reach of our imagination, it will have established dominion over us all."[4]

But now the devil is no longer invisible. Now we understand how profoundly real evil is — and how terribly human he may be. What happened exactly that this came to be? How do we understand such diabolic human evil, that of a terrorist, that (potentially) of any person?

The Rabbis of Old teach that when the angels learned that God intended to create the image of His own being and then breathe the breath of His life into that image, they conspired with one another to hide that image of Divinity. One angel suggested hiding it on top of a mountain. A second angel wondered about putting it at the bottom of the sea. But the cleverest angel of all said, "Look, let's hide the Divine image by putting it in man and woman, because that's the last place anyone would think to look for it."[5]

This tale is brilliant, realistic, and liberating. It acknowledges human evil and our potential to traffic in it, yet also acknowledges that we're made in the image of the Divine. This tale is true.

The Rabbis, by implication, present the basic human problem and challenge quite clearly: what do we do with the Divine image within us? Shall we hide it or respond to it? Ignore it or feel commanded by it? Destroy it or be elevated by it?

Shall we read the words "[The human] is created in the Divine image," either innocently or willfully, to mean we're basically good? Or shall we understand, as the Rabbis believe, that the verse means we're like God in knowing good and evil, that we possess inclinations to walk the road toward either, but which path we trod is entirely ours to decide? And, ultimately, for all our potential — for good and for bad — everything is in that choosing. Or to put it slightly differently, either path, either choice, is each within "the reach of our imagination," as Andrew Delbanco has it.

And would human beings come to learn that, as the Rabbis taught until they were tired, you can't choose intelligently if you don't know the world as it is? You can't choose rightly if you don't look clearly. You can't choose appropriately if you're not prepared to stand before human judgment or that of the Divine.

The two great rabbinic schools of their day, Hillel and Shammai, debated the nature of human beings at length before narrowing things down to one fundamental question: should human beings have been created? Eventually, they reached consensus: it would have been better had human beings not been created, but since they were created "let them investigate their past deeds, and let them examine what they were about to do (that they live a righteous life)." The Rabbis spoke like this because they knew the desire to have ultimate faith in people, while understandable, was deeply problematic. Ultimate faith is reserved for God alone. Yes, show faith in humans — by supporting them and challenging them as appropriate — but save faith and trust finally for God.

This isn't a pessimistic view, but a liberating one because it frees one from the burden of ignorance. In other words, we don't think people are depraved, but we know depravity is a possibility. We don't think people are inherently evil, but we surely know evil is a possibility. We are, most of us, not murderous, but murder is a human possibility — in *all* people.

This we know better than ever now. Don't we?

About the evil of that day — that horrific evil that slaughtered thousands of lives and ripped out the hearts of many thousands of families, that shocked us, that startled the West from its slumber — the task now is to name it, to confront it, and to fight it.

With my father, Morris Moscowitz, in St. Louis, Missouri, 1956.

With my father in Los Angeles, 1995.

Caught again, St. Louis, 1958.

St. Louis, 1959, with my parents and brothers.

I'm in the middle, second row. Also included here are rabbis who serve across the United States, a respected academic, Reuven Firestone of HUC-JIR in Los Angeles (first row, third from left), and the current head of the Reform movement, Rick Jacobs, president of the URJ (back row, far right).

With my brother, Jim, and my father in Toronto, 1997.

*With Barry Borden, Holy Blossom's president,
at my installation as senior rabbi in 2000.*

With Yossi Klein Halevi in Jerusalem, 2001.

In Jerusalem on a Holy Blossom Temple congregational trip, 2001.

Jerusalem, 2004, with rabbis David (left) and Donniel Hartman (right).

*Speaking at the Union for Reform Judaism Convention
in Toronto, 2009.*

In the Maasai Mara, Kenya, 2009.

And to say it was wrought not by an amorphous force but by specific human beings animated by a murderous ideology.

Yes, I said to fight it. But not in the heat of the day when passions are intense and the mind can be tricked and trapped. Rather, in the long cool of the night when minds can think and plan, imagine and collaborate.

So that we can match their brilliance with our brilliance, their cool intelligence with ours, their passion for hate and totalitarianism with our passion for democracy and human dignity. So that passion for life prevails over passion for death.

Jeff Jacoby, who has observed Osama bin Laden and his colleagues for years, wrote in the *Boston Globe*:

> Now, after the worst massacre in U.S. history, only the willfully blind can fail to see that the front line is here. The war between freedom and slavery, between hope and hopelessness, between the decent and the indecent, will be won or lost in America. For it is America that stands for everything our enemies hate.[6]

Our task, our obligation — yours and mine — is several fold:

1. To support those who, in the long, cool night of years, will have to do their work (our work) with the intelligence, the patience, the precision to match the mind of evil — to match it and then to prevail.

2. To give support, too, to those who hurt and whose loved ones evaporated within an hour or two of saying, "Bye, honey, I'll see you later. Don't forget the cleaning ..."

3. To not presume that Radical Islamic fundamentalists are a denomination of Islam but to understand their virulent ideology as a powerful and combustible mix of fascism and Islamic fundamentalism, one that seeks to reign over the world. So this is a test of our alertness to an evil that is real, potent, growing in numbers — and hates virtually all that we and so many others in common cause hold dear.

4. To realize also that this is a test of our "intelligent tolerance." Even as we won't pretend away the perversion that is Radical Islam, we won't demonize in any way whatsoever Muslims as a whole, Muslims in our midst who, too, fight evil. Islam is one of the great religions, even if some of its adherents believe — and act — otherwise.

5. And to recognize, finally, that we Jews have obligations specific to our history. This means understanding that our place in a new war no one wanted is both unique and not. Just as radical fundamentalist Islam first targeted our brethren in Israel and then cast its eye on the democratic West, so, too, not so long ago, did another utopian hatred.

As a member of the Israeli Knesset, Benjamin Netanyahu observed: "Nazism ... also started as a local movement, and ... in just a few years became a world force. Nazism 60 years ago, like fundamentalist Islam today, was also initially directed only against Jews and other local minorities. It quickly became clear, however, that its passionate hatred was directed against our entire civilization."[7]

Our special task because we have been in the front lines and because our tradition is unafraid to name and confront evil is to help encourage — literally give courage to — those who might otherwise explain or contextualize or relativize evil away.

We've been there: *Zachor et asher asa l'cha Amalek* ... who doesn't remember the evil done by the biblical Amalek who cut down our weary and worn, our women and children, as we made our way out of Egypt?[8]

We've been there, and here we are again. We have the history and the vocabulary to name evil. We can't afford to fail now.

The World Trade Center was the centre of financial power, but it's not where the power most potent resides. Our mind — how we think, what we behold and then hold on to, what makes us human, humane, or inhumane — that's what animates evil and good. It is the place of the imagination. The human being from early on could imagine for evil and for good. Nothing has changed since. We are our imagination.

May this now become a moral imagination schooled by the wisdom of our tradition made keen and clear by our history — an imagination that forsakes illusions and names the truth and whose reach knows no bounds; that allows us to act and to survive rather than be frightened into silence or even death; and that emboldens us with courage into common cause for life and not death.

Those who died Tuesday will never have back their breath. But ours will return. Let us use it wisely for life and for good, to name and fight evil in any incarnation. Let us do it now until our breath runs out. Let us answer the monster's question, not with silence but with truth, not with the fog of ignorance but with the imagination emboldened, with resolve and moral alertness. Because we have to, for God's sake, for our sake, for the sake of those felled by Satan's wicked hand before our eyes and before their time.

EVIL — AND GOODNESS
Holy Blossom Temple Bulletin, October 12, 2001

It isn't really that September 11 changed the world forever. Rather, the horrific events of that morning made reality stunningly clear. As British Prime Minister Tony Blair put it, "This mass terrorism is the new evil in our world today. It is perpetrated by fanatics who are utterly indifferent to the sanctity of human life ..."[9]

Isn't it clear that evil is for real? We may be taken aback by such language, but the tradition is not. Judaism long ago identified Satan as real, as evil incarnate, often in human form.

Our tradition understands evil to hold its own category separate from sin. Evil destroys what God has created. Hitler and Stalin were evil, and so, too, is Paul Bernardo. Those who crashed airplanes — 130-ton human bombers — through steel and glass, literally cutting up thousands of lives, were no less evil.

Evil is cold-blooded and calculating in its destruction of innocent life and in its terrorizing of other lives. It is a conscious attempt to rip up all that is orderly and good, to strip away the normality of daily life, to make us fear what (or who) is around the next corner.

What Israel has known, now America knows. And as many have said in recent days, we are all Americans now.

Here is what is not negotiable or debatable: evil must be named, not avoided; condemned and fought with unprecedented intelligence and courage. Evil must not be contextualized or relativized or explained away. Judaism is not shy to say that evil is real — and neither should we be so shy. If we do not confront evil, it will prevail by tearing up the fabric that holds society together. Fighting evil allows us to live with hope and not hopelessness. It affords a sense of security and trust.

As evil is real, however, so, too, is goodness. It, too, must be named. It must be celebrated, taught as a virtue, and embodied routinely by adults to inspire our children. Society depends on simple acts of goodness, and so does God.

If those who destroyed buildings and buried lives on September 11 were evil incarnate, then those who rushed in to save lives were the embodiment of goodness. The firefighters and the police of New York City — those who rushed in to burning buildings as many fled for their lives — are our heroes today.

While they feared danger, the firefighters and police had a job to do: to rescue people and save lives. As the Talmud puts it, "He who saves one life — it is as if he has rescued the entire world."[10] By heroically modelling goodness in the burning fire of evil, the extraordinary New York firefighters and police taught us to fight back against evil and thereby to help save what is good — a world in which people might live in peace and dignity.

MAKING GOOD OUT OF EVIL
Holy Blossom Temple Bulletin, December 22, 2000

Excerpted from a December 2000 talk at a memorial service in memory of the fourteen women murdered in the Montreal massacre of 1989.

In the beginning, when all was good, power and dominion resided with God alone. *Bereshit berah Elohim et halhamayim v'et ha'aretz* — all was in God's hands. Soon thereafter God created many things: plants and fish, animals and more. Then, whether out of hope or loneliness or whatever else, God created Adam, the first human. However, as not done with previous creations, God yielded some power to Adam: to bless and to make things, to wield power in unique ways. Human mastery was thus born.

This mastery was designed to exploit the world, to inhabit it, and to civilize it — for good. This exploitation wasn't intended to destroy or wreak havoc but rather to wield for good, to construct, to enhance. What God saw to be good was to be even better with the work of the human hand.

But it didn't all work out that way. In giving Adam free will, God also provided humans the opportunity to wreak violence. Sure enough, in only the second generation of human history, the first murder occurred. How telling. How awful.

And ever since, similar things have occurred. Violence in every generation, every culture — in every heart we should say — has shadowed human history. It has been a long time since all was good.

Yet this is but part of the story. For in creating free will, God also allowed for goodness. We then understand that power and dominion aren't negative but neutral. Therefore, how human beings employ our mastery will tell whether it will be for constructive or destructive power, for good or for bad, for virtue or for violence.

That means we have it in our hands not to yield to violence but to contain and lessen it. We do so by remembering those who have died or been trampled upon by the hands of violence, to work in their memory for the mastery of the good over the misery of the evil.

We gather together this evening, all too aware of the brutal deaths eleven years ago of fourteen women. We gather, aware of the violence by the hands of one person, yet all too aware of the violence in every human heart. We gather to remember and to work for good over evil knowing that, while all will never be good again, there can yet be much good still to come. It is in our hands to make this so.[11]

THE SCHOOL MASSACRE WAS HUMAN EVIL, NOT TRAGEDY (2012)
Globe and Mail, December 18, 2012

Most everywhere you turn these past few days, the horrifying killing of twenty-six people, primarily small children, is pronounced "a tragedy." It isn't a tragedy — it's evil. Even once the killer is determined to be ill, there's no avoiding that the unspeakable massacre of Newtown was born of human evil.

Those who permitted the all-too-lax gun laws to prevail and those who sold the weaponry participated in evil and in murder. So did the killer. Shooting your mother four times in the head, then spraying innocent children with bullets — if we're not prepared to name that for what it is, we'll neither comprehend it nor diminish the chances of its reoccurrence.

So how should we understand what happened in Connecticut? The Greeks, who gave us the notion of tragedy, understood it as a great suffering, or a fall from grace in which the one who so suffers aids his own demise. Former CIA director David Petraeus's recent fall from the heights has a tragic dimension. Suicide often bears the mark of tragedy. The children and others murdered in Connecticut had no part in their terrible end. They were victims of evil, not of tragedy. Read the Greeks and Shakespeare to know what is tragic. Read the Bible and look around with discernment to be clear about evil.

Why the confusion between the two? Why is the language employed to describe Friday's murderous rampage off base?

Muddled and misguided thinking. We refuse the discussion of evil because such language flies in the face of our need to see ourselves as essentially good and decent, the ill and the aberrant among us only reinforcing the majority's generous self-regard.

To think otherwise is to risk running afoul of the orthodoxy of modern liberalism, which requires unstinting flattery of others in public, and of ourselves in private. (Which, tellingly, is often reversed.) No wonder then that there is such clouded thinking and obfuscating language about what really matters most: the nature of the being with the power to employ good or evil in daily affairs.

The Book of Genesis isn't so encumbered. It understands that goodness is real in human nature, but so, too, is evil. And that both must be named. Heartbroken over the actions of his crowning creature — Adam, the progenitor of us all — God is equally deeply regretful and realistic. "And the Eternal saw that the wickedness of Adam (the human being) was great on the Earth, and that his every intention was evil from morning until night."[12] Overstated to make a point? Likely, but the point is clear and unassailable: this is a deeply flawed creature, capable of both stunning goodness and horrific evil.

And, indeed, here is where tragedy comes in — the tragic figure being God, who made this complex creature, the human. By bestowing the human with a duelling nature, as well as with the power to choose how to act in the world, God unwittingly helped sow seeds of destruction, which we witness more than periodically. No wonder, upon grasping human nature, that God regrets the making of the man and woman,[13] which is where religion comes into play.

At their best the great religious traditions — Judaism, Christianity, Islam, Hinduism, Buddhism — recognize the flawed essence of humanity and organize their thinking and observance to constrain our destructive impulses, all the while encouraging our better angels. Which, in the wake of the murderous wrath in Newtown, means that consolation will only come in comprehending that evil is real and that it must be named in order to be constrained.

A decent start would be enormous and unrelenting pressure, bipartisan and across the board, on the White House to lead, and the U.S. Congress to follow suit, in vastly revamping American gun laws. Those twenty-six in Connecticut are dead and gone. There doesn't have to be another twenty-six; there doesn't have to be even one person who suffers this fate before we wake up. If we don't, that's a tragedy — like all tragedies, one of our own making.

RABBI JOSEPH B. SOLOVEITCHIK ON THE NATURE OF ADAM
December 16, 2010, Blog Post

Resting untouched on my bookshelves for years now are volumes such as *The Third Chimpanzee: The Evolution and Future of the Human Animal* by Jared Diamond and *Next of Kin: My Conversations with Chimpanzees* by Roger Fouts. I'd passed over these books for years, thinking little about evolution in general and the relationship between humans and primates in particular. My learning in that regard was about what it was in grade ten biology — not more.

That is, until I found myself in East Africa for other reasons and encountered animals up close and in the wild. There one spies the startling similarities between animals and humans, aided by very different eyes from those utilized, say, when visiting the zoo. By that I mean it's almost as though on the African savannah you gaze at the baboons, monkeys, lions, elephants, crocodiles, and more as might have our ancient ancestors. And hence, in seeing these dangerous and beautiful animals, you gain a sense of the challenges faced by early *Homo sapiens*: how to figure a way around the dangers these creatures present, all the while strategizing how to exploit them in order to survive.

This experience makes you think divergently, not just about our most ancient cousins, these various animals, but also about the nature of Adam, the human being. Hence, when I returned from East Africa the first time, I headed straight for the writings of Rabbi Joseph B. Soloveitchik, from whom I've learned — through his books — for many years now. I knew he'd expand my African experience.

Known as "The Rav," Rabbi Soloveitchik was arguably the pre-eminent rabbinic figure of the twentieth century. The Rosh Yeshiva at Yeshiva University in New York City and the founder of the Maimonides School in Boston, Rabbi Soloveitchik was an authoritative decider of *halacha* among Jews for several decades. The teacher — literally, the Rav — to many admiring and grateful students, he easily influenced more rabbis than any other in our time.

Although I'm a liberal rabbi, I took to the traditional Soloveitchik while in rabbinical school in the late 1970s. No one in the Jewish religious world so articulated the compelling ideas of the tradition as did Rabbi Soloveitchik. His depth, his clarity, his knowledge of the human condition, his existential openness and loneliness — these were most attractive to a hungry learner. Especially so when Soloveitchik holds forth on the nature of Adam and other such conundrums.

To our matter at hand. Soloveitchik notes that one kind of Adam is present in the very first chapter of Genesis while a rather different Adam is found in the second chapter. In the first chapter, Adam is, as Soloveitchik observes, "a child of nature

— as was the brute of the field. It is not coincidental that on the same day that He created man, God created a very large part of the animal kingdom. In this context, man appears as a natural being. He shares a common biology with the animals."

That's Soloveitchik's take on what he calls Adam I, he who is biologically driven, natural, and unreflective. For Soloveitchik, "Simplicity is to him preferable to complexity."

However, the second chapter of Genesis reveals another — shall we say "evolved" — nature in Adam: self-conscious and self-reflective, consumed with the desire to stand out within the group, to be unique, and especially so to God. Soloveitchik calls him Adam II.

On the contrast between the two kinds of early humans (or better, the two natures of Adam; or better still, the evolving character and ways of being Adam), Soloveitchik says:

> Natural man lives as an instinctive biological being. His existence is limited by natural laws with mathematical boundaries. He can make no leaps and is pragmatic to the extreme.
>
> Only when man breaks with nature and rejects boundaries, when he longs for boundlessness, when he dreams, can man reach greatness. The man described in the second chapter [of Genesis], who might be termed metaphysical man, reaches for the infinite and yearns for happiness. While natural man is complacent, metaphysical man is restless.

This restlessness, permit me to speculate, is at the core of the evolution from the primate to the human, maybe more so from our hominid predecessors to *Homo sapiens*. Natural man, less evolved but evolving all the time, at home among the creatures of the wild, was not dissimilar to primates and animals in crucial ways. This was the world of Adam I.

Yet because the will or the need to change was inherent in his very being, this Adam wandered, driven by restlessness. This Adam, while moving toward Soloveitchik's Adam II, developed divergent brain power, ways of eating, perceiving, and surviving — all toward an evolving nature, both increasingly distinct from and yet reflective of that of his predecessors.

There is more here, much more, but for the moment only this. Of what is it exactly that Soloveitchik reminds us of (so easy to see, so easy to miss) in early Genesis? Again: "It is not coincidental that on the same day He created man [Adam], God created a very large part of the animal kingdom…. He shares a common biology with the animals."

Nowhere, at least for me, are the truths of early Genesis, to say nothing of the nature of God's most evolved creation, more obvious than on the African savannahs. As I've been in Jerusalem dozens of times and will return regularly the rest of my life, so will I return to the beautiful wilds of the African plains. Each is Home.[14]

6

Jewish Principles and Public Matters

PREAMBLE

The Rabbis of the Talmud and related texts (circa 200–600 CE) fascinate, in part, by virtue of their sophistication. They were conversant in ways and in fields you'd think far from their expected precincts. The wiles of human nature, the allures of sexual beauty, other languages and philosophies and religions — little human was foreign territory for the sages.

Indeed, they were no strangers to the Greco-Roman world, the cultural Mecca that was the New York and Paris of that time. Unafraid of being swallowed up by proximity, the Rabbis knew the surrounding culture almost intimately at times; they went about learning how to draw from the beauty and knowledge of the Greeks with confidence, even pleasure.

It wasn't quite as rosy as that — the tensions often ran high, the defeats were more than a few — but the principle of learning from the larger world, while remaining Jewish, sustained Jews in the first millennium after the Temple destruction in 70 CE. The discussions in all of rabbinic literature so testify to this dynamic — a "creative tension," we would call it today.

Of course, all of this is no different from the main challenge posed us: how to simultaneously honour the tradition and its demands and accommodate the lures of the larger milieu. All of us, rabbis included, are required to navigate the waters of modernity, roiled equally by the mandates of a venerable tradition as by the constantly evolving reality of contemporary times. Usually modernity wins and easily, and the loss is ours whether we're aware or not. Sometimes the tradition holds its own and what was a challenge becomes an opportunity.

Hence, a few things in this part of the book reflect that challenge and opportunity. Most are brief pieces originally spoken at Kabbalat Shabbat and then put in the Holy Blossom Temple Bulletin. I hope they, too, reflect the attempt to honour two masters, including the fact that while I'm not *halachic* in observance I've long been inclined toward the tradition in how I think. But not always.

This part starts, after all, with the sermon that gained perhaps as much attention as any I delivered in twenty-five years — how and why I changed my mind about rabbis standing under the *chuppah* with a gay or lesbian couple, as with any other two Jews. I make no claim that my change of mind reflects giving equal weight to the thinking of Jewish tradition concerning the sociological reality of today. Hardly so, obviously. Nonetheless, I would say that while my evolution in this regard wasn't linear or predictable (to me, anyway), my arriving at a new view is derived no less from Jewish principles than from changing factors in an altered social world.

RABBIS AT GAY AND LESBIAN WEDDINGS: HOW I CHANGED MY MIND
May 25, 2012

En route to Los Angeles not long ago, I noticed that the customs agent at Pearson Airport wore an interesting name tag:

McCarthy-Quiroz was her surname. "Wow!" I said to her. "McCarthy-Quiroz — what a great name!"

"Yeah," she said, "you can imagine how hot-blooded our children are."

What an interesting time and place ours is. The sense of freedom is unparalleled, the possibilities of how to live, where, and with whom multiply daily. The boundaries — social, political, religious, sexual — are porous and shifting, some disappearing altogether.

When a McCarthy marries a Quiroz and kibitzes with a rabbi in a customs line composed of a rainbow of people scattering to the four corners of the earth, we're worlds removed from what once was. Only two or three generations ago, the McCarthys, the Quirozes, and the Moscoviccis were in Ireland, Mexico, and Romania; they had virtually no likelihood of encountering one another. In Canada we live cheek by jowl, if not with one another. Our social reality and experience — how we organize our lives, how we relate to one another, the groupings we join or are born into, how we fit into and understand the larger society, even how we think — is no longer divided but shared.

Social reality is like an amoeba. It morphs from one thing to another in front of our eyes. You don't necessarily perceive the changes except at certain moments: a red-headed, green-eyed, pale-skinned woman, whose name half claims and half belies her look, signals the world isn't what it once was. By the way, as our social reality changes, so do we.

One example: several months ago at a meeting of the Reform Rabbis of Greater Toronto, a visiting rabbi from the United States requested that each colleague share an observation about the Toronto Reform community — the better to understand us, he said.

Here was mine: despite the fact that the Reform Rabbis of Greater Toronto has cultivated, within the larger Reform rabbinate, a collective persona as the guardian of the tradition (no rabbis here officiate at interfaith weddings; we employ stricter standards for conversion; we express strong disagreement with the patrilineal stance of the Reform movement, and so on), nonetheless, I said, within five years we should assume that one or more of us will perform interfaith weddings. The days of our rabbis being known as the defenders of the faith, the guardians of the gate, are numbered.

I added that neither was I judgmental about rabbis performing interfaith weddings, nor was I making a veiled announcement about my own intentions. Rather, our social reality is in flux and so are rabbis. We shouldn't kid ourselves, and neither should we judge those rabbis who break ranks for whatever reasons. As well, we should anticipate that the reasons will be thoughtful and that the resulting actions will quite possibly be in the best interests of the Jews and of the Jewish future.

If McCarthy can readily marry Quiroz, don't you think Reform rabbis in this town will, before long in some circumstances, marry a Goldberg to a McCarthy or a Quiroz with nary a *beit din* or *mikvah* in sight? And don't you think the people are often ahead of the rabbis, for better and for worse?

Modernity, as Arthur Hertzberg famously put it, is the solvent of tradition. Tradition literally dissolves and is swept away by the power and the rapidity of the changes in contemporary society. But it's more than that, since a very personal dimension is involved here: when social reality changes, so do people, rabbis included. And as people change, so do their minds.

It's not entirely clear how that happens. Perhaps you arrive at a better way of doing things; or you perceive the world more clearly from before; or you listen to different voices from previously; or, all of a sudden, old voices announce themselves with new clarity. Sometimes your own voice emerges more forthrightly or you learn more and vary your reading. Regardless, it's not just that the social reality has changed, so have you.

I'm not the same person, the same rabbi, as upon my arrival here twenty-five years ago. In those days I was thrilled to join a coterie of rabbis on the traditional side of things, colleagues who accorded significant status to Jewish norms. No longer a rabbinic fish out of water on conversion, patrilineality, and other matters, I now swam in a more compatible rabbinic stream.

But, you know, things change. Over the next fifteen years or so, I grew rather less comfortable at what had come to feel like posing as a guardian at the gate. I grew too accustomed to saying no without wondering whether yes might not serve better. While satisfied at being true to the tradition and its ways, I grew vaguely discontented with my stance. I couldn't help but picture myself as a sentry at the gates. Something wasn't quite right, even if I couldn't put words to it.

However, and now I come to the heart of the matter for this Shabbat, I still had the words of the defender of the faith. I had them and, to be fair to myself, I believed them.

So in 1999 as the Central Conference of American Rabbis debated whether rabbis should officiate at same-sex marriages, I believed that *kiddushin* is just that — a marriage ceremony between a Jewish man and a Jewish woman. Here's exactly how I worded my own decision, and by virtue of my stance once I became senior rabbi a year later, that of my colleagues, rabbinic and cantorial, at Holy Blossom Temple:

> All human beings are made in the image of God;
> that sexual orientation is irrelevant to the human
> worth of a person; that the issue in Judaism is not
> sexual orientation but sexual responsibility; that
> demonization of gays and lesbians is not tolerable

— not in public, not in private, not in word, not in deed; and, finally, that gays and lesbians merit full civil and legal rights as accorded all citizens.

However, *kiddushin*, Jewish marriage, is not of a civil category but of a religious one. Rooted in the religious concept of covenant and in the related imperative of procreation, *kiddushin* reflects the historic understanding of the destiny of this minority people.

Jewish marriage requires a Jewish woman and a Jewish man to propel and fulfill the destiny of our people: to be God's partners in the ongoing work of creation. Therefore, Jewish marriage carries with it the hope — actually conveys the blessing — that children will result.

So I do not officiate at ceremonies for same-sex couples or for interfaith couples because the Jewish ideal is of a marriage between a Jewish woman and Jewish man with Jewish children resulting. We promote this ideal even as we also make clear that those who for whatever human and real reasons make other choices are not to be discriminated against.

Second and related, I officiate only at marriages between a Jewish woman and a Jewish man because whatever involves the totality of the Jewish people — its unity, its identity, its collective destiny — is of the highest priority to support and promote. The very core matters that define and maintain our sense of Peoplehood and destiny require that we must not sunder ourselves from the body of the Jewish people.

Finally, I will officiate only at the weddings of a Jewish woman and a Jewish man because my ordination as a rabbi is rooted not in the civil authority of today but in the religious sensibility of the past of our people. My rabbinic ordination, not my provincial clergy wedding permit, ultimately provides me licence to marry a couple.

But that was then. I've changed my mind. I did so a couple years ago. Not all at once. I had no epiphany. Rather, over some time, I thought about same-sex marriages and the role of rabbis not in a systematic way but episodically as the winds of change blew by. Those blowing winds were the social reality in transition. It dawned on me at some point that I was in intellectual flux.

It was two or three years ago now, having been bollixed about by my own internal ramblings and rumblings, and no less influenced by periodic conversations with friends and colleagues, gays and straights, that I came to realize I had taken the final steps of an intellectual migration. I no longer believed what I once had. I held back from saying so until now, since I didn't wish to entangle this matter with other issues internally at play here.

So let me say it clearly and loudly: I believe rabbis should officiate at gay and lesbian marriages; that such a marriage, while arguably different, is no less *kiddushin* sanctification than that of a Jewish man and Jewish woman. No caveats, no exceptions, no footnotes.

More about the implications for Holy Blossom Temple in a moment. But first permit me to share how I changed. I do so precisely because it's not terribly profound or dramatic. I can't claim to have climbed toward the high moral ground. As President Barack Obama said last week about his change of mind, it's more personal than political. My shift, like that of the president's, is reflective of a significant transformation in our social reality, and no less — and no less important — in ourselves.

Upon reflection I realized I'd changed my mind for three reasons. Here they are in order of the lesser important reason first, the most important one last.

First, the larger social reality is today so different from that of even a decade ago that liberal congregations refuse gay/lesbian weddings now only at their own peril. It simply runs counter to the interests of Holy Blossom Temple that when two Jewish men or two Jewish women — our members or those who wish to be our members — seek our support as they sanctify their love that we not say yes with the same enthusiasm we express to a heterosexual Jewish couple. My first reason, then, is pragmatic and in the best interests of this congregation, its members, and its future.

My second reason returns me to a previous matter. It's about rabbis, our role, and our responsibilities. Here I speak for myself alone.

While rabbis enjoy less authority these days than it appears (and, by the way, more responsibility than it seems), nonetheless, we do have authority, even power. Employing power is a delicate matter: it's all too easy to yield it, and it's not simple to wield it — not these days in this radically levelled world of ours. You go too far one way or the other and you find yourself in harm's way, especially so in communal institutions.

As for myself, then, as the years went by, more and more I felt like the guardian at the gate saying no entry, no way, even as the gates no longer held and had been broken through.

How does the saying go? The only thing worse than having to change is becoming irrelevant. As the winds of powerful and positive change swept past me, I felt not only irrelevant but wrong, at least in some of my stances. What I grew to believe about gay marriage and weddings, likewise, I came to feel about conversions and rabbis: too much no, too much posturing and policing; not enough yes and welcoming and affirmation.

My second reason, then, is about rabbis — at least about this rabbi. About our roles and our relevance; about the delicate art of employing power well. And, frankly, about the need to change when the facts — and sometimes the people — stare you in the face.

My third reason for changing my mind is the most important one. When he apparently forced the hand of the president last week, Vice-President Joe Biden said, "Freedom for one means freedom for all."

Freedom is a philosophical stance and a human necessity. Biden is right. You can't have freedom in the abstract if you don't have freedom in reality. You can't have freedom for one or some without freedom for all. You can't have one set of rules for whites and another for blacks, one way to recognize love and weddings and marriages for straights and another for gays and lesbians.

And here my own political/philosophical ways prevailed. If I align myself most comfortably with conservatives on matters of Israel and foreign policy because they largely get it right, I believe, and if I align myself most often with those on the left on economic matters because they largely get those matters right, as I see it, then on personal and social matters I've grown to strongly identify as a libertarian. I believe deeply that freedom is an absolute necessity for all human beings; I believe in freedom's redemptive and liberating capabilities for the individual; I believe that freedom is a religious value and right. Freedom is at the very core of our humanity and our dignity, our goodness and our godliness.

You simply can't afford full freedom to one group without doing so to all groups, to one person and not all people. I believe that rabbis and cantors, the Jewish tradition at their back, should sanctify the love of Jewish gays and lesbians, no less than that of any other two Jews. When any two Jews wish to formalize their love through the rites of *kiddushin*, the Jewish wedding ceremony, our place is under the *chuppah*, not at the gates.

You see why this last reason is the most important one. It's the most religious, the most Jewish in its essence, the most personal in its impact and reach. Personal for gays and lesbians most of all, but also personal for all in our community, rabbis included.

What does this mean now in our small community at Holy Blossom Temple? Just this: each of our rabbis, each of our cantors, will decide on an individual basis whether to perform same-sex weddings. Each colleague will be respected as he or she chooses — period.

Let me conclude this way. You would have noticed that I've not employed any Torah as a proof text to rationalize rabbinic standing at same-sex weddings. The reason is straightforward. You, as easily as I, can find texts to buttress one side or the other. I believe that in our liberal milieu it's, at best, intellectually problematic to go there; one text is as good as another. Which doesn't mean the tradition has nothing to say about this. Quite the contrary. But I'll come back to that in a moment.

Likewise, I came to understand over the past decade that in 1999 I tilted toward the tradition for reasons as much to do with my own worldview as anything else. Today I can say the same: I've chosen this decision, this way of regarding same-sex marriages, in significant part, because as the world has changed, so have I. My worldview today isn't what it once was.

How does one capture personal change? How do you explain it to others and to yourself? Permit me one more try at this, first through a recent e-mail exchange, and then with the aid of the pre-eminent rabbinic thinker of the second half of the twentieth century.

Ten days ago, when President Obama announced his own change of mind regarding same-sex marriages, Debra Bennett sent me a link to the president's announcement — Debra with whom I've discussed this issue and who knew what I was planning to say today.

I replied, "Well, nice, but why is he so late?"

To which Debra shot back, "Why is *he* so late? Why are *you* so late?!" And she added, "Just because Obama beat you to it, don't change your mind!"

It happens that Debra had also copied Rabbi Karen Thomashow in the exchange — she who also knew what I was going to say today. After approving of the humour, Rabbi Thomashow summed up this way: "It's rather powerful when the perspectives, the ideas, the faith of leaders change — and those leaders publicly share their [intellectual and religious] evolutions. It's very moving [to hear and know that]."

Rabbi Joseph Soloveitchik, to whose writings I habitually turn when in search of something akin to answers, also thought about how we humans make decisions, how change emerges and from where.

Borrowing from the Jewish mystical tradition, Soloveitchik writes of the *ratzon elyon*, the higher will (as opposed to the *ratzon tachton*, the lower will) of the human being. This will is an endowment, claims the Rav, that separates the human from the remainder of creation. More than that, the *ratzon elyon* makes decisions and does so spontaneously, passionately, incisively, and intuitively. And all the while it has no need to resort to the pragmatic part of the human intellect, the *ratzon tachton*, which weighs pros and cons and goes about its business laboriously.

Says Rabbi Soloveitchik: this upper will lights up from within with intuitive affirmations about the most important of human decisions — of marriage, of choice of profession, of acts of military genius, the pivotal resolutions that define and determine every human life.

Learning from the Rav: sometimes, as if out of nowhere, you realize you've been changing all along and now you finally have the words. The light from within has shone through with an affirmation you intuitively know to be true, to be right. You've already decided even though you don't quite realize it yet; you've changed within before you do so without.

Important as the intellect is, as much as it, too, is an instrument of holiness, the *ratzon elyon*, that upper will of ours, is the deepest and most Divine part of Adam, this creature of God's. Each one of us — of whatever stripe, of whatever background, of whatever sexuality, of whatever gender — is of equal standing before God. And not before God alone but also before one another. Each one of us is worthy of the rites and the rights of *kiddushin*, of the opportunity to sanctify our love of another under the *chuppah* — and to do so with the very other of our own choosing.

BARACK OBAMA: ROLE MODEL FOR THE JEWS
April 24, 2010

In his fascinating new biography of President Barack Obama (*The Bridge: The Life and Rise of Barack Obama*), David Remnick captures how a young Obama goes in search of himself and makes a deliberate, if at times halting, choice about his identity. This young man of mixed parentage — and, in some sense, of no parentage — chose to be an African American. He would merge his personal story with that of the larger American black

narrative. Barack Obama, by Remnick's account, essentially constructed his own identity.

Remnick describes Obama's process of exploration early on:
conscious, thoughtful, often awkward, as it is with the young in
pursuit of the self. Finally, an early sense of confusion yields to
clarity and a firm identity. This son of a white Kansas woman
and a Kenyan man, raised in the polyglot world of Hawaii, would
take back his given birth name (the boy known as "Barry" giving back — way — to the man "Barack") and make himself an
African American. Most assuredly, not a white man, not a man
of mixed race, not even an African. An African American — an
identity of his own choosing realized by concrete steps on the
road to maturity.

By his early twenties, then, the African-American story
would be Barack Obama's. Selma was part of his story; slavery
was not alien to him; the spirituals in the Black Church were
on his lips, if not in his heart. He made Chicago — the centre
of African-American life — his city. And for his wife, Obama
took the daughter of one of inner-city Chicago's black families —
indeed, the great-granddaughter of slaves. In Remnick's telling,
the cadences of Barack Obama's speech and the gait of his walk
would be reconstructed to better fit in with Black America.

All done consciously. Remnick's Obama is a young man
without sufficient tethering (after all, he was abandoned not only
by his father but for all intents and purposes also by his dream-
pursuing-at-all-costs mother) who, in the process of maturation,
got himself very well tethered. All by choice and by will. David
Remnick puts it like this:

> As a well-read student who is coming of age in
> the era of multiculturalism and critical theory,
> Obama is keenly aware of the academic notions

that identity is, in some measure, a social construction. Race is a fact, a matter of genetics
and physical attributes, but it is also a matter
of social and self-conception. A commanding
theme of the book [Obama's *Dreams from My
Father*] is a young man's realization that he has
a say in all of this; that he is not merely a "prod-
uct" of family history; he has to make sense of
his circumstances and his inheritances, and
then decide what he wants to make of it all and
who he wants to be. Identity and race are matters over which he has some influence.[1]

So, deliberately and consciously (with elements both
authentic and artificial), Barack Obama chose his identity and
then worked hard to make it all work. His learned and earned
strong sense of self, his decision as to whom to be, his sorting out what he believes and why — none of this is unrelated
to his remarkably successful life. Regardless of how one views
President Obama's policies on Israel and the Middle East or on
anything else, what he did to carve out an estimable life is most
admirable. He is an attractive model in this regard, and we have
much to learn from him.

Reading Remnick on Obama reminded me of my own
choice of identity at more or less the same age. Raised with lots
of Jewishness but little Judaism, I knowingly opted for Judaism
over Jewishness. Like Obama, I wished to be the author of my
own life. My application to rabbinical school at age twenty-
four wasn't for the purpose of being a rabbi; primarily, it was
an endeavour of self-construction: I wanted to be a literate,
knowledgeable Jew. I'd known little and I wanted to know a lot.
I wanted to feel authentic, even if my way there was necessarily

artificial. I didn't like the feelings of self-consciousness along the way, but my sense of wanting to feel at home as a Jew anywhere and everywhere was far, far stronger. My path there was not unlike Barack Obama's road to an African-American identity.

Ours, after all, is a world of a multiplicity of choices in which (unlike previous times) who we are may, in the end, be less determined by who our parents are and shaped more by what and who we wish to be and why. Some choose this passively with little thought; some do so assertively with much deliberation and planning. I'm on the side of the latter — exactly what Barack Obama did so effectively. I can't think of a better model for constructing a life of meaning and purpose — and, by the way, one of much satisfaction.

Which brings me to Holy Blossom Temple. Whatever else bequeathed us, few of us are well endowed as Jews. Our knowledge as Jews, our literacy, our comfort within the Jewish collectivity — it's on the spare side for the most part. We cannot pretend this fact away, but neither do we have to accept it as determinative. Not at all.

Our homes do not possess the adequacy of knowledge and experience, for instance, to allow us to recite the Shabbat Kiddush with ease and regularity; to *daven* without self-consciousness; even to know which values are actually Jewish and which are of the larger world. Our access to one of the world's great treasure troves of literature (ours!) is stymied.

Who among us feels comfortable in any Jewish situation — whether in a Reform or an Orthodox synagogue? Who among us feels at home when asked to carry the Torah, or recite Birkat HaMazon, or discuss matters of Jewish history? Who among us has a sense of the great world of the Rabbis of Old — who, likewise in an act of the deliberate construction, fashioned a tradition, one both venerable and relevant?

Our homes, for the most part, are not equipped to provide this fundamental adequacy of identity. Our lives are too busy and distracted, we are subject to so many competing ideologies, identities, technologies, possibilities that our heads are spun around until we are used to being dizzy. And then, of course, we're inclined to give up before we even begin.

A good synagogue is alert to this. It doesn't judge the confusion, but neither does it look the other way. It says, in effect, particularly to parents of younger children and teens, those still forming their lives: Come, let us help you choose your identity — as a Jew. Let's do it deliberately and well, and let us help you plan this. We know how to do it. (We really do!) We can give you the tools and show you the path. But you as parents, and you as young adults, have to do the choosing.

The rewards are immense: a strong sense of identity is the best anchor in a chaotic and confused world; it's a mooring that provides the satisfactions of deep knowledge, strong family and community, and a robust sense of self. And, because this is learned and earned through hard work, it comes out remarkably satisfying. See the confidence with which President Obama walks and talks? It doesn't come out of thin air.

This reconstruction toward the making of a strong sense of self, however, is not simply a matter of personal satisfaction. That's nice but hardly sufficient; it's not reason enough to put our resources into learning and the building of personal identity alone. Here is the thinking: since personal and parental construction of Jewish identity is ultimately an act of personal self-defence (and a very positive one at that), so, too, is this an act of collective self-defence. This is also very much toward the strengthening of the Jews as a people.

Barack Obama appears to have figured things out largely on his own. He understood his life depended on his choice of a deliberate reconstruction of himself. He didn't toss out who he was and what he inherited; he used it to build something different, an identity he admired and could slowly take as his own. Indeed, his rather extraordinary life is testimony to Obama's wise choice and successful (re)building.

We should do no less. For the lives of our children and grandchildren, and for the life of our people, for the Jews. Not everyone can do this to the same extent or at the same pace. We begin in different places; we are the possessors of disparate and distinct lives. Still, neither can we, individually and collectively, afford to forgo the remaking of our lives. Our future, our success, our satisfaction — all of this is dependent on which choice we make or don't. For ourselves and for our people.

WHY *MUNICH* STILL MATTERS
Holy Blossom Temple Bulletin, March 2006

Steven Spielberg's film *Munich* isn't only about the 1972 Olympics massacre and the Israeli response afterward. Maybe even more importantly, it tells us much about the naïveté of the Jews and the West.

Toward the conclusion of the film, the skyline of Lower Manhattan is portrayed as it was in the mid-1970s — World Trade Center and all. The violence of the story is over, there are no more words, and Avner, the film's chief character, is remaining in New York rather than returning to Israel.

Cultural critic Edward Rothstein suggests in the *New York Times* that in having the camera focus at length on the World Trade Center, Spielberg is warning us that "militant attempts to destroy terrorism lead not to peace but to cycles of violence, and that the 9/11 attacks may even be consequences of Israel's response to the Munich massacre."[2]

Evolution of an Unorthodox Rabbi

For Rothstein, Spielberg has gotten up on his moral soapbox, claiming that a war on terror will only cause more terror; that, more tellingly, each side in that war will grow to resemble the other; and that, consequently, the moral edge of those attacked is worn down in attempting to destroy the terrorist.

Rothstein has Spielberg right, but it's actually worse than he's willing to say. For here is someone with significant moral credibility — *Schindler's List* and *Saving Private Ryan* are two of the great moral films of our time — who's wasting his well-earned respect in asserting (more or less) a moral equivalency between the Palestinian terrorists at Munich and the Israeli team of commandos who sought to avenge their deaths. I know Spielberg says otherwise, but at the heart of his response is the belief that in attempting to eradicate evil — and, yes, to kill the evildoers — you lose your own moral credibility. Spielberg has fallen for the trite notion that violence always begets violence, and the violence that it begets is worse because it destroys the avenger's soul and moral stuff.

Hence, in *Munich*, Avner weakens under the weight of his lost moral credibility as he and his team take out the terrorists. So much so that ultimately defeated and despondent Avner opts for exile in New York.

For Spielberg, Avner's only other choice was to mirror the image of the Palestinian terrorists, which the film suggests he has come achingly close to doing, anyway. Spielberg's notion that in confronting evil you become like evil, while at times obviously possible, is in this case patently untrue. I wish Spielberg would have portrayed Avner as he was rather than as the soul-wracked moral equivalent of the terrorist he portrays in the movie.

Our Torah has something to say about such matters. It understands that one doesn't necessarily lose moral authority

190

in confronting evil. Only consider what Moses does at the very beginning of Exodus: "And Moses turned this way and that way, but he saw there was no man [no one willing to confront the evil taskmaster] so he struck down the Egyptians ..."[3]

In other words, there are times when there is no choice but to wreak vengeance upon evildoers — otherwise evil will rule. Because he smote the Egyptians, Moses earned the moral standing of the prophet, and therefore is one in whom God can invest. Moses earned this position by standing up against evil and on behalf of the vulnerable. The actions of Moses ultimately make for less violence, not more.

As I watched *Munich*, I reflected on the fact that while these events were occurring in September 1972 I was a young antiwar activist in Los Angeles. In my apartment I had hung a poster of the North Vietnamese negotiator Madam Binh, alongside a poster of the Israeli city of Tiberias.

For me these posters symbolized that vulnerability and power could rest comfortably enough together. I wasn't willing to see the world as divided between the vulnerable and the powerless on the one hand and the strong and the powerful on the other.

Both Madam Binh and Israel possessed power and moral credibility — and both were required to use them in the best interests of their people, specifically for survival.

I understood then that sometimes for survival you must compromise your values. But because survival and life are the highest values in our tradition, compromise is not only necessary but is at certain moments morally mandated.

Steven Spielberg got this wrong. Maybe he can afford to do so in a film. But Israel, the Jews, and the West, besieged by a fascist Radical Islam on the march, can hardly afford Spielberg's mistake.

TERRI SCHIAVO: A PERSONAL VIEW
Holy Blossom Temple Bulletin, May 2005

I paid little attention to the Terri Schiavo case until the very end. The fact that I call it a "case" betrays me. For me, Terri Schiavo was an abstraction, not fully human. Her family seemed to me, anyway, unduly involved with her in a way that didn't seem healthy. Little did I realize how deeply human their involvement with Terri was.

With only a bare awareness of Terri Schiavo's situation until her end, I had assumed she was hanging on only by artificial means and that the fuss was largely a political matter. What I didn't quite realize then was that while she may have been in a "vegetative state" and maybe even was supported only artificially, this didn't mean Terri Schiavo was no longer human.

I didn't really know then what a vegetative state was. I didn't know what it meant to have no consciousness and no electrical activity happening in the thinking portions of the brain.

But as I began to pay closer attention in the last couple of weeks of Terri Schiavo's life, I was taken by the intensity of what her relatives felt. I was taken by their passionate belief that they were relating to a real human being and that this real human being had in some way or another a consciousness of them and of life. Unencumbered by medical training or sophistication, I couldn't help but feel that here was a real person with real feelings, even in a dramatically diminished state.

There was another reason I no longer saw Terri Schiavo as an abstraction, but rather as a real person. At the same time that I was watching her die on television, my father was in a not dissimilar situation. At the end of his life, dramatically diminished by the ravages of Parkinson's disease, my father barely speaks and is rarely demonstrative of feeling.

Nonetheless, a very real human being, in a very flawed body, cried when I told him that his wife had died. Likewise, he responds to certain stimuli around him that seem to arouse the deepest part of his humanity: small children who are playful and curious; love that's palpable and passionate; and a bit of television, especially basketball. He seems to very much know the difference between those who love him (primarily his caregivers and his family) and those who visit out of duty (the hospice nurses).

What I'm getting at is this: there are medical ways to view people, there are political ways to view people, and there are also religious ways to view people. Sometimes the three come together and we are most deeply informed. But sometimes we tend to view people — or in this situation "medical cases" — only in one way or another. But the religious perspective, as always, is the deepest, the most human, and the most humane.

If anything good comes out of Terri Schiavo's death, it will be an understanding that, as God's children, our humanity is complex and not always knowable; that in illness as in health our humanity must be the deepest concern to one another, and the only way that we can have a bond with one another.

REPENTANCE:
LEARNING FROM CLINTON AND RAMBAM
Erev Shabbat Remarks, August 1998

I had no intention of bringing up a certain president's name tonight — but he made me do it! How could it be otherwise? This month of Elul is one of preparation and review in anticipation of the demands (and rewards) of Rosh Hashanah and Yom Kippur. Repentance and renewal are hardly likely for us during Tishrei if we haven't been awakened to the urgency of the task in Elul.

So President Bill Clinton's bungled and badly delivered "apology" alerts us to this: that though the act of saying "I'm sorry" and taking responsibility for our actions may seem straightforward, it's anything but. Tradition teaches this by providing us with this preparatory month of Elul, so when Tishrei arrives we might get things right.

Watching and listening to Clinton, we saw a stark reminder of how to get it wrong: pretend to apologize but don't; deflect blame onto someone else; dissemble, rationalize, avoid, explain away. We also saw, stunning as it was, how someone so gifted and intelligent, so emotionally in tune, can fail so miserably at apologizing for wrongdoing.

If Clinton stands before us now as an example of how to fail at making repentance, how exactly do we get it right?

Maimonides, in his Hilchot Teshuvah (The Laws of Repentance), teaches that we shouldn't get tricky, shouldn't look to give explanation, but make a straight-from-the-shoulder apology and confession. His words in twelfth-century Egypt do rather well for us in late twentieth-century Canada: "O God, I have done evil, I have rebelled against you and done this. I regret it now and am ashamed of my acts; I will never do it again."

And in case we think we can make a verbal confession to God or deliver an apology to a human being without it being heartfelt and sincere, Rambam says better think twice. Again, his words: "Anyone who makes a verbal confession without resolving in their heart to abandon their sin is like one who takes a ritual bath while grasping a defiling reptile. The bath is useless unless the reptile is cast away." Which is just Rambam's hyperbolic way of saying, "If we really don't mean it, if we aren't truly contrite, we shouldn't bother — we'll only land in more trouble." Listening, Mr. Clinton?

Rambam is saying what we know well: a direct and heartfelt apology is likely to help the restitching of bonds between people as between the individual and God.

As we prepare to greet these coming Days of Awe, God puts this challenge and opportunity before each of us. May we have the courage and foresight to so respond and make this a truly sweet year.

LISTENING TO MARSHALL McLUHAN: A SUGGESTION FOR GETTING SHABBAT RIGHT
Holy Blossom Temple Bulletin, January 19, 1996

In *Understanding Media*, Marshall McLuhan wrote that "we become what we behold."[4] Elaborating on this theme, John M. Culkin wrote in a 1967 *Saturday Review* essay: "We shape our tools and thereafter they shape us."[5] Culkin, of course, was explaining McLuhan's media philosophy, primarily referring to how television shapes us and rearranges our culture. Others later referred to McLuhan's ideas in gauging the Internet's impact on our culture and on ourselves.

I wish to use McLuhan's insight about the relationship between tools and culture differently. I do so with regard to how Jews employ and regard ritual. McLuhan was correct in suggesting that, to a large extent, we become what we behold. Or to put it differently, we Jews become what we do; our acts shape our character, our religious communal culture deepened or thinned out by what we do or don't do.

In reckoning what McLuhan has to teach about being Jewish today, let's go directly to the Shabbat dinner table. While there, please consider this: years ago it became the custom in many Jewish households — liberal and otherwise — to inaugurate the Shabbat not by blessing and sanctifying it but by blessing and sanctifying the wine alone (in other words, reciting the first short paragraph while omitting the main part of the blessing). Whether this was done to save time, to save face, or to save conflict is another matter. However, whatever the rationale for blessing the wine while forgoing blessing the Sabbath (thereby not marking off Sabbath as holy time), important messages were — and are — communicated.

These messages include the following: that the momentary sweetness of the wine takes precedence over the abiding depth and privilege of making Shabbat; that modern Judaism (or better, modern Jews?) allows convenience to crowd out commandment; and maybe most consequently — since it has become the "custom" for children to say *borei pri hagoffen* in place of adults reciting Kiddush — in the contemporary Jewish home early and natural childhood fantasies about usurping appropriate parental roles might just actually come to be. In fact, it is the parents' role to say Kiddush and not the child's to do so. All in all, ideally, wouldn't we want our children and grandchildren home not so much for Friday night dinner but to make Shabbat?

What does McLuhan have to do with this? Simply this: perhaps more than any other place, it is at the Shabbat dinner table that we can best recognize that we become what we behold. If we shape our Shabbat observance, especially at its beginning, along minimalist lines, it will shape us along such lines more than we might know. And the reverse is also true: the more we do, even if tentatively and awkwardly at first, to expand and sanctify Shabbat, the more confident we are as Jews.

Learning and reciting Kiddush, performed by adults as are all *mitzvot*, will move us in the right direction toward beholding Shabbat rather than a Friday night dinner; toward thinking and acting Jewishly rather than in "Jewish style"; and toward making Judaism more integral to our lives and our family life.

Jewish Principles and Public Matters

Listening to Marshall McLuhan was worthwhile in the 1960s — and no less so today. So think about him at the Shabbat dinner table. His words teach much more than about media and culture; they can teach us about Shabbat, what kind of Jews we can be, and what kind of family life we can establish.

7

Remembrances

PREAMBLE

Over the years I wrote and spoke about all kinds of people on all sorts of occasions. These were appreciations of the living and the dead both, and took the form of book tributes and public testimonials, of private remarks and eulogies — and more. It's a wonderful privilege to say something about those you esteem and with whom you feel a kinship. I've limited myself here to seven remembrances — six people who have died, each of whom I admired, all but one close up and personal for me. The seventh piece is a different kind of memorial.

I wrote about Jackie Kennedy on the day of her funeral, about my teacher David Hartman a day or two after his, and about Christopher Hitchens as he was dying. The first represented the greatness and complexity of America; the second the enduring grandeur of the rabbinic tradition; and lastly, with regard to Hitchens, the thrill of learning to think for yourself in the form of a person who did it best.

Three others I knew well, each old-world men in the very best ways, whom I eulogized with affection and respect at their funerals: one of Canada's leading businessmen and philanthropists, Joseph Rotman; my office neighbour for thirteen years,

Rabbi W. Gunther Plaut; and my own father, Morris Moscowitz. Finally, while visiting Babi Yar in 1994, I felt as if I were visiting the ghosts of slaughtered Jews of decades earlier. I was, and that experience closes out these remembrances.

REMEMBERING DAVID HARTMAN (1931–2013)
March 4, 2013

At first glance Rabbi David Hartman appeared like most other rabbis. His was a *frum* family (his father from the Old City in Jerusalem, his mother from Safat's Old City) that migrated to Brooklyn in the 1920s; all three of his brothers were rabbis, as well (one of them, Hatzkel, was my grandparents' rabbi in St. Louis in the 1950s, markedly influencing my father for a period). And his rabbinic pedigree was as normative as it got for Orthodox rabbis in those days: from Brooklyn to Lakewood to Upper Manhattan, David Hartman learned in the right places and from the best. He taught Torah, he led a congregation or two, he loved Israel, and he loved the Jewish people. The normative rabbinic fare it would seem.

Not so.

For Hartman's reach was deeper and wider than perhaps any rabbi of our time. His sense of urgency to hone the intellect and penetrate the soul, most especially of the rabbis he loved, was relentless. His desire to learn from diverse sources — Dewey, James, Rambam, Soloveitchik, the Talmud (always the Talmud) — was unquenchable. David was a master teacher, a wonderful and colourful communicator of ideas, an animator for change but never, never for its own sake.

This driven, restless man could never have remained "orthodox" of any kind, and neither could any of his serious students. He changed lives and made them more interesting.

He challenged boundaries and broke them, or — as often as not — strengthened them. He ceremoniously paraded his contradictions.

For instance, unlike his intellectual hero, Mordecai Kaplan, he favoured the tradition, not modernity, with veto power; yet, unlike his rebbe, Joseph Soloveitchik, he eventually jettisoned normative Orthodoxy. This unorthodox Orthodox rabbi put on tefillin every morning until the end — all the while arguing with the Talmud, with Soloveitchik, with visitors of all sorts. You had a heartbeat and Hartman wanted to argue, engage, teach, and sometimes harangue. You had a mind and he would make you think differently, usually better. He demanded and his students responded.

I first came upon David Hartman in the late 1970s through his books. In 1991 I encountered Hartman in person at his institute in Jerusalem. Whether up close in the years since, or at a remove through his writings, Rabbi Hartman's voice — his Torah, his teaching, his passions — bellowed with urgency and overflowed with ideas. You couldn't ignore Hartman even if you wanted to; he wouldn't let you and he wouldn't let up. And, as for his way of thinking, once it got hold of you, well, there was no going back. He grabbed you, he shook you, he changed you. We, his students, loved him even when we didn't.

Which brings me back to the word *encounter*. As Martin Buber taught, to encounter someone is to have found a teacher and thereby to have gained knowledge beyond measure; indeed, to truly encounter someone is to be changed by them. Rabbi David Hartman was such a person for me, as well as for many others. I count myself fortunate and different from how and who I would have been, as a rabbi in particular, without encountering this singular kind of rabbi.

WATCHING CHRISTOPHER HITCHENS
(1949–2011)
Blog Post, August 30, 2010

Watching Christopher Hitchens reflect in various interviews these days on life with cancer puts one in the (digital) company of an impressive man. Thoughtful and honest, stoic but vulnerable, Hitchens knows his place in the world. He neither pretends away his hold on a life of significance (to say nothing of one of enjoyment), nor that human mortality (his own included) isn't essential for human progress. The rabbinic notion that we best consider ourselves but little lower than the angels, all the while not much above the dust of the earth, either, finds a ready example in Christopher Hitchens.

Which brings me back to being in Hitchens's real company during his last visit to Holy Blossom Temple a couple of years ago. Two university students had written the morning of his talk, seeking a few minutes with their intellectual hero for a video interview. Likely not, I responded, given the brevity of his visit and the packed schedule. But drop by my office at such and such a time and let's see …

The students didn't show up at the suggested time. After the lecture, however, they caught my attention, asking if an interview was still possible. By now Hitchens was downstairs, greeting many of the nine hundred or so people who had come by to hear him. He'd be signing books and chatting for quite a while, and given his early flight in the morning, I doubted an interview was in the offing.

Still, I mentioned the students' wish to Hitchens. "Of course," he said. "Let me finish the signing and then I'll sit with them."

Around 11:00 p.m. Hitchens greeted the two nervous students in his avuncular, somewhat intimidating, but equally warm way. What I assumed might be five minutes went on for well over forty. Earnest and serious queries were met in kind, and with kindness, by Hitchens.

Christopher Hitchens didn't have to do this. Most others would likely have begged off or given two twenty-year-olds a few perfunctory minutes. The way in which Hitchens appears to regard those he might otherwise easily ignore (I had seen the same when Christopher was with us previously), surely says something impressive about the man. This is, in part, what brings me to take him seriously on matters of life and death.

A footnote to this story: when Hitchens spoke at Holy Blossom, I asked him to put on a yarmulke, as I do all who speak in our sanctuary. He did so without reservation and with respect. Well after his lecture — into the book signing downstairs and still during the late-night interview — Hitchens wore his yarmulke (actually, one of mine that I gave him for the night, which to my mild disappointment he chose not to keep when I offered it to him).

So, not long afterward, when our students somehow got their interview slotted at the top when Christopher Hitchens was Googled, there he was, sitting in the Rabbinic Library of Holy Blossom Temple wearing a yarmulke. On came the vitriol from his atheist compatriots: "What in the world is Christopher Hitchens doing wearing a yarmulke! Is he selling out his atheist principles?"

No, not exactly. Rather, Hitchens gets *minhag hamakom*, the Jewish principle that suggests the importance of respect for the custom of a given community. He gets it without showing off or showing up anyone.

I like Christopher Hitchens, and if I'm not praying for him exactly, it's out of respect for his own ways and thinking. But I'm very much hoping for his restoration to health, for his own sake and that of his family, to be sure, but also for ours: We need more years of this leading intellectual figure in public, and no less, a worthy gentleman in private.

EULOGY FOR JOSEPH ROTMAN (1935–2015)
January 30, 2015

There are those so robust and full of life, so gifted and esteemed, that we're inclined to believe them impervious to the ways of man. They will not die, or if they do, not before their time and certainly after ours.

Who would doubt that Joe Rotman was the best among us? We admired him greatly; we loved him; we liked him. We wanted more time with him. He deserved it and we needed it. The Rabbis of Old, the shapers of a brilliant intellectual tradition (which Joe admired even while dubious of its theology), join us in our lament: *Olam k'minhago noheig,* they said — we have far less control over things than it usually appears. Joe understood that. At this moment we do, too.

A citizen of the world, a proud son of Canada, a lover of Israel, Joseph Rotman possessed qualities not normally found together in one person: excellence and elegance; brilliance and kindness; passion of heart and precision of mind. Joe was the ultimate outside/ inside man: For all of his intense care for matters of the public sphere, his real place was the private hearth. The life and family he and Sandy began all those years ago — one in which Sandy, Janis, Ken, Amy, and his grandchildren held the keys — mattered most to Joe. This great man of the world was a good man of family and friends. He cherished his family, his friends, and others — a love returned in spades.

The many, many people Joe helped weren't abstractions to him. Once he left me courtside tickets to the Toronto Raptors, and a week or so later when I told him I'd given away his tickets, that a family in hurt occupied his seats that night and enjoyed an evening's respite from pain, Joe's face lit up as only his could and would so often and readily. His eyes went bright and alert, and that smile of his went wider than a mile. He shook his head up and down in joy and approval, then the husky voice bellowed with pleasure: "That's perfect. That's what I would have wanted!"

Joe knew intimately those of renown, but he thought more about those whose lives depended on his talents and drive to provide hope. Even if he didn't know them personally, they weren't faceless — not for this man who knew his own vulnerabilities and refused to pretend them away.

Some years ago when my father died Joe asked to see the eulogy I'd delivered at my father's graveside. I sent it to him, and twenty minutes later he wrote back (a rare occurrence for a man who hated e-mails) just one sentence: "Tears are streaming down my face ..." That's what I mean when I say Joe was the best among us: a man who shook hands with kings and queens but had the touch — and the heart — of the commoner. He may have had a head for business and civic betterment, but he had the heart of a healer.

Kishmo ken hu, say those same Rabbis. Literally: "as is his name, so is he." Yosef ben Menachem was his name: Yosef — he who adds and gives of himself; Menachem — he who brings comfort to those who so need.

Joseph Rotman, Yosef ben Menachem, added much to this world. And in so doing he comforted and bettered its people. Sandy, Janis, Ken and Amy, Paul, Phoebe and Harrison, and Jenny — none will forget your Joe. Not you, not us. Not now, not ever. He was the author of a great, great life, and now you — and we — are the authors of his memory.

EULOGY FOR MORRIS MOSCOWITZ (1914–2006)
August 18, 2006, St. Louis, Missouri

As we lay our father to rest here in the city of his birth, here next to our mother, here less than a mile from the resting place of his parents and other family members, we, his family, wish to recall at least these things.

Morris Moscowitz was the son of Louis (Leib) and Bertha (Bryna Sirka); the older brother to Hyman and Sylvia; and the grandson of Chaim and Sheindel (Jenny) Fleg, Zvi and Rayza Moscovicci. His parents were East European immigrants, having arrived in this country in their late teenage years — his mother with her parents and his father alone. Both had fled the impoverishment and constraints of the Old World, and at least in his father's case, gravitated toward the appeal of the New World. As a boy, our father was caught between the traditional mores of his mother and the intrigue modernity held for his father. Our father's first language was Yiddish, but his sight was on the New World, not the Old. Morris Moscowitz was his father's son.

His was the boyhood of the immigrant Orthodoxy of the inner city of those days, of the cheder, of the *melamed* who dealt harshly with a ruler; yet also of a public school that exposed an alluring and available world. His larger family context, on and around Ridge Avenue, included various cousins and friends, all of whom lived nearby, many of whom he would know for much of his life.

Armed with imagination and ambition, he left home with a vengeance at age fifteen. He set out for an inviting male world of girls and gambling, of weekend adventures, keen for the freedom to sail his own waters. This leaving home at fifteen — ostensibly for university but, in fact, for life itself — set the stage for the man he would become: fiercely independent, even if quietly so, and possessed of his own mind, some of which he would share and much of which he would not. Dad was from those early days on generous and thoughtful. He was easy to be with and never demanding. He would grow to be wise — he wasn't there yet — and had already begun to chart his own course.

So, five years later, at age twenty, having finished his Washington University courses along with all the requisite law school classes, Dad strode into his final law school exam (after which he stood to earn his B.A. and a law degree). He took a quick look at the exam and decided then and there that the conventional world of law wasn't for him. Almost immediately he jumped the rails for the fun and adventure of Los Angeles, the farthest edge of the New World.

While on his way, with two friends in tow, he got himself lost or perhaps in trouble. An official letter from the deputy sheriff of Wilcox, Arizona, dated August 9, 1934, reads as follows:

> To whom it may concern: these boys Morris Moscowitz, Melvin Newmark, and Cruvant Altman were stranded through no fault of their own in Wilcox, Arizona. They are not hobos and are just trying to reach their home in St. Louis, Missouri. Any co-operation in this respect will be appreciated by me.

The note, signed by the town's constable and deputy sheriff, suggests the young male wandering ways of our father and his friends, including, tellingly, that they obviously fibbed to the deputy sheriff. In August 1934 they weren't trying to reach St. Louis; they were bound for good times in Los Angeles.

Our father stayed in Los Angeles for a year, working some, but by his own telling mostly lounging on the beaches in Venice and

Evolution of an Unorthodox Rabbi

Santa Monica. A letter from his father dated July 1935 suggests in rather strong language that Morris better get his act together, stop being a bum, return to St. Louis, and make something of himself. Even as our father did return, California had gotten into his blood. It never left and eventually coursed through us, as well.

Once back in St. Louis, Dad never returned for those degrees. Instead, he headed straight to work for his father. First in the Munger Linen Service business and later in buying a diaper service business, he seized good opportunities and made them grow larger. His business acumen and the good times enabled him and our mother to live the kind of life they would want over the next several decades. Years later, when he would go into real estate and dabble in the movie business, this was icing on the cake.

Our father and mother met at a dance in St. Louis in 1937, our mother's father having been transferred here from Chicago for about six months of work. Marilyn Barr was a dark, prepossessing beauty, seventeen years old, a working-class girl who would somehow carve out for herself an authentic elegance. Although each had come to the dance with their own dates, Morris and Marilyn couldn't take their eyes off each other. As he crossed the dance floor, she watched him approach while their respective dates made their way to the sidelines.

Our mother moved back to Chicago shortly thereafter. Then, for a year or so, they visited back and forth, but meanwhile — this is 1938 — our father, ever with wanderlust, decided to go off to Tahiti for a year of play with his friend Cruvy Altman. Our mother would have none of it: it's either Tahiti or me, she told him. They were married on March 19, 1939, at the Blackstone Hotel in Chicago.

For many years their marriage was very happy and passionate. Then came periods of rockiness, of being out of sync with each other, and then once again of feeling strongly bonded. It would be like that always.

Our mother and father knew how to enjoy life. They found equilibrium, satisfaction, and pride in each other as they constructed an almost singular life. Morris and Marilyn Moscowitz had much to enjoy and the capability to do it, whether, when fuelled with imagination but not much money, they built a rather unique house and home at 9255 Clayton Road; or, in the many travels their curiosity took them on, especially Europe in the 1960s, Italy, Paris, and London, their favourite haunts; or in their love of and collecting of art and artists and art critics (to say nothing of all the other fascinating people who graced our home and provoked the curiosity and sometimes bewilderment of our parents' sons). They loved being quiet together, sharing books and long walks.

Yes, their difficulty in understanding each other's ways and woes would sometimes bedevil them. But all in all, our father would say — and I'm certain our mother would concur — that nothing was more important than their marriage. They remained drawn to each other, tied together perhaps as much at the end as at the beginning.

The end — our mother's death in February 1974 — was a deep shock to our father. It's not clear even as he went on (for that was his way) that he ever got over her death.

But what he did then was the most important thing our father ever did: he made certain that Robert, already ill and in the hospital in Boston, would have a life, indeed a life of dignity. He literally saved Bob's life: spiriting him out of the hospital when the doctors warned against it; setting him up in his own apartment in Santa Monica in 1980; providing him with expert medical attention, the requisite balance of dependence and independence, a sense of self and a place in the world. I don't think it's an exaggeration to say that our father saved Robert's life. He would never want attention for all that he did — for Robert or, for that matter, for anyone else.

Our father loved his three sons equally, but he loved Robert best — and Jim and I are grateful. We wish Bob could be with us today, but, in fact, he is; he feels Dad's death as deeply as anyone. Bob learned his own strength, dignity, and courage at his father's feet — a silent and compelling teacher always, our father.

Sometimes we, our father's sons, felt close to him and sometimes, perhaps responding to his sweet distance, we loved him but from an emotional distance that he established. Nonetheless, our love for him, our respect for him, our appreciation for his wisdom and generosity, all ran deep and constant. We were quite aware that others took to our father, they, too, responding to that generosity, the wisdom and his sweetness, to his irony and his intellect and his capability at business. All of that drew many to our father over the years.

No wonder, in the midst of the Six Day War in 1967, Dad was asked to chair the Federation Emergency Campaign for Israel. Nor should it be surprising that he was sought for various positions requiring judgment and the regard of others. His advice, always given with quiet words, with discretion and without any desire for credit, was sought often. Most of the time we knew little of it.

Perhaps what most intrigued us was his ability to sail his own waters. Jim and I speak often about our father's decision to retire at age forty-nine — and the life, first in St. Louis and then in Los Angeles, he was able to stake for himself: one of enjoyment, of independence, of travel, of reading, of exercise, and more. We remain intrigued and admiring that for all the financial success he had — he could have had much more but didn't particularly want it. He wanted life and independence more than he wanted money and prestige.

Remembrances

Our father had charm without attitude, humour without hurting, and capability without pretension. His wisdom was thoughtful and practical and never judgmental. When at age twenty-three, I told him I wanted to go rabbinical school, his first response was to look at me quizzically and ask, sincerely, had I thought about law school? He wasn't being judgmental but rather knowing. He worried that rabbis had too many bosses, something he cautioned wouldn't be a good thing. But when after a while I found myself quite satisfied in the rabbinate, Dad was happy for me.

His marriage to Madeleine was for us often painful and agonizing. But we weren't unaware of the benefits: she did provide companionship to our father; he did love her and perhaps she him; and, maybe most importantly, Madeleine was good to Robert all the years they lived together in the same building.

Dad loved being a grandfather. When Jim and Amy married and Tali, Kira, and Dori came into the world, our father's life brightened considerably. Nothing brought out his sweetness like the company of his granddaughters. They were to him not only a delight but also deeply respectful and loving. Tali, Kira, and Dori, you brought your grandfather much happiness.

Our father lived very well, despite the various curves thrown his way, until his early eighties. He was vigorous and handsome and clearly enjoyed his life. Quiet as he was most often, you couldn't miss him if you crossed paths.

And then about ten years ago the Parkinson's struck, first slowly and then with a vengeance, robbing him of his capabilities, physical and mental, and eventually taking his life. Nonetheless, even with these difficult last years, he would profess his good fortune. He enjoyed his family, he knew success and esteem, and had a very good run for a long time — better and longer than most by far.

In these past five months Jim knew the great privilege of having Dad in the same city, of being with him every day, of providing the kind of support and love a son feels satisfied and honoured to give a father. Jim and Amy, Tali, Kira, and Dori brought Dad much comfort in these last five months of his life.

When we brought our father to Minneapolis in March, once the nurses at the Gianni Home had settled him comfortably in his room, he took a nap. When he awoke, Jim, Amy, and I were sitting nearby. He opened his eyes, looked around the room groggily once or twice — this his last room of his life — and finally turned to us and said slowly, "I kind of like my new executive office." In those words were everything: his appreciation of what we had done to make certain he would be comfortable in his last days; his irony; his humour; and, ultimately, his acceptance of his lot in life.

The Rabbis say, "Who is the one who is most happy in life? It is he who is happy in his lot." Morris Moscowitz, born all those years ago in 1914 in this city, whom we now lay to rest ninety-two years later, was ultimately happy with his lot in life. It may be the greatest gift he left to us, his family.

We don't know exactly why our father held on to life as he did in his last couple of years, indeed in his last couple of weeks. Perhaps it was because, as one of the nurses said, "The stubborn hold on the longest." Or perhaps he was simply grateful for being with his family in those last days. Not long before he died, Dad spoke the final complete sentence of his life. Always one to feel gratitude but rarely one to express it, he looked at Jim — just over a couple of weeks ago now — and said slowly with some difficulty but clearly, "Thank you for everything."

We, his family, are grateful that the end of our father's life was one of peace. He let go of life feeling the love of his family.

Now he is with God, always in peace. For this we are grateful as we bring our father and mother together to rest here at this spot in God's good earth.

EULOGY FOR
RABBI W. GUNTHER PLAUT (1912–2012)
February 13, 2012

In the first chapter of the Second Book of Samuel, when David learns of the death of Saul and Jonathan, he proclaims, "They were swifter than eagles, they were stronger than lions."[1] And two chapters later when David learns of the death of Avner, he declares to his soldiers and to all of Israel, "Know well that a Prince and a great man of Israel has died this day."[2]

W. Gunther Plaut, father and husband, son and grandfather, brother and uncle, eminent man of letters, a rabbi of the word and the deed, was swift like the eagle, strong like the lion. He was a prince and a great man of Israel, and now he has died.

The eagle soars above all; the lion is mighty on land. One is master of the skies; the other will never yield the ground. Each is esteemed by the Bible, one bearing the next generation on its wings, the other a symbol of pride and courage.

Moreinu HaRav: W. Gunther Plaut was our teacher, our rabbi. He soared above, scoping out our history as Jews. And he stood his ground, reminding Jews of our responsibilities born of that history. Eagle and lion, Rabbi Plaut embodied it all: grace and power, the privileges and sorrows we've known, the obligations incumbent on the fortunate.

Holy Blossom Temple felt that he was ours, and rightly so. But we also knew that he wasn't ours alone. From the first, Gunther Plaut was a man of the world, and so he would always be. A Middle European driven by the gathering storm of extremism into the arms of America, he became a patriot twice-fold, first in love with America, then enamoured of Canada.

He knew how to adapt to the new and to embrace the many. A rabbi to his congregations in Chicago and St. Paul and finally in Toronto, Rabbi Gunther Plaut was a man of the larger community as activist, animator, spokesman, and leader. Many claimed him as friend and as moving spirit — no wonder the lamentations in quarters near and far these past few days.

Moreinu HaRav: Gunther Plaut was foremost our teacher of the Torah. In his hands the Bible opened itself up to those who had put it down, his elucidations making a complex text alive with meaning.

He loved, Rabbi Plaut did, to teach and to preach, and he did so as few have or will. With verve and vigour, with substance and style, he held us — his congregation, his rabbinic colleagues, his community — in his (intellectual) hand.

For this was a most serious man, one whose inner world was sustained and stirred by learning, a rabbi who brought the ideas and intellectual excitement of his rabbinic forebears to the congregation and beyond.

He was a teacher par excellence, most often a preacher without parallel.

It is of such a rabbi that the tradition has conceived the notion of a *Rav Muvhak*, one's distinct rabbi, one's primary teacher. Such a teacher — his presence, his spirit, his mind — shines forth a clear light, illuminating the way, the path one should walk, even how one should think.

For many Rabbi Gunther Plaut was such a *Rav Muvhak*. He taught out of his biography and out of the story of the Jews. He taught out of the Torah, which he made his and ours. He taught as the senior rabbi of this congregation and as our senior scholar. He taught out of his writings and activism. He taught from the bimah, the classroom, the lecture hall, the rally platform. Always, the spirit of this *Rav Muvhak* shone through: a bright light of intelligence, experience, and Torah learning.

Rabbi Plaut instructed about living and dying. About how to live as a Jew in the modern world. About the centrality of the State of Israel for the Jews. He preached responsibilities to one's own, and no less, to others. He lived what he spoke: for Gunther Plaut, the word was the deed, for he knew the texts of the Jews as he did the Jews.

He had faith, but he understood those without. He was a liberal Jew at one with traditionalists; a European who made North America his home; a Jew in dialogue with the Christian, the Muslim, the Sikh, the Hindu, and the religiously unhoused. He wrote many books and played many sports. Gunther Plaut uniquely reached across many divides. And he did so out of his theology.

He wrote:

> I believe I was created as a Jew to be God's tool. I believe that my purpose on earth is to serve not only my people, but to serve humanity and do so as a Jew. Others may see only themselves and their goals, private and national. We Jews see our goals as more than private goals.

This public man served the Jews and humanity out of his personal experience and that of his people's story. He did so with distinction and urgency. His achievements, his bridging of divides — social and religious, ethnic and racial — were born of his and of our past. Gunther Plaut brought pride to his congregation and his community, the public he sought to serve.

But ultimately he belonged singularly to his family: to Jonas and Selma (Muti) Plaut; to his late brother, Walter, and family; to, most of all, Elizabeth, she who made Gunther a rabbi of both word and deed, she who was his anchor, this warm, intelligent, no-nonsense commonsense woman; to Judith, Jonathan, and Carol, who cared for both parents with unflagging loyalty and the fiercest kind of protection; to Daniel and Amy, Deborah and David; and to Steven and Jeffrey.

The Rabbis of Old, Rabbi Plaut's teachers and ours, took note of these words in that love poem, the Song of Songs: "The lips of those that are asleep, they move gently." Which the Rabbis took to mean, "His lips move from a place of eternal rest and speak to us through the Book."

The eagle has landed, the lion has lain down, but *Moreinu HaRav*, W. Gunther Plaut will long speak through the Torah of his life, the Torah of his teaching.

Family and friends, congregation and community, a prince, a great man of Israel, has now died. We are sad and impoverished, yet we are grateful and buoyed: the man, our rabbi, is gone, but his Torah will long live. May his memory and his life be for a blessing.

HER CHARACTER AND OURS:
ON JACKIE O (1929–1994)
Holy Blossom Temple Bulletin, June 9, 1994

Permit me, a rabbi in Canada, to reflect on the death of a Roman Catholic in the United States. I write on the morning of the funeral of Jacqueline Kennedy Onassis, wondering along with many: why does her death evoke such apparent nostalgia, sadness, and genuine appreciation?

First the nostalgia. For anyone who remembers President Kennedy's death, Jacqueline Onassis's death — all too sudden, at all too young an age — closes the circle on a time of longed-for innocence. While alive, beautiful, dignified, gracious as ever, Jackie symbolized that earlier time before the violence and the fraying of an America that once seemed the hope of the world. Her death is a reminder of how wrenching her husband's death was, how Dallas 1963 served as a portent of things to come.

And yet the response to Jacqueline Onassis's death is much more than about a loss of an earlier innocence. In an age of total revelation, false "sharing" of the personal, confession of the trivial, and blurring of boundaries, she maintained her sense of self. In an age of confession, she wouldn't confess. In an age of no boundaries and false boundaries, she kept hers. In an age in which all is supposed to be public, she was private.

Jacqueline Kennedy Onassis had character, and this is why we so liked and admired her. Character is knowing who you are and maintaining your sense of self in the midst of forces that tear away at this. Mrs. Onassis had this in abundance. Hers was a character undiminished by the flaws of family and husbands, by tragedy, by the public's relentless desire that she be "a legend when all she wanted was to be a person," as Edward Kennedy said.

Beyond our interest in this remarkable woman's life and death, of what meaning is Jacqueline Onassis for us? It is that she had — and apparently instilled in her children — exactly what we Jews want for our children and ourselves: the gift of character. Her identity was secure because she cultivated and honoured an internal private world of family and friends, of books and arts, of language, of humour, and of religion, which ultimately shielded this most public person from being known by strangers. Even the paparazzi were in awe of her, remaining at some distance as she apparently went about dying on her terms over a few months. Would that we and our children have identities and lives as enriched as Jacqueline Kennedy Onassis enjoyed, regardless of money and fame.

STANDING AT BABI YAR
October 15, 1994

This isn't a normal sermon. It may not be easy to listen to. It doesn't reflect normal circumstances or normal times. But it is about a real place and a real time.

The first thing you notice about the place is its quiet. A flat, grass-covered area above a ravine serves as a park. But unlike most parks, little seems to happen here. Some trees sway gently, though most are still. A few birds fly solo, silently, overhead. There are almost no people. It is a place of utter stillness. It is quiet.

Down below, in the thickly forested ravine, you sense more is going on. But beyond the trees and brush, you see nothing. And as you stare into this ravine, you hear nothing, too — nothing except the noiseless sound of the wind, and the noise of your own imagination.

Your own imagination — what does it bring up at this place of places? What does memory know about things here that words can never say? What does the heart know about what occurred here that monuments can't tell?

You can't imagine it all — or don't want to or dare not — and, thankfully, inevitably, your imagination yields to the overwhelming silence of this place. Simple, eloquent, and complete silence.

But if you listen closely enough, if you still your troubled imagination, if you stare long enough into that dense green ravine ... the silence yields and you can finally hear it all. You can imagine everything that happened in this place: the screams, the shots, the nightmare of three days and nights of death ... the utter and unspeakable horror of it all ... and finally, finally, the total silence that once engulfed this place, forever stilling what occurred here, stilling it but not erasing it — for this place is Babi Yar.

This place, Babi Yar, just on the outskirts of Kiev, some fifty-three years ago, witnessed over three days and nights the killing of some thirty thousand plus Jews. Men, women, and children were herded here on pretense. They were shot and shoved into the ravine and barely buried. Like Auschwitz, like Dachau, like numerous places, Babi Yar became shorthand for untold horror, for what the imagination didn't wish to bear, for what history didn't want to own.

This place, Babi Yar, like countless places on the European continent, some well known, most not, is where the earth is forever soaked in human blood. Much of this blood is from Jewish people, the blood of many whose names aren't even remembered. This is what Ukraine, Belarus, and such areas feel like — still, in some odd and morbid way, as Jewish as ever because the feel of blood and the smell of memory yet haunts the landscape.

This place, Babi Yar: standing at the edge of the ravine, wanting to grasp what occurred here, only able to picture a small part of it, you can't help but hear the words of Bertolt Brecht — "The imagination is the only truth."

It's not the only truth, but short of everything else, imagination is necessary at Babi Yar. Necessary because its truth, its events, became shut down, buried along with the lives of those who sleep beneath the quiet surface of that ravine.

So you understand what the Russian poet Yevgeny Yevtushenko was trying to do, some twenty years after the event, when he wrote in his famous poem "Babi Yar":

No monument stands over Babi Yar.
A drop sheer as a crude gravestone.
I am afraid.
   Today I am as old in years
as all the Jewish people.
Now I seem to be
   a Jew.[3]

What was the poet attempting to do? Only to put into words what one should not but must: the utter and stark horror of events that all prefer to forget — the perpetrators because they were murderers; the victims because they suffered enough; the bystanders and those who would suppress memory because they were murderers, as well.

But why do we put words to such events? Why do we, especially in "normal" times, under "normal" circumstances choose to remember? Why do we insist, as is now the case, that places such as Babi Yar have monuments?

We do so for the dead and for the living, both. The dead because the least we can do is respect and mark their lives — giving them in death what they couldn't know at the end of life.

We the living remember Babi Yar because tradition presumes a profound and lasting relationship between evil and the loss of memory. Haman, the demonic figure in Jewish history, matched only perhaps by Adolf Hitler as a symbol of evil, is said to have been a slave who, when he rose to master, forgot his former status and suppressed his experience of oppression. He then required others to kneel before him, to suffer his boot as a way to boost him up; anything else would lead him to violence and killing.

So the experience of oppression must be recalled lest the victim assume a false identity — pretending, manipulating, and using others as a way to feel a sense of importance. Without the memory of oppression the victim, too, can rise up to do evil.

Precisely for this reason the Bible doesn't censor our history as slaves: remembering one's helplessness, especially once overcome, serves as a basis for renewal, for recovery, for thanking God for the possibility of redemption.

This act of remembering and the sense of renewal that ensues leads one back to some measure of faith and hope, a belief that evil may loom but will not sustain; that, though not powerful enough to prevent all evil, God lessens evil — lessens it, liberates the oppressed, and gives them the capacity and the command to remember.

The prophet Isaiah, writing in Babylonian exile, imagining the ruins of Jerusalem, says much the same in our *haftarah*:

> Why do you say, O Jacob,
> Why declare, O Israel,
> "My way is hid from the Lord,
> My cause is ignored by my God"?
> Do you not know?
> Have you not heard?
> The Lord is God from of old,
> Creator of the earth from end to end,
> He never grows faint or weary,
> His wisdom cannot be fathomed.
> He gives strength to the weary,
> Fresh vigour to the spent.
> Youths may grow faint and weary,
> And young men stumble and fall;
> But they who trust in the Lord
> Shall renew their strength
> As eagles grow new plumes:
> They shall run and not grow weary,
> They shall march and not grow faint.[4]

In his own way, in his own words, that's what Yevtushenko is saying in "Babi Yar." Somewhere in my memory I had his words running through my mind, first charging, then stilling my imagination as I stood at Babi Yar three weeks ago. I stood there with three friends, understanding that testimony can, in some small way, counter the overwhelming helplessness one feels at that place. Yevtushenko writes toward the end of "Babi Yar":

> The wild grasses rustle over Babi Yar.
> The trees look ominous, like judges.
> Here all things scream silently, and, baring my
>   head,
> slowly I feel myself turning grey.
> And I myself am one massive, soundless scream
> above the thousand thousand buried here.
> I am each old man here shot dead
> I am every child here shot dead.
> Nothing in me shall ever forget![5]

There really is nothing to say — with the possible exception of "Amen."

8

Appreciations

PREAMBLE BY RICHARD ROTMAN

Different from the norm as a rabbi, John Moscowitz, as he tells it, was the last person anyone would have predicted for the rabbinate. To this day, he still seems different — not easy to predict or categorize. From an avant-garde home in St. Louis, he became part of a seismic shift in politics and society in California that defined the next several decades.

John understood he wasn't to everyone's taste, but he also understood that the rabbi's purpose isn't to cultivate personal popularity but to teach Jewish tradition and speak truth as he saw it. That sounds like an ideal, but it produces a different kind of rabbi who chose to do just that. Those differences attracted many members of the congregation and many friends and colleagues. Read the variety of his colleagues' and friends' comments about John here for a fascinating portrait of a rabbi who served his community and Jews so well and with such dedication for twenty-five years.

My own story parallels and accompanies John's. I first came to Toronto from Chicago in June 1987, joined Holy Blossom Temple (HBT), and was told there was "a new young rabbi, also from the States." We soon met and discovered we had entered

Canada at the same time, were both from the U.S. Midwest, and were exactly the same age, with birthdays one month apart on the twenty-fourth. We had friends in common through summer camps, and our fathers had improbably met at an industry convention.

After John became the senior rabbi at Holy Blossom, I joined one of the most exciting experiences at any institution of higher learning I had attended — Rabbi Moscowitz's Shabbat morning Torah class. I spent more than ten happy years in the class. John has many gifts, but his role as a teacher is one of his most outstanding.

When he persuaded Gerry Schwartz and Heather Reisman to sponsor the Holy Blossom Lecture Series, it was a high point in the temple's history. We became like a small university with many distinguished professors. John invited such luminaries as Amos Oz, Thomas Friedman, Victor Davis Hanson, Naomi Levy, David Wolpe, Abba Eban, Samantha Power, Michael Oren, Charles Krauthammer, Leon Wieseltier, Daniel Gordis, Paul Berman, Ruth Wisse, David Hartman, and many others.

The lecture series, which typically drew from several hundred to a thousand people and on occasion well over that, wasn't meant to appeal to HBT members alone. Rather, Rabbi Moscowitz intended to bring many others into the building and thereby bring the Jews of Toronto together. The great intellects and authors — leading figures of the day all — helped the rabbi do that. Holy Blossom became for a time the centre of Toronto Jewry. Those were exciting days.

That, in essence, is the legacy of Rabbi John Moscowitz at Holy Blossom Temple. He reached out and connected the numerous strata, person to person, old and young, thought to thought, the high and the low, influencing movers and shakers to help more, all to strengthen the synagogue and ultimately bring us closer to God. I can think of no greater accolade to a rabbinical tenure.

DR. MICHAEL B. OREN
Israeli Ambassador to Washington, 2009–2013, Member, Israeli Knesset

I first met Rabbi John Moscowitz in the spring of 2002 in Jerusalem through mutual friends. Soon thereafter John invited me to Holy Blossom Temple for the Toronto launch of my recently published book *Six Days of War*. He made me feel thoroughly at home and in the company of an old and trusted friend. Imagine my embarrassment, then, when speaking before the congregation — the largest audience I'd ever addressed — I suddenly felt overwhelmed by fatigue and thought I'd mixed up my notes. But, no, John assured me, my remarks had been totally cogent, and he couldn't wait to hear more.

Over the years, I returned several times to Holy Blossom where John provided a bimah for launching my latest ideas about the challenges confronting Israel and the Jewish people. Before and after my speeches, John and I would talk for hours about pressing Jewish issues. The incisiveness of his mind was only matched by his heart's courage. He was utterly unafraid to take on conventional assumptions and to go against intellectual trends. I found him invariably informative, wise, and inspiring.

John and I would frequently continue our conversations while in Israel at the Shalem Center and the Hartman Institute, at my home, and in Jerusalem's cafés. He enriched my life and gave me strength during those periods when Israelis needed strengthening.

I will always cherish my relationship with Rabbi John Moscowitz and look forward to continuing our friendship and, above all, our conversations.

LAURIE SAPIR
Kibbutz Sarid, Israel

Backtrack more than forty years when I first met John during our undergraduate years at Pitzer College in Claremont, California. Our initial conversations grew out of his sharing with me that he had just lost his vibrant mother, way before her time. He was quiet and devastated, and amid our talks, we developed a love that carried us through our college years. (In truth, we each had had a crush on each other for months before we ever spoke ...)

We visited each other's families, celebrated Rosh Hashanah and Pesach with my family in Seattle, and explored the beauty of the great Northwest before my departure for Israel, which separated our paths.

How telling: John was one of the first people I knew who felt the tension between being part of the New Left, now seething with hatred for Israel, and being a Jew in America. I believe that dilemma propelled him onto his spiritual and intellectual journey of self-discovery, culminating in his rabbinical studies and in the many achievements through which he has distinguished himself.

As college students, we bore witness to the catastrophic Yom Kippur War of 1973. Who could have imagined that the situation could get any worse for Israel and the Jewish people? Many of us now tremble at what lies ahead for Europe, the West, Israel, and for those striving for freedom under the dark veil (literally) of barbaric Radical Islam.

John "woke up," as he says, to this in the 1990s. Perhaps it has all been leading up to this moment. Having been tested and strengthened from his experiences at Holy Blossom Temple, John has become our clear voice, speaking truth in an increasingly frightening international reality that Jews have not encountered since the Holocaust.

I fear the day will come (again) when future leaders will have to ask themselves where they were and what they did to stop the terrible downward spiral of events. I have no doubt that John's courageous stands will be viewed as what distinguished him as a conscience for our people. I now await the books John was meant to write.

GREER AND ASHER KIRSHENBAUM; JOSH SALTZMAN
Toronto

Holy Blossom Temple was our second home during our child-hood, and Rabbi Moscowitz was the centre of our unique experience. Even though we were kids, a small part of a larger congregation, he always found the time to make us feel special. We knew he cared about us. During our bar and bat mitzvah preparation, Rabbi Moscowitz guided us to find our own original ideas. He pointed us toward a path we could walk on our own, toward being independent original thinkers like him. He always encouraged us to explore our Judaism in our own way. The environment of equality and acceptance he founded at Holy Blossom greatly influenced our identities as individuals and Jews. Women, men, and children were all equally important in lessons, services, and prayers, and this message will be part of us forever. Rabbi Moscowitz understood that the future of the congregation was to be rooted in the younger congregants, and always connected to each of us in a meaningful way.

Especially on the holidays we anticipated his wise words in his sermons and his unique view on the issues of our time. Rabbi Moscowitz continues to be a very important person in our lives. He was and is a guiding light with a warm smile — whether at our b'nai mitzvah, or as he performed the first marriage of our generation in our family. We hope he will continue to play a part in our simchas to come. He is our connection to *our* Judaism, and a beloved mentor.

FERN AND STEPHEN MORRISON
Toronto

> *I like to listen. I have learned a great deal from*
> *listening carefully. Most people never listen.*
> — Ernest Hemingway

John Moscowitz likes to teach, and unlike all but the very best teachers, he truly likes to listen, and he listens carefully. Despite possessing one of the best informed and most thoughtful rabbinic minds that we have ever encountered, John is a constant seeker of fresh information, knowledge, wisdom, and perspectives. When presented with a new idea or a new slant on an old idea, he delights in revealing, without embarrassment, "That never occurred to me before!"

The breadth of John's curiosity is also something to behold. He is fascinated both by the teachings of Joseph Soloveitchik and the lyrics of Bruce Springsteen, by the evolution of the African continent and no less by the world of sports, or the inner life of Laurel Canyon in the 1960s. A close friend of Israeli intellectuals, journalists, and writers, he is equally interested in the perspectives of a black taxi driver in his hometown of St. Louis, Missouri. John is more concerned with the substance than the source.

Although now a centrist by inclination, John has never completely outgrown his activist roots. In the religious realm he exhibits a deep respect for traditional values, but also an openness to discard practices when, after careful consideration, he concludes they are ultimately out of touch with contemporary values he also values.

As long-time members of Temple Sinai, John was never our "rabbi." In fact, for most of his tenure at Holy Blossom Temple, he was someone we knew casually through our involvement with the institutions of the broader Reform community in Toronto. We only came to really know John as teacher and friend as a result of a chance encounter during his sabbatical when we learned of his volunteer involvement with a recently formed *chevra*, Nefesh HaChayim, a loose collection of unaffiliated and otherwise affiliated couples and individuals sharing a common interest in adult Jewish study and a more intimate environment for Shabbat prayer.

That was more than two years ago. It is not all that common to make new friends in one's sixth decade, so it was a particular delight to discover a kindred spirit at this relatively late stage in our lives. But better late than never!

RABBI AMMIEL HIRSCH
Stephen Wise Free Synagogue, New York City

Dear John:

I am honoured to be part of this wonderful tribute to you. You have inspired me since the day we met many years ago. You are a rabbi's rabbi, among those rare colleagues we turn to when we want genuine counsel and truthful advice. You are authentic; you are sincere.

You have a brilliant, fierce, first-class intellect. You take ideas seriously. You have personal and intellectual integrity. These qualities led you to become a serious, studious student of Judaism. As a result, you are now a great teacher, a terrific writer, and a powerful communicator.

The rabbinate for you has never been about ritual and ceremony alone. There are plenty of colleagues who do just fine in these rabbinic responsibilities. What sets you apart and makes you very special is your understanding that, as individuals and as Jews, we are part of something larger, and that it is our task as rabbis to instill this sense of grandeur in fellow Jews. You have strong beliefs. How refreshing and how rare! You are a principled man. You have the courage of your convictions.

And what profound convictions! The animating principles of your life are completely, joyously, unreservedly, and unabashedly Jewish: love for the Jewish people and our supreme creation in this age — the State of Israel; love for Jewish tradition that you feel so responsible to learn, teach, and pass on; and most of all — love for our fellow human beings and the consequent obligations to act with kindness, compassion, and respect, and being created in God's image, to honour, preserve, and enhance human dignity.

It is these qualities that brought you to one of the pre-eminent synagogues in the world. Your quarter century of leadership has honoured Holy Blossom Temple, which has been enriched beyond measure by your rabbinate.

Keep teaching, John. Keep writing. You have much yet to do, and so much more to contribute.

In abiding friendship,
Ammi

CANTOR BENJAMIN MAISSNER
Holy Blossom Temple, Toronto

Aseh l'cha rav, u'kneh l'cha chaver.

Pirkei Avot 1:6 (Ethics of the Fathers) states: *Aseh lecha rav, u'kneh lecha chaver, v'haveh dan et kol adam lekaf zechut* — "Make for yourself a Rav and acquire for yourself a friend, and let it be such that you always judge each person according to their merits." One must find a rabbi to call your own, for both strictly legal and personal matters. Everyone needs a mentor, someone to turn to for guidance. However, what has become clear to me recently is that the Mishnah is asking for more than that. The Rav referred to is a true role model that is a real live person whom one can have a human relationship with — a person who you respect and who respects you in turn. Someone who you can both see as a model to live by and as someone you can critique and who feels equally comfortable doing the same for you. This is a lofty ideal to reach, but it fits perfectly with my relationship with Rabbi John Moscowitz.

We had the unique privilege of working together, serving our congregation for over twenty-five years. We saw each other develop and grow into our professional sacred callings of rabbi and *hazzan* at Holy Blossom Temple. John revealed himself as an erudite liberal-thinking rabbi. His intellectual wisdom and personal guidance always helped me personally to aspire to the highest goals and to strive for excellence. John always appreciated the highest qualities of authentic traditional Jewish music and respected the musical legacy of our local heritage. He was and is a loyal personal friend, which was always reflected both on the bimah and in our personal lives. I will treasure our friendship forever.

RABBI NAOMI LEVY
Nashuvah and Author, Los Angeles

In Pirkei Avot, the compendium of rabbinic wisdom, we find five rabbis attempting to answer a critical question: what is the highest quality a person should seek to acquire? One rabbi says, "A good heart." His colleague chimes in: "To be a good friend." A third replies, "To be a good neighbour." Another rabbi suggests: "To be able to anticipate what is coming." But one rabbi offers an answer that encompasses all these noble attributes: "A good eye."

What exactly is a good eye? It's the opposite of an evil eye. If an evil eye is a curse cast by a jealous person, then a good eye is the blessing that a humble person spreads — a person who sees the best in others and wants them to succeed and flourish; a person who lifts others up. My dear friend Rabbi John Moscowitz has been graced with the full measure of what it means to have a good eye.

John Moscowitz is kind and gentle to the depths of his soul. He is curious, wise, and a lover of the Torah and Israel. He is forever learning and growing and evolving, collecting friends wherever he goes. I am honoured to be one of the friends in John's orbit. He invited me to speak at Holy Blossom Temple several years ago, and there was an instant connection, a meeting of souls.

John and I have had long conversations, long walks, and long meals in Toronto, Los Angeles, and Jerusalem, too. It's so easy to talk to John because you never feel like you are being judged. He listens with an open heart and values opinions even when he doesn't share them. He is a voracious reader with a prodigious memory, yet he carries his intellect so very lightly without ever needing to impress. He is a rabbi in the best sense of the word, a natural-born teacher who leads by example and who lives by his word.

"A good eye" also implies a visionary, and John is most definitely a man of vision. He sees true potential and holy possibility in all his friends, in all his students, and in the Holy Blossom community that flourished under his leadership.

When God chose Abraham, God said, "You shall be a blessing" — not you shall offer blessings but your very presence will sow blessings wherever you go. Rabbi John Moscowitz has planted many blessings. When you read his words and teachings in this volume, you will certainly be blessed. Through him perhaps you, too, will acquire a good eye.

MARC AND CRAIG KIELBURGER
Founders of Free The Children and Me to We, Toronto

We feel incredibly blessed to have received mentorship and wisdom from community elders across numerous cultures through our work and travels. Rabbi John Moscowitz has been a most valuable adviser and supporter of Free The Children and Me to We, counselling us through the big challenges we've faced and being readily available for conversations on the little things, too.

For the young people of the Holy Blossom Temple community, Rabbi Moscowitz helped forge a lifelong connection between the local and the global. He has modelled the spirit of giving and engaged youth and families in service to their home community and their peers overseas — inspiring a generation to see beyond their own lives to their place in the larger world.

Our fondest memory of Rabbi Moscowitz is a trip we shared to Kenya's Rift Valley where we invited him as an elder of our Toronto community to meet elders from our adopted communities among the Kipsigis and Maasai people. He humbly participated in the everyday activities of these communities, building new school rooms, beading jewellery with the local mamas, and carrying heavy water jugs on his back for miles from the closest well.

In the evenings we listened with awe as he exchanged wisdom and stories with the Kenyan elders — struck by the instant camaraderie and good humour between them. On one occasion they shared insight into the rites of passage in their respective traditions. In Maasai culture these customs include showing unflinching strength by lying on a bed of stinging fire ants, resilience by being burned by hot coals, and courage by hunting a lion. Before his turn telling about the Jewish tests of bar and bat mitzvah, Rabbi Moscowitz jokingly began, "Well, that sounds just like us."

RABBI JEFFREY K. SALKIN
Temple Solel, Hollywood, Florida

From the moment I first met John Moscowitz, I knew we would become friends. It was during the summer of 1976, and we had both just begun our studies at Hebrew Union College–Jewish Institute of Religion in Jerusalem. Given the New York–centrism of my youth, John was the first person from St. Louis I had ever met, making him totally exotic.

We hung out with each other, often going on impromptu mini-*tiyulim* (tours) through obscure places in Jerusalem. One afternoon we hiked deep into the Valley of Hinnom below the Old City, finding an ancient Greek Orthodox monastery, at that time inhabited only by equally ancient nuns. The young Palestinian caretaker proudly took us on a tour, proudly showing us a room piled with skulls and skeletons of long-deceased monks. It was like something out of Stephen King. John, with characteristic grace, complimented him: "You've done a great job of cleaning up in here."

Our friendship endured over the years, surviving and even thriving despite physical distances and the vagaries of career movement. I have always been grateful for our friendship — not least of all because we have been kindred spirits. While good food and wine have always been staples of our friendship, it has been our ongoing conversation that has truly sustained us.

Appreciations

Everyone who knows John's biography knows of his political and social "internship" on the extreme Left, associating with the likes of Jane Fonda and Tom Hayden. And everyone who knows John also knows of his political pilgrimage toward the centre — or, to be more precise, away from the left.

In the true sense of Reform Judaism, John has always been willing and eager to reform his own thinking. John embodies an intellectual iconoclasm that refuses to accept the pieties of both the right and the left. He has little patience for sloppy and/or sentimental thinking. Like our ancestor Abraham, John has never been afraid to be *ha-ivri*, the one who stands on the other side.

During moments when it seemed that the current tide of Jewish thinking and endeavour was moving away from a firm embrace of Israel — land and people — John has stood up and he has stood fast in his commitment to Jewish nationhood. Even and especially as the senior rabbi of one of the world's most prominent Reform congregations, John has maintained and championed a fierce spiritual independence, lovingly questioning the direction of the Reform movement.

John reads voraciously and widely. He says and writes what he believes. He has never been afraid to be lonely in his positions — and, in fact, rarely has been, because his intellectual honesty has won him friends from all over the Jewish spectrum. John is generous with his friendships; on more than one occasion he has served as a "matchmaker" for me, introducing me to people whom he thought I should know and learn from. It is an amazing and rare gift.

I mentioned that John and I have had now more than thirty-five years of conversation. It has been a long, extended, ongoing conversation, one that might stop at a point and then pick up again months later. We have seen each other through various challenges, and his is among the first numbers I will call if need arises.

I no longer know what a "typical" Reform rabbi is or should be. But this I know to be true: whatever that is, it's not John Moscowitz. I'm proud to be his classmate and colleague. I am even prouder to be his friend.

RABBI KAREN THOMASHOW
Isaac M. Wise Temple, Cincinnati, Ohio

> *Just as a person is commanded to honour a parent and hold that parent in awe, so, too, is that person obligated to honour a teacher and hold that teacher in awe.*
> — *Mishneh Torah* 5:1

I hold Rabbi John Moscowitz, my teacher, in awe. For six years at Holy Blossom Temple, he was always my mentor — a relationship that continues to impact my own rabbinate today.

Three illustrations of how John taught me.

On my first Sukkot morning at Holy Blossom, I arrived, by accident of my misunderstanding, half an hour late and sheepishly took my place on the bimah next to Rabbi Moscowitz. He waited for me to settle in (and down) before he leaned over and said, "You will make yourself more upset about this than anything I might say, so we are fine." He never said another word about it — he didn't need to. Rabbi Moscowitz was always fair and honest.

And protective, which brings me to the second illustration. The first time I was slated to officiate at a funeral, the family called him and complained that they didn't want a woman officiating; they asked that a male rabbi officiate in my place. Rabbi

Moscowitz refused; I would officiate, he said. He always believed in me, protected me, and went to bat for my best interests.

Finally, Rabbi Moscowitz called me every day from Africa when I was in California with my family facing some early scary days regarding the health of our little one. I was grateful for his constancy, and I learned from that how to pay attention to those burdened by illness.

I am grateful to John for his mentorship and friendship — then and now. *Mazel tov*, my teacher, whom I hold in awe.

JULIE AND LARRY SCHWARTZ
Toronto

By virtue of our birth year and country of origin, John Moscowitz and I were fellow travellers through the 1960s, even though we actually only met each other here in Canada.

Like many American Jews, I had a secular upbringing devoid of rabbinic interaction — and predicated on the stereotypical image of rabbis as old men with long beards.

Enter John Moscowitz — a beardless rabbi my own age, an ex-pat American to boot, and a person in authority who said the word *schedule* with a *k* and pronounced the word *prah-ject* my way.

Rabbi Moscowitz's talent for teaching was grounded in his ability to lead the learner to the discovery. I was once going on about how lucky our son, Jonathan, was to get Shoftim as his Torah portion. I explained that because it laid out the rules of fair fighting, this portion made a good sports metaphor ... and thus would resonate with Jonathan. When I pronounced Shoftim a "great parsha," Rabbi Moscowitz gently suggested that they are all great portions.

Throughout John's tenure at Holy Blossom Temple, Larry and I always found him to be thoughtful, wise, intellectually courageous, and compassionate ... and never more so than when he helped us through the too-early death of our son, Joel. There aren't enough ways to thank a rabbi who eulogizes your son with such a wonderful blend of respect, familiarity, and care.

As tragic as the circumstances were is exactly how fortunate our family has been to have John in our corner.

RABBI DANIEL GORDIS
Senior Vice-President, Shalem College, Jerusalem

One of life's great pleasures and unexpected blessings is the opportunity to meet someone long after the stage when one makes most of his or her friends, someone who feels like a long-lost friend even though you've just encountered them for the very first time. That pleasure, that blessing, is precisely how I think about the now-treasured friendship I have with Rabbi John Moscowitz.

John represents for me a model of precisely what the Jewish world needs. An avid reader and careful thinker, John is deliberate. A man of passionate convictions and deep commitments, he nonetheless continues to ponder and occasionally to change. In a world in which people are often either immovable or entirely uncommitted, his is a model of thoughtful conviction and intellectual nimbleness that we all ought to model.

John is a Reform rabbi, and I am not a Reform Jew. But John is the kind of Reform Jew our world needs. I still recall the day John told me he had (at that point) three requirements of the members of his rabbinic team: (1) they could not publicly use money on Shabbat; (2) they could not perform intermarriages; and (3) they had to be publicly supportive of Israel. I remember that day because I remember thinking: *If only there was an entire movement of such people, how different and rich would the Jewish world be!*

Not that those had to be the particular criteria, of course. I can easily envision a world in which Reform Jews differ on principle regarding how to revere Shabbat, and it is, to be sure, not entirely clear to any thinking person what loving and supporting Israel entails, especially when our hearts are so often breaking when it comes to the Jewish state. But the notion that there are standards, that Jewishness entails limits, that community is built in large measure through shared disposition and shared practice — a liberal Jewish world founded on these would enrich us all.

John's intellectual world, his life of kindness and thus deep commitment to both principle and people, his willingness to stand for things even as he continually rethinks them is, especially in an era such as ours, not only a breath of fresh air but a model to which to aspire. Thus, it is largely out of individual and collective selfishness that I wish him many more years of productive leadership and the health and vitality that will enable him to continue to enrich us all.

MICHAEL AND JANETTE DIAMOND; JESSE, COLE, AND ARI
Toronto

Rabbi Moscowitz built strong and enduring relationships with each member of our family. Those relationships were built through caring and empathy. He shepherded us through our son Jesse's bar mitzvah at a most difficult time for our family and did so with kindness and firm support. He made efforts to empower and support our children as Jews and as people. And for me, he opened doors to learning continually. He was always a teacher, whether in private conversation, on a mission to Israel, or through his sermons, which often took us into areas of thinking that were challenging but necessary.

More than any other rabbi I am aware of in the progressive movements, he shared possibilities and opinions that needed to be shared and that have turned out, in the fullness of time, to have been in many ways prescient and well considered. He also has an understanding of the Jewish people and our role both in the world and within and among ourselves, which is full and complete and which he has shared to the great advantage of all of us.

Rabbi Moscowitz is also a social entrepreneur — he considered and then agreed to provide critical support for a pilot *shinshinim* program at Holy Blossom Temple that ultimately provided the platform for the Israel Engagement Shinshinim Program, one of the community's most successful programs.

I have always felt comfortable and trusting around Rabbi Moscowitz and continue to do so. In his quiet but enlightened way, he has opened up my eyes, and the eyes of many others, to new ideas, thoughts, and considerations. And while so doing, he has been instrumental in helping Janette and I, as parents, to build as much Jewish identity in our sons as possible.

RABBI JOHN ROSOVE
Temple Israel of Hollywood, Los Angeles

I have been close friends with John Moscowitz since 1975. We were two of maybe five men (among more than two hundred women) attending a conference on Jewish feminism at the University of California, Los Angeles. We were curious about what Jewish feminism meant for us and the Jewish people.

John had just been engaged in political work with Tom Hayden and Jane Fonda, and in 1975 he was now turning to his Jewish core.

The best part of that conference for me was meeting John. We talked deeply, thoughtfully, broadly, and personally. He credits me in his decision to enter the rabbinate. Ever since, we have been the dearest of friends, sharing much in our personal and professional lives. Over these four decades of friendship, we have been each other's confidants and greatest fans.

I love John's heart, his *menschlikeit*, his thoughtfulness, his dignity, his dry humour, and his commitment to living his life honestly and with integrity as a Jew. His commitment to study, teaching, and writing, to the people and state of Israel, to his friends and congregants, to his family, to everything decent, defines him as a man, as a Jew, and as a rabbi.

I cannot imagine my life without his friendship, and I am so happy that his congregation is saluting him. He immensely deserves this tribute, and I am thrilled to add my own words.

BARRY BORDEN
Past President of Holy Blossom Temple, Toronto

Rabbi — a Jewish scholar and teacher, one who studies and imparts the words and meanings of the Torah.

Rabbi John Moscowitz embodies this definition, but to those, like myself, who have been fortunate to see the other side of this person, John Moscowitz is much more.

My relationship with John began as with most — as a congregant and a rabbi. However, when I became president and Rabbi Moscowitz was transitioning from associate rabbi to senior rabbi, I was privileged to not only witness first-hand his strengths and positive approach but also quickly realized how effective he is as a rabbi and how he could relate, care, and project all in a clear, concise, and meaningful way.

As senior rabbi, he focused on the big picture. He quickly developed his vision based on utilizing the three pillars: Torah, *Avodah, Gemilut Chasidim* — the three pillars that would support and help define the future of Holy Blossom. Understanding that individuals have different needs and desires at different times, he tried to define a philosophy for Holy Blossom as an institution with many doors of entry — you would enter the door of your choosing into the larger house. Once inside, involvement would expand, ultimately leading to an atmosphere that would allow for individual differences and requirements. This very positive approach would ultimately help define not only his overall feelings for Holy Blossom, but also his caring for the congregation and the community, his love for Israel, and his knowledge and compassion for other world issues.

Having an understanding of human nature, Rabbi Moscowitz has much to teach — his strengths and abilities are easy to describe and his personal friendship is indeed valued.

MICHELLE KATZ
Toronto

Eighteen years ago, inspired by your *divrei* Torah, each Erev Shabbat, a new member then to Holy Blossom Temple, something drew me to you. I asked if you taught anything else at temple. You encouraged me to come to Torah study on Wednesday mornings.

That was the beginning of my getting to know you as a friend, a teacher, and truly as a spiritual guide. I use that term *spiritual guide* intentionally, as I believe it is no accident that I was pulled in your direction — compelled by your teachings, pushed by my own will, of course, but definitely driven by some greater Guiding Force.

I arrived each Wednesday morning, not quite sure what I was doing there, and I'd leave each Wednesday morning looking forward to the next week. I was drawn by something deep, and those weeks evolved into years and eventually included Shabbat mornings, too.

Gradually, I noticed myself changing. Your teaching was changing me. My learning, my understanding of Judaism, was becoming deeper and more thoughtful. I recall you saying once, "Life is not about happiness. It's about meaning and purpose." I was slowly beginning to understand that a life of ideas and learning is exactly that: meaningful, purposeful, and deeply satisfying.

John, it is truly a gift and a blessing to know someone like you: serious, profoundly thoughtful, provocative, complex, kind, gracious, and decent — these are deeply attractive attributes.

In addition as a teacher, your attention to detail and preparation, your memory of the knowledge that you acquire, internalize, and live by through your voracious appetite for reading — all of this is inspiring and challenging for those who wish to learn more. Most of all, John, you have a big heart and a generosity for sharing your ideas so that those who choose to better themselves intellectually, morally, and spiritually may also benefit.

RABBI AARON FLANZRAICH
Beth Sholom Synagogue, Toronto

Yehoshua ben Perachia lived twenty-two hundred years ago. That means that Yehoshua saw the Second Temple in Jerusalem, that he lived under Hasmonean rule, and perhaps even lived when the Maccabees recaptured the Temple from the Seleucids. We also know that this means Yehoshua lived before Hillel and Shammai, though in a similar intellectual and moral oeuvre as them.

Despite the special status that Yehoshua ben Perachia has in Talmudic history — he is one of the five *zugot* responsible for the transmission of the Torah through the generations — we have little in his name and few laws and ideas attributed to him.

Some scholars note, based on evidence found in ancient papyri, that Yehoshua ben Perachia had a reputation as a faith healer, exorcist, and incantation writer. But Yehoshua is best known for this terse and beautiful reflection in Pirkei Avot:

> Yehoshua ben Perachia and Nittai the Arbelite received the Torah from them. Yehoshua ben Perachia says, "Make for yourself a Rav. And get yourself a friend. And give everyone the benefit of the doubt."

Yehoshua's guidance remains relevant today. I offer his words to celebrate this collection of writings and sermons by Rabbi John Moscowitz. John has a passionate interest in what makes humans so human, which when you get to know John isn't at all surprising. Because what strikes you immediately with John is the tireless support he gives to others, the pleasure he gains from helping people reach their goals, and in the open and easy rapport one easily strikes with him. This is the John Moscowitz I call my friend, and this is the John Moscowitz you will discover in these pages.

Here is what we uncover through a careful reading of Yehoshua ben Perachia's words: "Make for yourself a Rav and you will gain a friend. And be sure to give everyone the benefit of the doubt." He is saying when you find a Rav you will find for yourself a friend, too. Armed with a spiritual guide and a friend we will acquire love and joy in our lives. With love and joy we can be open of heart and soul and thus be fair and kind to others. I know this has been true for my life, as I am sure it has been for others.

The truth of this is seen in the work of my *Rav vhaver*, teacher and friend, Rabbi John Moscowitz. His work blends word and passion; it mixes idea with humanity. His skill is in knowing we need both — the strength of teaching and the love of a friend to nurture the growth of the souls who come to seek, discover, and struggle in pursuit of spirit.

Rabbi Abraham Joshua Heschel, z"l, wrote, "In our own lives the voice of God speaks slowly, a syllable at a time ..." saying that by hindsight we can see a majestic tapestry of how God has inspired and touched the things we have said and done. I know this book will reveal the "slow speech of God" in John Moscowitz's writing and teaching, of seeing God's words in ways that are eloquent and meaningful through the hand and heart of a *Rav vhaver*.

YOSSI KLEIN HALEVI
Shalom Hartman Institute, Jerusalem

My deep friendship with John began during the Second Intifada of the early 2000s. In Israel we were experiencing the suicide bombings as a turning point in the conflict — much like the Arab world's rejection of partition of 1947. Israel, after all, had just offered to create a Palestinian state with Jerusalem as its capital, and the response was the worst wave of terror in Israel's history. Most Israelis concluded that the conflict wasn't about 1967 but 1948 — that is, not about the occupation of the Palestinians but the creation of Israel. The problem wasn't the absence of a Palestinian state but the existence of a Jewish state within any borders.

As a result of the Second Intifada, the Israeli left all but collapsed. Israeli newspapers published confessions from dis-illusioned left-wing leaders who had devoted their lives to Israeli-Palestinian reconciliation but who now saw their work destroyed by Palestinian intransigence.

But when I lectured in North American Jewish communi-ties, especially liberal communities, I found confusion. Wasn't the Oslo process supposed to bring peace? Diaspora Jews wondered. What went wrong? Surely, this was only a misunderstanding, a temporary distraction on the road to an inevitable peace agreement.

I felt a profound disconnect between Israelis and Diaspora Jews, an inability by many liberal Jews abroad to appreciate the depth of Israel's shattering. And then I met Rabbi John Moscowitz. Every true leader has a historic moment, a time of testing one's courage and vision; John's moment was the Second Intifada.

John was that rare Jewish leader who didn't wait for consensus or approval — not from colleagues, not from his congregation. Instead, John became a vocal defender of Israel and its policies. In his Shabbat sermons, John insisted that the moral balance in the Palestinian-Israeli conflict had shifted in Israel's favour. Jews, he noted, couldn't afford wishful thinking. He began inviting speakers to Holy Blossom Temple who challenged some of the most cherished notions of the left. (I was one of them.) And he scandalized much of the liberal Jewish world by organizing an advertisement in the Jewish *Forward*, signed by a small group of fellow courageous Reform rabbis who broke rank and supported the policies of President George W. Bush and Prime Minister Ariel Sharon.

John paid a price for his courage, earning enemies at home and abroad. But he never hesitated from speaking the truth as he understood it.

In Judaism there is the notion that one can earn one's place in the world to come in an instant. For all the many acts of service to the Jewish people that have defined John's career, I believe that he earned his world to come in that moment of clarity and courage when he stepped out of line and reminded us all that confronting reality takes precedence over loyalty to comfortable ideological beliefs.

Books I Love

In my early teens, when I gave up the ghost of being a baseball player and laid down my glove, I didn't remain empty-handed for too long. By my early twenties, I'd walk around with a book, one I was reading or intending to read, or one that just made me feel good. A book in my hand, not entirely unlike a baseball glove, was a guardian spirit of sorts. It's no different today.

What have books meant to me and why do they preoccupy me? Why in this digital day do I still line the walls of my house with books?

It's simple, actually. Books are often emotionally laden reminders of past experiences (and people) to which we wish to remain tethered. Books also expand our world: they transport us to places intellectually and geographically, to the past and the future we can't otherwise inhabit or visit. Good books inspire; they are about possibility and promise; they can rearrange your perspective and even change your life. Reading, as said by many before me, is "everything." And at least for me, that means a physical book, not a digital reader.

Who doesn't have their favourite books? I do, and here's my idiosyncratic and incomplete list, and in no special order. These books range from childhood favourites to what occupies me today, though I've excluded traditional Jewish texts, a different category. I've limited this list to about 100 books.

CHILDHOOD BOOKS

This first group includes those books I loved best between the ages of eight and eighteen: *The Yearling*, Marjorie Kinnan Rawlings; *Oliver Twist*, Charles Dickens; *To Kill a Mockingbird*, Harper Lee; *The Red and the Black*, Stendhal; *Exodus*, Leon Uris; *Black Like Me*, John Howard Griffin; *The Bridge of San Luis Rey*, Thornton Wilder; *Ethan Frome*, Edith Wharton; *A Portrait of the Artist as a Young Man*, James Joyce; *Giants in the Earth*, O.E. Rølvaag; *In Cold Blood*, Truman Capote; *The Greek Way*, Edith Hamilton; *The Call of the Wild*, Jack London; *The Scarlet Letter*, Nathaniel Hawthorne.

FICTION

This next section includes the fiction I've loved, though admittedly most of these I read in my twenties and early thirties. It was about then that the lure of history, biography, and politics took hold. Fortunately, fiction has begun to capture my attention once again: *The Sun Also Rises* and *A Farewell to Arms*, Ernest Hemingway; *Man's Fate*, André Malraux; *Sophie's Choice*, William Styron; *Song of Solomon*, Toni Morrison; *The Secret Agent*, Joseph Conrad; *Bread and Wine*, Ignazio Silone; *Fathers and Sons*, Ivan Turgenev; *The Brothers Karamazov*, Fyodor Dostoyevsky; *The Great Gatsby*, F. Scott Fitzgerald; *Finnegan's Wake*, James Joyce; *Goodbye, Columbus*, Philip Roth; *Fear of Flying*, Erica Jong; *Darkness at Noon*, Arthur Koestler; *The Trial*, Franz Kafka.

POLITICS AND MORE

Next come politics, public matters, and other interests I gained as a child and have never lost. Here is that very truncated list:

Ghost Wars, Steve Coll; *Chasing the Flame*, Samantha Power; *The Canadians*, Andrew Malcolm; *The Neoconservative Imagination*, Irving Kristol; *The Dream Palace of the Arabs*, Fouad Ajami; *The Sixties*, Todd Gitlin; *Power and the Idealists*, Paul Berman; *City of Quartz*, Mike Davis; *The Penguin Essays of George Orwell*, George Orwell; *Pedagogy of the Oppressed*, Paulo Freire; *New Art City*, Jed Perl; *Fallingwater Rising*, Franklin Toker; *The Brain That Heals Itself*, Norman Doidge; *The Drama of the Gifted Child*, Alice Miller; *The Family Crucible*, Augustus Napier and Carl Whitaker; *The Interpretation of Dreams*, Sigmund Freud.

JUDAISM AND JEWS

I've read books about Judaism and Jews extensively since my early twenties. The following are a few books that comprise a list fairly reflective of my interests in Judaica (outside of classical texts): *Majesty and Humility: The Thought of Joseph B. Soloveitchik*, Reuven Ziegler; *The Lonely Man of Faith*, Joseph B. Soloveitchik; *Renewing the Covenant*, Eugene B. Borowitz; *Between Berlin and Slobodka*, Hillel Goldberg; *After Emancipation*, David Ellenson; *The Ordeal of Civility*, John Murray Cuddihy; *Why Faith Matters*, David J. Wolpe; *Tormented Master*, Arthur Green; *Kaddish*, Leon Wieseltier; *The Uses of Tradition*, edited by Jack Wertheimer; *Judaism and Christianity: Essays by Leo Baeck*, translated by Walter Kaufmann; *The Religion of Israel*, Yehezkel Kaufmann; *On Jews and Judaism in Crisis*, Gershom Scholem; *Zakhor: Jewish History and Jewish Memory*, Yosef Hayim Yerushalmi; *The Rebbe: The Life and Afterlife of Menachem Mendel Schneerson*, Samuel Heilman and Menachem Friedman.

ISRAEL

Now to the most important books for me on the modern state of Israel. At the very least they must include: *A History of Zionism*, Walter Laqueur; *The Israelis*, Amos Elon; *Six Days of War*, Michael Oren; *One Palestine, Complete*, Tom Segev; *At the Entrance to the Garden of Eden* and *Like Dreamers*, Yossi Klein Halevi; *A Table for One*, Aharon Appelfeld; *The Jewish State*, Yoram Hazony; *The Zionist Idea*, edited by Arthur Hertzberg; *Menachem Begin*, Daniel Gordis; *1948*, Benny Morris; *Recovered Roots*, Yael Zerubavel; *Israelis and the Jewish Tradition*, David Hartman.

HISTORY AND BIOGRAPHY

Next, here are my mainstays in history and biography: *Einstein's German World*, Fritz Stern; *Rome and Jerusalem*, Martin Goodman; *Bloodlands*, Timothy Snyder; *Salonica, City of Ghosts*, Mark Mazower; *Fin-de-Siècle Vienna*, Carl E. Schorske; *The Great War and Modern Memory*, Paul Fussell; *Black Mountain*, Martin Duberman; *From That Place and Time* and *The War Against the Jews*, Lucy S. Dawidowicz; *The Promised Land*, Nicholas Lemann; *RFK: A Memoir*, Jack Newfield; *Founding Brothers*, Joseph J. Ellis; *Hitch-22*, Christopher Hitchens; *A Walker in the City*, Alfred Kazin; *Power Struggle*, Richard L. Rubenstein; *Memoirs of a Dutiful Daughter*, Simone de Beauvoir; *It Ain't No Sin to Be Glad You're Alive: The Promise of Bruce Springsteen*, Eric Alterman; *Lost in Translation*, Eva Hoffman; *Leo and His Circle: The Life of Leo Castelli*, Annie Cohen-Solal.

FOR A DESERT ISLAND STAY

Finally, what lover of books hasn't imagined being stranded on a desert island and allowed to bring a few books along? Were that me, what would I take? Which books do I most love and return to frequently because they are uniquely sustaining? I was going to limit myself here to five, but I have to opt for ten. And because it's a dire situation, I'll break my rule imposed on the overall list with regard to Judaism's sacred texts — hence, the last three listed below are equally necessary for intellectual nourishment on that island: *Africa: A Biography of the Continent*, John Reader; *A Tale of Love and Darkness*, Amos Oz; *Joy and Responsibility*, David Hartman; *Shiurei HaRav: A Conspectus of the Public Lectures of Rabbi Joseph B. Soloveitchik*, edited by Joseph Epstein; *Civilization and Its Discontents*, Sigmund Freud; *Bacchae and Other Plays*, Euripides; *The Complete Works of William Shakespeare*; The Bible; *Genesis: The Beginning of Desire*, Avivah Gottlieb Zornberg; *The Beginning of Wisdom*, Leon R. Kass.

Afterword by Dr. Norman Doidge

These remarks from Dr. Norman Doidge, author of The Brain That Heals Itself, *were delivered at a gathering celebrating Rabbi John Moscowitz in September 2012.*

What in the end surprised me is how long and what a productive run you have had, given that you were, as far as I am concerned, bettering the synagogue each year you were there, fully knowing that these projects always mean spending political capital, which is never infinite.

I always felt good, and will feel good, knowing that you had somehow managed to do so many good things as you did, for so long a time. Apart from serving Holy Blossom Temple, you gave the Toronto Jewish Community an intellectual centre. You filled a huge gap. Since most of Toronto is not Reform, the fact that you managed to do so at Holy Blossom is remarkable. Your subtle work, more than anyone else's within the community, has been the most effective in giving the community unity in some very embattled years. You have, to my mind, been the most able defender of Israel within our community because you truly educated it on some key things it had to know at this moment in history, which was a prerequisite for it to be effective as a group.

There have been tidal shifts in the habits of mind of our community in the past decade and it has become far more able to protect Israel, and you are responsible for much of that. That this hasn't been yet fully recognized by others has to do with the centuries of trauma to the Jewish people, which have given some of our people many psychological complexes precisely around the area of how we survive as a people, as you well know. By my minimalist Jewish moral aesthetic (for Jews often submerge our aesthetic impulses into morality for better or worse) to be able to do the right thing, as you have, often without outside support, or understanding, against opposition, or in the midst of indifference, is a magnificent and beautiful thing.

I think that part of what has occurred is that you tried, with great success, not to allow the community to live in denial of painful truths. This is generally a thankless job, but it, in our time, has been arguably the most important task, and thus noble. What most impressed me is that you didn't waste your time at the pulpit merely trying to protect yourself and your place at that pulpit. You really used it as it should be used.

I know of others who feel as you do but who didn't dare express those feelings and views to keep their place protected and in the end put their interest ahead of their people. Had you not acted as you did, I imagine you might have been there still longer than this extraordinary run but done far, far less. You had the imagination to realize that there are special obligations that go with being the rabbi at the oldest congregation in the city, and one so established and seen from the outside as representing the community or key aspects of it. Thus, you've shown both a good sense of reality, and courage, to do what you believed was right.

As a result, you've had influence on a generation and directly influenced the largest Jewish community in this country, allowing people to hear what they would not otherwise have and to think what they might not have thought. You helped to bring Reform and the other mainstream groups closer together than they had been. I go over the many fine lecturers you brought to our attention, and I just feel sad for the Jewish community that these may not continue at Holy Blossom.

And, in a more personal vein, people think they know and can judge the complexity of the feelings and thoughts of public individuals, but since it's mostly projection, I won't project my feelings and thoughts onto you. All I dare presume, knowing you, is that your reactions are complex, and sophisticated, and emotionally deep.

I'm hard to please when it comes to rabbis; there have only been a few that impressed me, I confess. But that is not because I think myself superior; it is because I was spoiled by a wonderful early encounter. Fackenheim was my rabbi beginning when I was a teenager, and we had Seders and Shabbats together; he married me and my wife; he comforted me when I was bereaved; he taught me philosophy. And I merely cut his grass and babysat his children. But very soon into our relationship we began to fight on the same side. He wasn't my *shul* rabbi, and there were no dues to pay; he was just my rabbi based on compatibility.

So spoiled, I haven't had a *shul*. I would have joined Holy Blossom because you were there, and I lobbied my family many times to do so, but they wanted something more traditional. But in the end I didn't have to join, for, as my family knows, I have a rabbi, which is all I need. For, without your consent or knowledge, I considered you my rabbi, anyway, and for what that is worth, I still do.

Acknowledgements

My most basic gratitude is to the members of Holy Blossom Temple in Toronto for their willingness to listen and to consider, whether in agreement or not, when its rabbis speak. Holy Blossom has long expected its rabbis to read and have ideas and to put those ideas forward with substance and some degree of style. That's a measure of a serious congregation. The congregation's rabbis have normally grown intellectually and gained otherwise by virtue of the high expectations. I have and I remain as grateful today for this as when I arrived in Toronto in 1987.

My sincere thanks goes to those friends who made the publication of this book possible — much as they have been instrumental in realizing many significant accomplishments in Canadian and Jewish life over the past couple of decades. They are a remarkable group, not the least because, to a person, they never seek attention for their contributions from which many benefit. Each is a model for how to do good things in the public realm. I thank with pleasure: Senator Linda Frum and Howard Sokolowski, Gerald Schwartz and Heather Reisman, Lawrence and Francis Bloomberg, and Joseph (z"l) and Sandra Rotman. I thank also Robert Lantos and Senator Irving and Gail Gerstein for their generosity, and, as well, Michael and Laurie Davis, Michael and Janette Diamond, Michael Bregman and Katie Osborne.

It is said that rabbis have at most but three sermons to weave and then deliver — and everything else is spun from the cloth of one of those three. Perhaps that's true, but what's beyond doubt is that what a rabbi says and writes is shaped not by one but by many. I'm most pleased to thank those whose thinking has invariably made mine better, and who have extended their friendship along with the intellectual fare.

First, those with whom I spent many hours of conversation in my twenties, when passions, mine, anyway, hadn't yet matured into ideas and principles. I'm pleased to be able to still learn from most today, even those who have died (in every case, way too young): Bill Berk, Ben Beliak, Bill Cutter, Laurie Fein (Sapir), Marc Feldman z"l, Janis Goldman, Jim Haas z"l, Devorah Jacobson, Jonny Jacoby, Gary Kates, David Katz, Lucian Marquis z"l, Norman Mirsky z"l, Bert Myers z"l, Sandy Ragins, and John Rosove.

I'm grateful to still others, likewise for their intellectual probing and friendship in more recent years. Through their pushing, the passions grew more refined and the principles more clear, though the errors remain mine alone. I thank, too: Barbara Amiel, Paul Berman, Larry Blumenthal, Barry Borden, Norman Doidge, Sarita Dotan, Seymour (Epi) Epstein, Arthur Fish, Aaron Flanzraich, Linda Frum, Yoel Glick, Danny Gordis, Yossi Klein Halevi, David Hartman z"l, Tova Hartman, David Hazony, Ammi Hirsch, Lloyd Hoffer, Michelle Katz, Fern Kirshenbaum, Naomi Levy, Beny Maissner, Carole Meyers z"l, Char Miller, Fern Morrison, Stephen Morrison, Jim Moscowitz, Michael Oren, W. Gunther Plaut z"l, Jacqueline Printz, Larry Ritchie, Richard Rotman, Jeffrey Salkin, Steve Saltzman z"l, Barry Silver, and David Weil.

Finally, I'm grateful to Anna Porter and Julie Kirsh for their advice, and to Michael Carroll for his deft editorial hand. I thank as well those at Dundurn Press who shepherded the book through the publishing process: Carrie Gleason, Kathryn Lane, Beth Bruder, and Publisher Kirk Howard. Hayley McAdam,

Acknowledgements

Tania Blumenthal, and Elissa Hermolin were most helpful with administrative matters. Each, in no small part due to their humour and grace, aided me at what I've tried to do — as rabbi, and now in putting together this book. I'm most appreciative, too, of Joan Garson, Russ Joseph, Harvey Schipper, and Yael Splansky for their support of this book. To those who wrote the heartfelt things you did about me here, thank you for your kindnesses, both here and elsewhere. With regard to your accuracy — that will be but one part of our continuing conversations.

Notes

WHERE I COME FROM

1. Paul Mendes-Flohr, "The Retrieval of Innocence and Tradition," in *The Uses of Tradition: Jewish Continuity in the Modern Era*, ed. Jack Wertheimer (New York: Jewish Theological Seminary of America, 1992), 283.
2. Haym Soloveitchik, "Rupture and Reconstruction: The Transformation of Contemporary Orthodoxy," *Tradition* 28, no. 4 (Summer 1994): 64–130. The questions here are inspired by Soloveitchik's essay.
3. John Murray Cuddihy, *The Ordeal of Civility: Freud, Marx, Lévi-Strauss, and the Jewish Struggle with Modernity* (New York: Basic Books, 1974), 10.
4. Franz Kafka, "Letter to His Father," trans. Ernst and Eithne Wilkins, rev. Arthur S. Wensinger, in *Franz Kafka: The Sons* (New York: Schocken Books, 1989), 147–48.

AT THE OPEN GATE: REMARKS ON THE HIGH HOLY DAYS

1. David Remnick, "We Are Alive: Bruce Springsteen at Sixty-Two," *The New Yorker*, July 30, 2012, 42.
2. Judah Goldin, Introduction, in S.Y. Agnon, ed., *Days of Awe: A Treasury of Jewish Wisdom for Reflection, Repentance, and Renewal on the High Holy Days* (New York: Schocken Books,

1995), xxviii.

3. Maimonides, Hilchot Teshuvah 2:4.

4. A popular story about Rabbi Joseph B. Soloveitchik told regularly by his students.

5. Viktor E. Frankl, *The Will to Meaning: Foundations and Applications of Logotherapy* (New York: Plume Books, New American Library, 1970), 156–57.

6. Details about the Middle School No. 1 attack are taken from C.J. Chivers and Steven Lee Myers, "Russian Rebels Had Precise Plan," *New York Times*, September 6, 2004.

7. David Brooks, "Cult of Death," *New York Times*, September 7, 2004.

8. Victor David Hanson, *Ripples of Battle: How Wars of the Past Still Determine How We Fight, How We Live, and How We Think* (New York: Doubleday, 2003), 255.

9. The comment is that of the sixteenth-century Italian Jewish commentator Obadiah ben Jacob Sforno concerning Genesis 4:8.

10. Karen Armstrong, *In the Beginning: A New Interpretation of Genesis* (New York: Ballantine, 1996), 35.

11. Clifford Stoll, *Silicon Snake Oil: Second Thoughts on the Information Highway* (New York: Doubleday, 1995), 1.

12. Matthew L. Wald, "Conversations/Clifford Stoll: A Disillusioned Devotee Says the Internet Is Wearing No Clothes," *New York Times*, April 30, 1995.

13. Stoll, *Silicon Snake Oil*, 3.

14. Soloveitchik, "Rupture and Reconstruction," 83.

15. Ibid., 85.

16. Talmud Bavli, Brachot 17a.

17. Talmud Bavli, Avodah Zarah, 54b.

18. Abraham Joshua Heschel, *A Passion for Truth* (New York: Farrar, Straus and Giroux, 1973), 2.

19. Adapted by John Moscowitz from one of the many stories about Avraham Yehoshua Heschel, the Apter Rav.
20. See Joyce Carol Oates, "The Deadly Sins/Despair: The One Unforgivable Sin," *New York Times*, July 25, 1993. I have paraphrased certain ideas from Oates's essay.
21. See Harold Kushner, *Who Needs God* (New York: Fireside Books, Simon & Schuster, 2002). I have paraphrased here from Kushner's book.
22. Yosef Hayim Yerushalmi, *Zakhor: Jewish History and Jewish Memory* (Seattle: University of Washington Press, 1982), 8.
23. See Yerushalmi, *Zakhor*, where the distinction between ancient Greek and Judaic approaches to history are spelled out in more detail by the historian.

ISRAEL: WHEN YOUR LOVE REMAINS THE SAME AND YOUR VIEWS CHANGE

1. Numbers 14:20.
2. Ruth Wisse, "Welcome to Freshman Disorientation," *Wall Street Journal*, August 27, 2012.
3. Charles Krauthammer, "At Last, Zion," *The Weekly Standard*, May 11, 1998.
4. Yossi Klein Halevi, "The Crisis," *The New Republic*, March 16, 2010.
5. Ibid.
6. For more discussion about the events of March 2010 in Israel and the U.S. reaction, see Daniel Gordis, "Will Obama Ignite 3rd Intifada?" *The Jerusalem Post*, March 26, 2010.
7. Daniel Gordis, "Anything You Say Can and Will Be Used Against You," *The Jerusalem Post*, November 5, 2009.
8. John Moscowitz, e-mail message to unspecified correspondent, September 17, 2009.

9. Gordis, "Anything You Say Can and Will Be Used Against You."

10. This article originally appeared as John Moscowitz, "Unequal Mideast Equation," *Globe and Mail*, February 12, 2004.

11. Charles Krauthammer, "He Tarries: Jewish Messianism and the Oslo Peace" (Distinguished Rennert Lecture for 2002, King David Hotel, Jerusalem, June 10, 2002), www.freerepublic.com/focus/f-news/699375/posts.

12. Ibid.

13. Ibid.

14. Exodus 13:17–18.

15. Leon Wieseltier, *Kaddish* (New York: Vintage, 2000), 414.

16. Fouad Ajami, "Arafat's War," *Wall Street Journal*, March 29, 2002.

17. Ibid.

18. Ari Shavit, "Naming the War," *Haaretz*, March 13, 2002.

19. Yossi Klein Halevi, "'Cycle of Violence' Is a Middle East Lie," *Los Angeles Times*, January 23, 2002.

20. Shavit, "Naming the War."

21. David Hartman, "The God of Surprise!" in *A Different Light: The Big Book of Hanukkah*, eds. Noam Zion and Barbara Spectre (New York: Devora Publishing, 2000), 187.

THE TORAH SPEAKS IN ITS LANGUAGE AND IN OURS

1. Pirkei Avot (Ethics of the Fathers) 5:26.

2. Mishnah Eduyot 2:9.

3. Wieseltier, *Kaddish*, 256–59.

4. The interpretation of *plastir* is found in the Midrash Petirat Moshe (Midrash on the Death of Moses).

5. Pirkei Avot (Ethics of the Fathers) 1:2.

6. Christopher Hitchens, *Hitch-22: A Memoir* (London: Atlantic Books, 2011), xi.

7. Adapted from John Moscowitz, "Noach (6:9–11:32): What Kind of Father Was Lamech?" *The Modern Men's Torah Commentary: New Insights from Jewish Men on the 54 Weekly Torah Portions*, ed. Jeffrey K. Salkin (Woodstock, VT: Jewish Lights Publishing, 2009), 11–15.

8. Genesis 5:29.

9. Armstrong, *In the Beginning*, 41.

10. Genesis 9:20–21.

11. Sigmund Freud, *The Interpretation of Dreams*, in *The Basic Writings of Sigmund Freud*, trans. and ed. A.A. Brill (New York: The Modern Library, Random House, 1938), 260.

12. Sigmund Freud, *Civilization and Its Discontents*, trans. James Strachey (New York: W.W. Norton, 1961), 19.

13. Leon Kass, *The Beginning of Wisdom: Reading Genesis* (New York: Free Press, Simon & Schuster, 2003), 204.

14. Deuteronomy 7:16–24.

15. Deuteronomy 10:18–19.

16. See Yehezkel Kaufmann, *The Religion of Israel: From Its Beginnings to the Babylonian Exile*, trans. Moshe Greenberg (Chicago: University of Chicago Press, 1960).

17. Deuteronomy 7:26.

18. Proverbs 16:5.

19. Talmud Bavli, Sota 4b.

20. Yerushalmi, *Zakhor*, xxxiv.

21. Ibid.

22. Deuteronomy 25:17–19.

23. Benno Jacob, *The Second Book of the Bible: Exodus*, trans. Walter Jacob (Hoboken, NJ: KTAV Publishing House, 1992), 489.

24. Nahum M. Sarna, *Exploring Exodus: The Origins of Biblical Israel* (New York: Schocken Books, 1996), 120–21.

25. Stanley Kauffmann, "Spielberg Revisited," *The New Republic*, January 24, 1994.

ABOUT THAT MATTER OF EVIL ...
(AND OUR EAST AFRICAN HOME)

1. Andrew Delbanco, *The Death of Satan: Americans Have Lost Their Sense of Evil* (New York: Farrar, Straus and Giroux, 1995), 19.
2. Thomas Harris, *The Silence of the Lambs* (New York: St. Martin's Press, 1988), 21.
3. Delbanco, *The Death of Satan*, 19.
4. Ibid., 9, 234.
5. Adapted from Harold M. Schulweis, "The Image of God," Keruv Program Lecture, 8–9, http://hmsi.info/2014/03/03/the-image-of-god-a-keruv-program-lecture-by-rabbi-harold-m-schulweis.
6. Jeff Jacoby, "Our Enemies Meant What They Said," *Boston Globe*, September 13, 2001.
7. Benjamin Netanyahu, as quoted by *The Free Lance-Star* (Fredericksburg, Virginia), September 24, 2001, from a Netanyahu article that appeared in *The Jersualem Post* the previous week.
8. Deuteronomy 25:17–19.
9. Tony Blair, as quoted in *The Guardian*, September 12, 2001, from a speech the British prime minister gave the night before at the Trades Union Congress in Brighton, England.
10. Talmud Bavli Sanhedrin 37a.
11. Excerpted from John Moscowitz's talk at Holy Blossom Temple on December 6, 2000, at the memorial service commemorating the Montreal massacre and recognizing the continued threat of violence against women.

12. Genesis 6:5.
13. Genesis 6:6.
14. All quotations in this blog post are taken from Joseph B. Soloveitchik, "Adam and Eve," in *Shiurei HaRav: A Conspectus of the Public Lectures of Rabbi Joseph B. Soloveitchik*, ed. Joseph Epstein (Hoboken, NJ: KTAV Publishing House, 1974), 137–42.

JEWISH PRINCIPLES AND PUBLIC MATTERS

1. David Remnick, *The Bridge: The Life and Rise of Barack Obama* (Toronto: Random House Canada), 242.
2. Edward Rothstein, "Seeing Terrorism as Drama with Sequels and Prequels," *New York Times*, December 26, 2005.
3. Exodus 2:12.
4. Marshall McLuhan, *Understanding Media: The Extensions of Man* (Cambridge, MA: MIT Press, 1994), 19.
5. John M. Culkin, "A Schoolman's Guide to Marshall McLuhan," *Saturday Review*, March 18, 1967, 70.

REMEMBRANCES

1. Second Samuel 1:23.
2. Ibid., 3:38.
3. Yevgeny Yevtushenko, "Babi Yar," in *The Collected Poems, 1952–1990*, ed. Albert C. Todd with the author and James Ragan (New York: Henry Holt and Company, 1991), 102.
4. Isaiah 40:27–31.
5. Yevtushenko, *The Collected Poems*, 104.

Index

Abbas, President Mahmoud, 87, 88
Abel, 53–55
Abraham, 94–95, 99–101, 141, 232, 235
Adam, 53, 132, 154, 166, 168, 169–72, 184
Africa, 237
Ajami, Fouad, 108
Akiva, Rabbi, 122
Am Yisrael, 25, 120
Amalek, 141–46, 163
Arab Legion, 87
Arab Spring, 83
Arafat, Yasser, 51, 76–77, 82, 83, 99, 102, 104, 108, 109, 117–18
Armstrong, Karen, 54, 132
Atta, Mohamed, 153
Augustine, Saint, 158
Auschwitz, 219
Avnery, Uri, 76
Axelrod, David, 88, 89
Azariah, Rabbi Menachem, 122

Baal Shem Tov, 64–65

Babi Yar, 200, 218–22
Baeck, Rabbi Leo, 52
Baltimore (Maryland), 16
bar Yochai, Rabbi Shimon, 140–41
Barak, Ehud, 111
Barcas, Hamilcar, 134
Beerman, Rabbi Leonard, 12
Begin, Menachem, 21, 76
Beilin, Yossi, 81–82
Beit Jalla (West Bank), 112
Beit Yisrael Quarter (Jerusalem), 110
Belarus, 219
Ben Bag Bag, 121, 122
ben Perachia, Yehoshua, 243–44
Bennett, Debra, 183
Berman, Paul, 24, 224
Bernardo, Paul, 151, 152, 164
Beslan (Russia), 49–51
Beth Sholom Synagogue (Toronto), 243
Bible, 60, 70, 79, 136–40, 142, 145, 147–50, 154, 167, 213, 214, 220
Deuteronomy, 139, 142–45

Ecclesiastes, 105
Exodus, 13, 29, 75, 92, 106,
    119, 143–44, 191
Genesis, 53–54, 99, 132, 136,
    151, 154, 168, 170–72
Numbers, 79
Proverbs, 140
Biden, Vice-President Joe, 88–89
    181
bin Laden, Osama, 53, 153, 158,
    161
Binh, Madame Nguyen Thi, 28,
    191
Blair, Tony, 164
Borowitz, Eugene, 123, 124
Boston (Massachusetts), 43, 44,
    170, 209
Brecht, Bertolt, 219
Brooks, David, 51
Buber, Martin, 201
Buddhism, 168
Burg, Avram, 102
Bush, George W., 84, 246

Cain, 53–55
Caleb, 79–80, 85
Camp David (Maryland), 117
Canaan, 141
Canaanites, 138–40
Carter, Jimmy, 99
Central Conference of American
    Rabbis, 32, 177
Chesed, 130–31
Christianity, 168
Christians, 31, 134, 215

Claremont (California), 226
Claremont Colleges, 9, 27
Clemons, Clarence, 39
Clinton, Bill, 77, 84, 193–95
Clinton, Hillary, 88, 89
Coastal Road massacre, 87
Cuddihy, John Murray, 20
Culkin, John M., 195

Dachau, 219
Dallas (Texas), 217
Damari, Tina, 104
Days of Awe (Yamim Noraim),
    37, 38, 49, 65, 156, 195
Delbanco, Andrew, 157–59
    The Death of Satan, 157–58
Dewey, John, 200
Diamond, Jared, 169
    The Third Chimpanzee: The
        Evolution and Future of
        the Human Animal, 169
Doidge, Dr. Norman, 253–55
    The Brain That Heals, 253
Dome of the Rock (Jerusalem),
    87
Dreyfus, Alfred, 100

E Street Band, 39
East Africa, 26, 154, 155, 169,
    170
East Jerusalem, 88, 90
Easter, 31
Eban, Abba, 24, 224
Egypt, 70, 79, 106, 138, 140, 142,
    143, 149, 163, 194

Index

Ellenson, Rabbi David, 21–24, 124
European Union, 88

Fatah, 104
Faulkner, William, 13
  Requiem for a Nun, 13
Fayyad, Salam, 87, 88, 93
Federici, Danny, 39
Flanzraich, Rabbi Aaron, 243–45
Fonda, Jane, 15, 26–29, 235, 240
Fouts, Roger, 169
  *Next of Kin: My Conversations
    with Chimpanzees*, 169
Frankl, Viktor E., 46
Free The Children, 233
free will, 139, 166
French, Kristin, 151
Freud, Jacob, 135
Freud, Sigmund, 32, 133–35
  *Civilization and Its
    Discontents*, 134
  Interpretation of Dreams, The,
    133–34
Friedman, Thomas, 88, 224
Frum, Senator Linda, 9–10

Gaza, 76, 112
Gemilut Chasidim, 94, 128, 130,
  241–42
Geneva Accord, 101
Germany, 105
Gibson, Bob, 29
Globe and Mail, 29–31, 101–04,
  152, 167–69
Goldstein, Baruch, 102

Gordis, Rabbi Daniel, 23, 95, 100,
  224, 238–39
Great Rift Valley, 154, 155, 233
Green, Rabbi Arthur, 24
Grossman, David, 76

Haaretz, 111–12, 118–19
Habakkuk, 46
Haifa (Israel), 75, 87
Hair, 75
halacha, 170
Halevi, Yossi Klein, 23, 90–91,
  113–14, 245–46
Haman, 145, 220
Hamas, 88, 102
Hannibal, 134
Hanoi (Vietnam), 28
Hanson, Victor Davis, 24, 52–53,
  224
Harper, Prime Minister Stephen,
  84
Harris, Thomas, 157
  The Silence of the Lambs,
    157–58
Hartman, Rabbi David, 22–24,
  119–20, 124–25, 199,
  200–01, 224
Hartman, Rabbi Donniel, 23
Hasidism, 34, 64
HaTzaddik, Shimon (Simon the
  Just), 127–31
Hawaii, 185
Hayden, Tom, 9, 24, 27–29, 235,
  240
Hazony, Yoram, 23, 116

Hebrew Union College, 21, 32, 122, 123, 234
Hebrew University (Jerusalem), 139
Hebron (West Bank), 75, 98
Herodotus, 72
Hertzberg, Arthur, 176
Herzl, Theodor, 96
Heschel, Abraham Joshua, 64–65, 245
    A Passion for Truth, 64–65
Heschel, Avraham Yehoshua (Apter Rav), 65–66, 71
Hillel, 94–95, 100, 121, 160, 243
Hinduism, 168
Hirsch, Rabbi Ammiel, 229–30
Hitchens, Christopher, 24, 130, 199, 202–04
Hitler, Adolf, 53, 145, 164, 220
Hollywood (California), 27, 240
Hollywood (Florida), 234
Holmes, Oliver Wendell, 58
Holocaust, 105, 226
Holon (Israel), 96
Holy Blossom Temple, 9–12, 15, 16, 23–25, 29, 37, 101, 116, 126, 127, 177, 179, 182, 187, 202, 203, 213, 223–27, 229–33, 236, 237, 240–42, 246, 253, 255
Homolka, Karla, 151
Hurva Synagogue (Jerusalem), 87
Hussein, Saddam, 53

Ignatieff, Michael, 24
Information Age, 37, 57–64
interfaith marriage, 176, 178, 238
Internet, 58–60, 62, 63, 195
Iran, 85
Ireland, 175
Isaac, 94
Isaac M. Wise Temple (Cincinnati, Ohio), 236
Isaiah, 221
Islam, 50, 97, 162, 168
Islamic, 102, 162
Islamo-Fascists, 152
Italy, 35, 209

Jackson, Henry "Scoop," 84
Jacob, Benno, 144
Jacoby, Jeff, 161
Jakarta, 50
James, William, 200
Japan, 84
Japheth, 133
Jerusalem, 17, 18, 50, 75–77, 81, 87–89, 91, 95–98, 110, 116, 120, 128, 147, 152, 155, 172, 200, 201, 221, 225, 232, 234, 238, 243, 245
Jerusalem Post, The, 95
Jewish Institute of Religion, 234
Jewish Theological Seminary, 17
jihad, 50, 56, 102
jihadist, 50, 52, 80, 85
Joshua, 79–80, 85, 144
Judaism, 10, 18, 20–22, 27, 29, 31, 33, 34, 62, 68, 73, 85, 95,

Index

97, 105, 119, 121, 123–26,
139, 141, 164, 168, 177, 186,
196, 221, 228, 229, 243, 246
Conservative, 22
Orthodox, 18, 187, 200, 201,
206
Reform, 9, 19, 21, 22, 34,
78, 81, 82, 175–76, 187,
229, 235–36, 238–39,
246, 253, 254
Judt, Tony, 99

Kaddish, 113, 114
Kafka, Franz, 16–17, 21, 26
"Letter to His Father," 21
Kansas, 185
Kaplan, Mordecai, 201
Kass, Leon, 135
Kaufmann, Yehezkel, 139
Kauffmann, Stanley, 145–46
Kennedy, Edward, 217
Kennedy, John F., 84, 216, 217
Kennedy, Robert, 29
Kenya, 154, 233
kibbutz, 75, 104
Kibbutz Metzer, 104
Kibbutz Sarid, 226
Kiddush, 187, 196
kiddushin, 177–79, 182, 184
Kielburger, Craig, 233–34
Kielburger, Marc, 26, 233–34
Kiev (Ukraine), 219
King, Stephen, 234
Kinneret Agreement, 116
Kipsigis, 233

Klute, 27
Knesset, 162, 225
Kol Nidre, 13, 65, 78–79, 86
Kotzk (Ukraine), 64
Krauthammer, Charles, 23, 85,
91, 93, 104–05, 224

Labour Party (Israel), 89
Lamech, 132–37
Leo Baeck Temple (Los Angeles),
15
Levin, Danny, 18–19, 22
Levy, Rabbi Naomi, 224, 231–33
Lewis, Stephen, 24
Lieberman, Joe, 84
Likud Party (Israel), 89, 90
Livni, Tzipi, 90
London (England), 31, 96, 209
Los Angeles, 9, 11, 15, 21, 27,
174, 191, 207, 210, 231, 232,
240
Los Angeles Times, 113–14
Luria, Rabbi Isaac, 40

Maasai, 233, 234
Maccabees, 243
Machpelah (West Bank), 94
Mahaffy, Leslie, 151
Maimonides (Rambam), 41, 42,
193–95, 200
Hilchot Teshuvah (The Laws
of Repentance), 41, 194
Maimonides School (Boston), 170
Maissner, Cantor Benjamin, 57,
230–31

Marmur, Rabbi Dow, 11–12
McCain, John, 81
McLuhan, Marshall, 195–97
    Understanding Media, 195
Medinat Yisrael, 25
Meir, Golda, 96
Meiser (Israel), 104
Mendel, Menachem (Kotzker
    Rebbe), 64
menschlikeit, 241
messianic, 91–92
messianism, 105
Mexico, 175
Mezbizh, 64
Midianites, 94
Midrash Tanhuma, 132
mikvah, 176
Minh, Ho Chi, 28, 29
Minneapolis (Minnesota), 44,
    212
Mishnah, 231
Mishneh Torah, 236
Modern Men's Torah
    Commentary, The, 132
Montreal massacre, 151, 165–67
Moscow, 50
Moscowitz, Morris, 28, 44–46,
    192, 200, 206–13
Moses, 70, 78–79, 91–92, 126,
    143, 146, 149, 191
Mount Sinai, 92, 93, 122–26, 140,
    143, 148
Mughrabi, Dalal, 87
Munich (Germany), 190
Munich massacre, 189–91

Munich (movie), 189–91
Muslim Brotherhood, 82–84

National Liberation Front
    (Vietnam), 28
Nazi, 32, 105, 145, 146
Nazism, 162
Nefesh HaChayim, 229
Netanyahu, Prime Minister
    Benjamin "Bibi," 84, 88–91,
    99, 162
New Left, 24, 27, 226
New Republic, The, 145
New York City, 43, 44, 50, 95, 97,
    100, 155, 156, 165, 170, 173,
    189, 190, 200, 229, 234
New York Times, 51, 67, 88, 153,
    189
New Yorker, The, 39
Newtown massacre, 151–52,
    167–69
Noah, 132–37
North Vietnam, 29
Nusseibeh, Sari, 83, 103

Oates, Joyce Carol, 67–68
Obama, President Barack, 81, 84,
    89–91, 179, 183, 184–89
    Dreams from My Father, 186
Onassis, Jacqueline Kennedy,
    199, 216–17
Oren, Michael, 23, 224, 225
    Six Days of War, 225
Oslo Accord, 76–77, 81, 104, 116,
    246

Index

Oz, Amos, 23, 76, 105, 224

Palestine, 46, 98, 99
Palestinian Authority (PA), 87,
91
Palestinian Liberation
Organization (PLO), 76, 81,
82
Palestinians, 13, 76, 81, 83, 87,
88, 90, 91, 93, 98 101–05,
110–15, 117, 190, 234,
245–46
Paris (France), 28, 115, 173, 209
Parkinson's disease, 44, 45, 192,
211
Parsons, Talcott, 20
Peck, Gregory, 29
Pennsylvania, 155
Peoplehood, 13, 21, 23, 26, 107,
178
Peres, Shimon, 109, 115–16
Pesach (Passover), 31, 106–09,
119, 226
Petraeus, David, 167
Philistines, 106
Physicians for Human Rights,
105
Pirkei Avot (Ethics of the
Fathers), 230, 231, 244
Pitzer College (Claremont,
California), 226
Plaut, Rabbi W. Gunther, 12, 200,
213–16
Power, Samantha, 24, 224
Prague, 16

Purim, 142

Rabin, Yitzhak, 76–77
Radical Islam, 51, 156, 162, 191,
226
Ragins, Rabbi Sandy, 12, 15, 16,
31–35
Ramallah (West Bank), 87, 96, 112
Ramat Shlomo (Jerusalem), 88
Rashi, Rabbi, 133
ratzon elyon, 183–84
ratzon tachton, 183
Rav Muvhak, 15, 214, 215
Reisman, Heather, 224
Remnick, David, 39, 184–86
  The Bridge: The Life and
    Rise of Barack Obama,
    184–86
Romania, 175
Romans, 63, 134, 173
Rome, 63
Rosh Hashanah, 16, 37, 38, 39,
40, 48, 49, 56, 57, 86, 117,
151, 152, 155, 193, 226
Rosove, Rabbi John, 240–41
Rothstein, Edward, 189–90
Rotman, Joseph, 199, 204–05

Salkin, Rabbi Jeffrey K., 43, 132,
234–36
Saltzman, Josh, 227–28
same-sex marriage, 12, 13,
174–84
Santa Monica (California), 29,
208, 209

Sarah, 94, 99
Sarna, Nahum M., 145
Saturday Review, 195
Saul, 213
Saving Private Ryan, 190
Schiavo, Terri, 192–93
Schindler, Oskar, 141–46
Schindler's List, 141–46, 190
Schorsch, Ismar, 17
Schulweis, Rabbi Harold, 12
Schwartz, Gerry, 224
Schwartz/Reisman Centre, 24
Seattle (Washington), 226
Second Intifada, 77, 117, 152, 245, 246
Sefat Emet, 86
Seleucids, 243
Selma (Alabama), 185
September 11 (9/11), 52, 152, 154, 155–65, 189
Shabbat, 15, 37, 95, 96, 99, 116, 126, 142, 174, 177, 187, 193, 195–97, 229, 238, 239, 242, 243, 245, 246, 255
Shakespeare, William, 167
Shalem Center/Shalem College (Jerusalem), 116, 225, 238
Shalom Hartman Institute (Jerusalem), 245
Shammai, 160, 243
Sharon, Ariel, 102, 111, 116, 246
Shavit, Ari, 111, 118
Signer, Michael, 123
Simon, Ernst, 16, 26
Six Day War (1967), 210

Soloveitchik, Haym, 62
Soloveitchik, Rabbi Joseph B., 22–24, 43, 124, 125, 155, 169–72, 183, 184, 200, 201, 228
Spielberg, Steven, 145–46, 189–91
Springsteen, Bruce, 39, 43, 228
St. Louis Cardinals, 29
St. Louis (Missouri), 9, 29, 30, 200, 207–08, 210, 223, 228, 234
Stalin, Joseph, 53, 164
Stephen Wise Free Synagogue (New York City), 229
Stoll, Clifford, 59–62
Silicon Snake Oil, 59–60
suicide bomber, 105, 115
suicide bombing, 245
Sukkot, 236
Sullivan, Craig, 29–31

Tahiti, 208
Talmud, 34, 43, 63, 165, 173, 200, 201
Tanzania, 154
Tehran (Iran), 83
Tekoah (West Bank), 98
Tel Aviv (Israel), 75, 87, 115
Temple (Jerusalem), 56, 87, 173, 243
Ten Commandments, 92
terrorism, 51, 55, 108, 113, 115, 164, 189
terrorists, 49–50, 87, 104, 108,

Index

114–15, 159, 190
teshuvah, 41–43
Thomashow, Rabbi Karen, 183,
236–37
Tiberias (Israel), 28, 191
To Kill a Mockingbird, 29, 153
Tojo, Hideki, 53
Torah, 55, 62, 63, 72, 91, 92, 94,
106, 121–50, 153, 182, 187,
190, 200, 201, 214, 215, 216,
224, 232, 237, 241, 242, 244
Torah mi-Sinai, 124, 126
Toronto Raptors, 204
Tzaddik, 34
Tzaddikim, 34
tzedakah, 41
tzitzit, 17, 19

Ukraine, 64, 219
Union for Reform Judaism, 81
United Nations, 24, 115
United States, 23, 75, 84, 88, 89,
175, 216
University of California, Los
Angeles (UCLA), 11, 240
Uris, Leon, 29, 75
Exodus, 29, 75

Valley of Hinnom (Jerusalem),
234
Venice (California), 27, 29, 207
vidui, 48
Vienna (Austria), 32
Vietnam War, 27, 28
Washington, D.C., 155

Washington Post, 104
Washington University, 207
Weekly Standard, The, 85
Weizmann, Chaim, 96
West Bank, 50, 87, 89, 90, 98
Wiesel, Elie, 24
Wieseltier, Leon, 24, 106, 122, 224
Kaddish, 106, 122
Wilcox (Arizona), 207
Wilf, Einat, 23
Will, George, 24
Wisse, Ruth, 81, 224
Wolpe, Rabbi David, 224
World Trade Center (New York
City), 163, 189

yarmulke, 203
Yerushalmi, Yosef Hayim, 72, 141
Zakhor: Jewish History and
Jewish Memory, 141
Yeshiva University (New York
City), 43, 170
Yevtushenko, Yevgeny, 219–21
"Babi Yar," 219–22
Yiddish, 81, 206
Yizkor, 73, 106–09
Yohanan, Rabbi, 140
Yom Kippur, 37, 38, 44, 49, 56,
68, 72, 78, 86, 193
Yom Kippur War (1973), 226

Zion, 22, 26, 85
Zion, Noam, 23
Zionism, 116

VISIT US AT

Dundurn.com
@dundurnpress
Facebook.com/dundurnpress
Pinterest.com/dundurnpress

CPSIA information can be obtained
at www.ICGtesting.com
Printed in the USA
LVOW05s1318110116
469733LV00007B/9/P